The John Harvard Library

ON RELIGIOUS LIBERTY

Selections from the Works of Roger Williams

Edited and with an Introduction by

JAMES CALVIN DAVIS

THE BELKNAP PRESS OF
HARVARD UNIVERSITY PRESS
Cambridge, Massachusetts
London, England
2008

Library of Congress Cataloging-in-Publication Data

Williams, Roger, 1604?–1683.
  On religious liberty : selections from the works of Roger
Williams / Edited and with an Introduction by James Calvin Davis.
      p.   cm. — (The John Harvard Library)
  Includes bibliographical references and index.
  ISBN-13: 978-0-674-02622-3 (cloth : alk. paper)
  ISBN-10: 0-674-02622-5 (cloth : alk. paper)
  ISBN-13: 978-0-674-02685-8 (pbk. : alk. paper)
  ISBN-10: 0-674-02685-3 (pbk. : alk. paper)
  1. Freedom of religion.   I. Davis, James Calvin.   II. Title.
  BV741.W55 2008
  323.44′2—dc22   2007014202

For Jae William

Contents

Acknowledgments

Several individuals and institutions provided valuable assistance to this project. I am indebted to the *We the People* initiative of the National Endowment for the Humanities for two research grants that underwrote the bulk of the work. I also wish to thank Middlebury College for generously granting me a sabbatical leave during the 2004–2005 academic year, and especially President Ron Liebowitz, Dean of Faculty Development and Research Carol Rifelj, and Grants Coordinator Franci Farnsworth for their enthusiastic help and support. I am grateful to the staffs of the Middlebury College Library and the Bailey/Howe Library of the University of Vermont for helping me to procure copies of Williams's treatises. Two student research assistants, Phil Koretz and Celia Cohen, were indispensable in transcribing large amounts of those texts for this collection. Colleagues at Middlebury College and elsewhere who read portions of the manuscript or who otherwise lent their support to the project include Laura Lieber, John McWilliams, Amy Feely Morsman, Justin Stearns, Charles Swezey, and Mark Valeri. Finally, I thank my wife, ElizabethAnne, who not only carefully read the introduction but also provided much-needed support and encouragement in what turned out to be a larger project than I first anticipated. The book is dedicated to our son, Jae, who came into our lives from South Korea while I was working on it, and whose insistence on playtime with Daddy provides a pleasant distraction from old texts and weighty ideas.

Editorial Method

The intent of this volume is to provide an accessible edition of important selections from Roger Williams's writings on religious liberty. Toward that end, I have relied on the Narragansett edition (New York: Russell and Russell, 1963) of Williams's works for most of the treatises and letters, with some comparative analysis of textual alternatives (for instance, Edward Bean Underhill's version of *The Bloody Tenent* [London: J. Haddon, 1848]). Most of Williams's public works are represented in this volume, with a few exceptions. As historically important as it is, no attempt was made to include selections from *A Key into the Language of America*. The *Key* is still in print, and it does not lend itself to dissection for a volume of excerpts. For both its theological and anthropological insights, the *Key* is better studied as a whole. Neither does this volume include Williams's *Experiments of Spiritual Life and Health*, a brief piece he wrote as encouragement for his wife that says nothing about religious liberty. Finally, only a few of Williams's private letters are included in this volume, for Glenn LaFantasie has edited a remarkably exhaustive collection of Williams's correspondence.

My aim in including *The Bloody Tenent* and most of the smaller tracts was to retain as much of the development of Williams's argument as possible by taking a minimalist approach to deleting passages. The result in these cases is more an abridgment of the text than an assembly of short, crudely excised selections. The passages that have been deleted from these texts involve redundancies and tangents not germane to Williams's central arguments (for instance, moments of excessive biblical exegesis). By contrast, *The Bloody Tenent Yet More Bloody* is often hopelessly repetitive and tangential, and *George Fox Digg'd out of His Burrowes* is only incidentally about religious liberty. In these treatises, what needed to be eliminated far exceeded what was necessary to retain, so the selections from them read more like a series of excerpts than an abridgment.

Most of the external structure for these texts is my own imposition. I have eliminated the marginal notes from the original texts, since they rarely contribute anything useful. I also abandoned the chapter divisions in the larger treatises, substituting instead section titles (in italics) that I trust better represent the transition from one conceptual theme to another. I also have added subtitles (again, in italics) to some of the smaller treatises to clarify the development of the argument. I recognize that this will make it harder for the interested reader to match texts in this volume with the Narragansett editions, but I believe the sacrifice makes for a more readable text.

In terms of editorial strategy, I have modernized nearly all spelling and have adjusted grammar and punctuation in order to clarify passages, eliminate run-ons and fragments, and adhere to modern expectations for sentence structure. Occasionally I have divided a sentence that in the original was a confusing ramble. In addition, I have eliminated or completed the numerous open-ended parentheses in Williams's works according to the needs of the sentence. I have eliminated Williams's copious use of "etc.," normally replacing it with an "and" before the last item in a series, and have dispensed with almost all of the original italics, which seldom contributed meaningfully to Williams's point. The deletion of single words is rarely noted, but three ellipsis dots mark the deletion of a phrase, sentence, or passage. When I have needed to add a word for clarity, the addition is enclosed in brackets, and when that addition is a substitution for a word, the original is normally noted in a footnote. On the rare occasion that I needed to reword or rearrange an entire phrase or sentence, the original rendering is also included in a footnote. The remaining notes provide historical background for persons or events mentioned in the text, clarify Williams's argument or those to which he is responding, define obscure words, provide biblical references, and insert interpretive commentary on arguments raised in the text.

On Religious Liberty

Roger Williams and the Birth of an American Ideal

Roger Williams was America's earliest pioneer for religious liberty, but although he retains his place in cultural lore as the founder of Rhode Island and a curious voice in the Puritan wilderness, he is largely overshadowed in contemporary discussions of religious freedom by the legacy of enlightened patriots from the eighteenth century. One hundred fifty years before one of those patriots, Thomas Jefferson, penned a similar phrase, Williams was advocating a "wall of separation between the Garden of the church and the wilderness of the world." Generations ahead of James Madison, Williams commended freedom of conscience as being in the best interests of both religion *and* state, protecting not only the integrity of belief but civil peace as well. But what makes Williams essential to the American tradition of religious liberty is not just that he was the first to argue for such liberty, but that in many ways his vision of religious liberty was superior to the one we have inherited from the Enlightenment. In contrast to John Locke, Williams argued not just for toleration but for liberty; he recognized that religious freedom must be understood as a fundamental human right and not legislative discretion. Williams also extended the protection of conscience farther than Locke could imagine, applying it to Catholics, Jews, Muslims, and even atheists. And unlike Jefferson, Williams understood religious expression to amount to more than opinions, which compelled Williams to advocate for a sphere of protection around religious practices while also recognizing that the pursuit of the common good might occasionally justify the violation of that protection. In these and other ways, Williams's vision for religious liberty is richer in both scope and depth than that of more prominent defenders.

What is astonishing is that Williams derived this higher vision not from agnostic rationalism or political pragmatism, but from a radical commitment to Puritan Calvinism. As a Puritan, Williams was committed to a classically Calvinist worldview that emphasized the sovereignty of God, the utter sinfulness of human beings, the necessity of divine grace for salvation, the primacy of the Bible as religious and moral authority, and the importance of a pure church. Like his fellow Puritans, Williams also maintained a certain exclusivity in his religious convictions; in other words, Williams believed that because the Puritan worldview was "true," many (if not all) alternative religious perspectives were "false." He and his fellow Puritans abhorred the Quakers' theology and practices, they insisted that the Catholic Church was the arm of the Antichrist, and they assumed that Native Americans worshipped the devil. In fact, Williams's intolerance was too radical even for his fellow Puritans, for he was sure that most of his brethren in the Church of England were going to hell. Indeed, his rejection of that institution as an apostate church helped lead to his banishment from Massachusetts.

Remarkably, however, the same religious dogmatism that made Williams so theologically intolerant eventually would inspire him to work tirelessly for a civil policy of religious liberty in both England and New England. The Calvinism that made him so confident in his own beliefs also commended to him the integrity of conscientious conviction and warned him of the dangerous consequences of a society's attempting to coerce religious compliance from its citizens. His insistence on absolute purity in worship sensitized Williams to the importance of protecting religious practice as a necessary expression of genuine religious belief, even when that practice conflicts with widely held social and legal norms. Williams desired religious liberty for everyone, including the very groups whose religion he most despised. In establishing Rhode Island as a safe haven for conscientious conviction, he argued that such liberty should extend not just to Christians but also to Jews and Muslims, not just to believers but also to atheists, not just to Puritans but also to Catholics, Quakers, and Native Americans. At the same time, he also recognized better than most how hard it would be to establish this universal liberty, precisely because the expressions of conscience most in need of protection—those of a dissenting minority—have the potential to be most disturbing to the equally noble concern for social order. Because his principled defense of religious freedom grew from a sophisticated and personal understanding of religious experience, a deep respect for human dignity and the integrity of the conscience, and a genuine appreciation for the importance of social obligation and cooperation, Williams was better prepared to deal with the "hard cases" of conscientious social deviance than were Enlightenment thinkers, whose proposals characteristically were based on a thinner conception of religion. The conceptual richness that informed Williams's writings on religious liberty was provided by his religious worldview. Williams did not come about his defense of religious liberty *in spite of* his own dogmatism, but in many ways *because* of it.

This introduction and the texts that follow tell the story of this underappreciated prophet of religious liberty. Williams's beliefs intersected with the events of his life to yield an apology for religious freedom that would distinguish him not only from the defenders of uniformity in Massachusetts, but also from later, more famous advocates of toleration. In the eighteenth century, Williams's theological defense of religious liberty would profoundly influence the efforts of religious activists whose own efforts would be essential to the passage of the First Amendment. Since then, Williams has occasionally inspired and eternally symbolizes the distinctive contribution of religious figures, traditions, and communities to the consideration of freedom of conscience in America. Roger Williams reminds us that the American doctrine of religious liberty is not inherited from Enlightenment rationalism alone, but is equally indebted to the religious foundations of American culture.

Beginnings in Puritan England

Roger Williams was born in Smithfield, England, probably in 1603, the year Queen Elizabeth I died and James I ascended to the throne. Though few Londoners appreciated it at the time, this royal transition marked a fateful new chapter in the religious and political tensions that had been simmering during Elizabeth's long reign. In 1527 King Henry VIII, in response to the pope's refusal to annul his marriage to Catherine of Aragon, had torn the Church of England from the Catholic fold. With the Act of Supremacy in

1534, Henry declared himself "Supreme Head" of the Church of England, dissolved the extensive property holdings of Catholic monasteries in the country, and consolidated control of the church under the crown. England was thus made officially a Protestant nation, but because the reformation was largely political rather than theological, and because Henry removed himself from obligation to the papacy but not necessarily from the Roman character of his own personal faith, changes to English religious life were minimal. During the brief reign of Henry's son, Edward (1547–1553), the theology and worship of the English Church took a decidedly Calvinist tone, but in 1553 Edward was succeeded by Mary, the Catholic daughter of Henry and Catherine. Fueled by her memory of a spurned and humiliated mother, Mary brutally restored Catholicism to the English church, making martyrs of the Protestant leadership in the process. When Mary's reign ended in 1558, English Protestants in exile on the continent returned home with the hope that the new "Virgin Queen" Elizabeth would restore Protestantism to England and complete the reformation.

Restore Protestantism she did, but Elizabeth was shrewd enough to know the value of keeping all her subjects somewhat satisfied. She was intent to repair the national rift between Calvinist Protestants and high-church Anglicans by offering something to nearly everyone, giving everything to no one, and centralizing her power in the process. Elizabeth navigated a middle way, but the result was a church that exhibited few of the radical reforms the Calvinists had hoped to see. In their eyes, the liturgical practice of the church still resembled too much the "papist" trappings of Rome, with its priestly vestments and fixed prayers and a calendar of feast days that encouraged (to their mind) excessive occasions for revelry. Furthermore, the doctrine propagated by Elizabeth's advisors provided a theological latitude that offended Calvinist sensibilities, while the structure of the church—with its priests, bishops, and archbishops—remained virtually unchanged from Catholic days. Increasingly during Elizabeth's long reign, Calvinist detractors voiced concern over the residue of Catholicism and the shortcomings of Protestant reform in the Church of England. Many of those who clamored for more aggressive doctrinal and liturgical reform were pejoratively labeled "Puritans," and although Elizabeth managed to keep the peace, the Puritans' struggle for reform became more vocal, more organized, and more popular throughout her reign.

When Elizabeth died in 1603, the Puritans looked to the transition from the Tudor line to the Stuart kings with cautious optimism. James was king of Scotland, after all, where Calvinist Presbyterianism thrived; surely he would have greater sympathy for the Calvinist cause than Elizabeth's careful politics had allowed. While Elizabeth had failed to satisfy the Puritans' long-ings, however, they quickly discovered that the Stuart kings were much worse. Tolerant of the Puritans early in his reign, James had little stomach for their fastidious theology and became increasingly frustrated with their nagging for reform. As the antagonism between king and Puritans became more acute, James moved to squelch the dissent. Persecution of the Puritans was made official in the final years of James's reign, and after Charles I suc-ceeded his father to the throne in 1625, hostility between royalists and Puri-tans reached an apex. Charles married a Roman Catholic, responded weakly to the growing threat of Catholic France, and favored the anti-Calvinist forces in the English Church. In 1633 Charles would elevate one of these en-thusiastic enemies of the Calvinists, William Laud, to the post of Arch-bishop of Canterbury, entrusting him with the responsibility to stamp out Puritan dissent in England. By the end of the 1630s, Puritans and royalists were engaged in open conflict.

Roger Williams grew up amidst this hostility, and one of his biographers even suggests that he might have witnessed the execution of a few Puritans from the windows of his home on Cow Lane.[1] While there is no evidence to suggest that Puritan sympathies ran in his family, Williams hints of a con-version to Puritanism in his boyhood, perhaps around the age of eight or nine.[2] Of course, such a boyhood conversion had little public consequence at the time. More immediately important to the trajectory of his life was his apprenticeship (perhaps around the age of fifteen) to Sir Edward Coke, the premier jurist in seventeenth-century England. Coke and Williams's family frequented the same parish church in Smithfield, and it is perhaps there that Coke discovered young Williams, diligently taking notes on the Sunday ser-mon as his schoolteachers required him to do. Coke needed a secretary, so he took on Williams as scribe for his business in the Star Chamber, a court of inquisition in which Williams would have a clear view of the persecution of Puritans. In his role as Coke's assistant, Williams not only perfected his

1. Ola Elizabeth Winslow, *Master Roger Williams: A Biography* (New York: Octagon Books, 1973), chapter 3. Winslow's biography remains the most detailed account of Williams's life, particularly of his boyhood in England.
2. Ibid., 28.

shorthand (a skill that would serve him well in his adult roles as ambassador for both a fledgling colony and the principle of religious freedom), but he perhaps also acquired some of his facility with logical argumentation, which he would later put to great use in debates over church and state with the New England authorities.

In the short term, the greatest gift Williams received from Coke was the means to higher education. With the jurist's sponsorship, Williams enrolled first at Charterhouse and then, in 1624, at Cambridge's Pembroke College. While Pembroke College was more loyal to the Anglican establishment, Cambridge as a whole was dominated by teachers with Puritan ties. Thomas Cartwright, William Perkins, and William Ames had held posts at the university, and the Puritan presence was so heavy that it is fair to say that Cambridge was at this time "the West Point of Puritan Calvinism."[3] Williams studied for the ministry at Cambridge, and upon graduation he signed the Subscription Book, a testament to the orthodoxy of his faith and his loyalty to the Church of England and the crown. By making this oath, he promised conformity to the established church's standards for doctrine and liturgical practice, hardly the bold mark of a Puritan in the making. But instead of taking a parish position, Williams (after lingering at Cambridge for a couple more years) chose to serve as chaplain at the estate of William Masham of Essex, a move more telling than his momentary bow to graduation requirements. It was common practice at the time for Puritan-leaning clergymen to serve as chaplains or lecturers for the estates of sympathizers in order to escape the direct supervision of ecclesiastical powers to whom they could not, in good conscience, conform. Masham was such a Puritan sympathizer, and Williams's decision to accept the offer to serve as chaplain at Essex suggests that by the time he left Cambridge in 1629, he was committed to the Puritan cause.

While at Essex, Williams made important connections with prominent Puritan leaders in England. When Charles ascended the throne in 1625, the political climate quickly became more dangerous for Puritans, and some who had labored domestically for church reform under Elizabeth and James now thought seriously about relocating. With England active in the exploration of the new world, some Puritan leaders were considering emigration to America, with the hope of establishing a Christian community that could

3. I am indebted to Charles M. Swezey for this image.

serve as a model for reform at home. In July 1629, several of these Puritan leaders gathered in Lincolnshire to discuss such a venture, and Williams attended the meeting. The next year a band of Puritans left England under the charter of the Massachusetts Bay Colony, and that winter Williams and his new wife, Mary, set out on the *Lyon* to join them.

Williams in Massachusetts

When Roger and Mary Williams arrived in Massachusetts in early 1631, they were greeted enthusiastically. Governor John Winthrop recorded the arrival of this "godly minister" in his journal, and Williams's emerging reputation as a minister of integrity and charisma soon led the leaders of the Boston church—the most prominent church in the colony—to offer Williams a position. Boston's current teacher (the Puritan title for an assistant pastor), John Wilson, needed to return to England to persuade his wife to join him in New England, and in his absence the church would need a new minister, a great honor they invited young Williams to accept. Williams, however, rejected the congregation's invitation on the grounds that they had not explicitly renounced the Church of England. To the surprise and bewilderment of the Boston leadership, Williams had "outed" himself as a separatist.

All Puritan dissenters in seventeenth-century England objected to the "Roman" (that is, Roman Catholic) vestiges in the official church's liturgy, theology, and ecclesiastical practices. But while they shared a common dissatisfaction with the official church, their responses to the abuses they observed divided them into two camps. Many of the Puritans considered themselves faithful members of the official church despite—or, more accurately, because of—their objections to the current state of the institution. These Puritans prayed and labored for improvement from within the church. Other Puritans, having given up any hope for internal reform, advocated the abandonment of the English Church and the formation of "true" congregations that followed more faithfully the pattern of early Christianity. These more radical Puritans were known as "separatists." According to the separatists' primitivist ecclesiology, true churches focused their worship on the preaching and hearing of the Word, disciplined themselves according to a close reading of scripture, and governed themselves locally without the hierarchy and trappings of higher offices (like bishops). To the minds of separatist Puritans, the Church of England was hopelessly entangled in Roman polity, elevated the importance of the Book of Prayer over that of the Bible, and evinced a lax sense of internal discipline. In order to protect the purity of the church, therefore, separatist Puritans believed that they must renounce the official church and gather in new, holier communities.

Both groups were English Puritans in their Calvinist theology, anti-Catholic ecclesiology, and interest in religious and moral reform, but blanket use of the term "Puritan" by modern students of the period risks obscuring the deep differences between these groups. In the seventeenth century, too, the term "Puritan" was sometimes used indiscriminately, and nonseparatist Puritans were particularly sensitive about being confused with their separatist counterparts. The nonseparatists generally believed that the separatists got their ecclesiology all wrong, that a purge of the church did not require the absolute rejection of the current institution and a reconstitution from scratch. More than bad theology, however, the nonseparatist Puritans were concerned with the unfortunate political consequences of being associated with separatism. In withdrawing from the established church, separatists denied the authority of its bishops and, by extension, that of the king who appointed them. A rebuff of the established church, then, was not only a theological statement but political rebellion as well, and those who rejected the church risked facing all the normal consequences of treason against the king. Nonseparatist Puritans thus had good reason to avoid association with their more radical comrades, lest their similar pleas for ecclesiastical reform be taken for complicity in the separatist cause. Compared to the separatists' rejection of the official church, the nonseparatist Puritans' demands seemed downright mild, but they correctly feared that royalists would fail to notice the subtle distinction. For this reason, these Puritans became nervous whenever someone close to them started sounding too much like a separatist.

This fear explains the traumatic reaction that greeted Roger Williams's revelation that he, a well-regarded Puritan minister whose arrival in the Bay Colony was celebrated in the highest ranks, espoused separatism. Massachusetts Bay Colony was governed by leaders and ministers who were mostly nonseparatist in ecclesiology and who preferred to maintain that reputation with the relevant powers at home. Despite their geographical removal from England, Bay Colony leaders envisioned their settlement as a model for the reform of English church and society, not as a symbol of their rejection of the mother church. Challenging the official church invited political retribution on the colony, revocation of its charter, and a premature end to the "holy experiment" its leaders set out to create. Williams certainly was not the only separatist in New England; the leaders of Plymouth Colony to the south of Massachusetts founded their colony explicitly on separatist principles. He was not even the only separatist in the Bay Colony, for the people of Salem had long held positions that sounded suspiciously separatist. But Williams was an especially prominent and vocal separatist, and he quickly became a thorn in the side of the Massachusetts leadership.

Having spurned the congregation in Boston for not removing itself from the Anglican fold, Williams began to petition publicly for the churches of Massachusetts to separate from and denounce the Church of England. While no record of his pronouncements from this period survives, Williams would later articulate his commitment to separatism in a debate of letters with fellow Puritan John Cotton. The early salvos in that exchange, too, have been lost, but during his first return to London in 1644, Williams published a response to Cotton entitled *Mr. Cotton's Letter, Lately Printed, Examined, and Answered.* In this treatise, which debated the circumstances surrounding Williams's banishment but was largely a defense of separatism, Williams argued that the Boston leaders, despite their objections to his theology, implicitly practiced separatism by physically removing themselves from the direct supervision of the Church of England and granting church membership only to persons "whom they carefully examine and cause to make a public confession of sin and profession of their knowledge and grace in Christ." Their objections to separatism amounted to hypocrisy, argued Williams, but they also betrayed the values of Puritanism itself, for separatism's concern for the purity of church and worship was simply the logical extension of important Puritan doctrines. Indeed, insisted Williams, Calvinist theology and the witness of countless faithful in church history testified to the necessity of a "hedge or wall of separation between the Garden of the church and the wilderness of the world." Williams counted the apostate Church of England among the profanations of the latter, and he insisted that godly Christians must explicitly reject the waywardness of the official church before they could establish true congregations.

After rejecting the Boston church's offer, Williams migrated to the town of Salem, where he served briefly as teacher for the more separatist-leaning congregation there. Eventually, however, Williams became dissatisfied with the degree of his Salem friends' commitment to separatism (or at least their willingness to live out that commitment within the larger context of non-separatist Massachusetts Bay). Later in 1631 he moved from Salem to the openly separatist Plymouth Colony, where he lived in apparent comfort of conscience for a short period of time. But eventually he wore out his welcome there, too, for reasons that are not altogether clear. Governor Bradford attributed Williams's problems in Plymouth to "strange opinions" he was espousing.[4] These opinions may have had to do with his radical separatism, which evidently surpassed even the commitment of the residents of Plymouth. (In particular, Williams objected to the habit of some Plymouth residents of worshipping in Anglican parishes on their return to London, in violation of their professed Puritan scruples.) More likely, however, the "strange opinions" that led to his undoing in Plymouth had to do with his increasingly vocal defense of the land rights of Native Americans.

While in Plymouth, Williams served no congregation, so he supported himself by operating a trading post with the local Native American tribes, principally the Narragansett. (Williams's father had also been a trader, and Williams may have learned some of the necessary skills from him.) Through his interactions with the Native Americans, Williams acquired a sophisticated knowledge of their language and customs and a profound respect for them as moral beings. He also developed deep friendships with several of their leaders, none more intense than his relationship with Canonicus, chieftain of the Narragansetts. It was Canonicus who would grant Williams the initial property for the Providence settlement, refusing to take payment in the transaction. In gratitude, Williams secured gifts and favors for Canonicus for the rest of the sachem's life, and their relationship ensured relative peace between the Narragansetts and the English, not only in Rhode Island but in the United Colonies as well.

On the basis of his interactions with Canonicus and his broader knowledge of the tribe, Williams compiled a guide to the Narragansett language entitled *A Key into the Language of America*, which was published during his first return to London in 1643. The *Key* is remarkable not only for its linguistic insight, but also as a sophisticated anthropological study of the Native Americans' customs. In addition, Williams peppered his observations in the *Key* with commentary on the apparent moral superiority of the Native Americans as compared with the so-called Christian English. For in-

---

4. William Bradford, *Of Plymouth Plantation, 1620–1647* (New York: Random House, 1981), 286.

stance, Williams testified of the Native Americans that he "could never discern that excess of scandalous sins amongst them which Europe abounds with. Drunkenness and gluttony, generally they know not what sins they be, and although they have not so much to restrain them (both in respect of knowledge of God and laws of men) as the English have, yet a man shall never hear of such crimes among them—robberies, murders, and adulteries [for instance]—as among the English."[5] Noting that their natural intellectual and moral capacity was on a par with Europeans, Williams observed "a favor of civility and courtesy even among these wild Americans, both among themselves and toward strangers" that served as an indictment of his allegedly more civilized countrymen.[6] His first published work, the *Key* not only would bring Williams fame in an English culture that craved information about the exotic (and potentially convertible) Americans, it would provide the earliest insight into Williams's conviction that common morality— *not* religious uniformity—was the secret to a stable and flourishing human society.[7]

Williams's good relationship with the local tribes would enable him later to serve as an effective mediator between the Native Americans and the English, and the leadership of Massachusetts would appeal to him for such service long after they banished him from their colony. But at first his affection for the Americans threatened the colonies, for during his stay in Plymouth Williams became increasingly vocal in his criticism of the king's charters on which the English colonies were founded. The land in New England belonged to the Americans, Williams asserted, so it was not the king's place to be granting permission for the English to settle on it; instead, the land should be purchased from the natives. Williams's attack on the royal charters concerned the New England leadership, of course, because this challenge to royal authority smacked of treason and jeopardized the health of colonies whose relationship with the crown was already tenuous.

Whether the precipitating disagreement was over the requirements of separatism or the question of the royal charters, eventually Williams became

5. Roger Williams, *A Key into the Language of America* (Bedford, Mass.: Applewood Books, 1997), 143.

6. Ibid., 10.

7. Williams's relationship with the Native Americans and his separatist theology would also inspire a treatise in which he rejected the mass conversion of Americans, entitled *Christenings Not Make Christians* (1645).

so disillusioned (or unpopular) with the residents of Plymouth that he returned to the Bay Colony in 1633. There he took up again with the people of Salem and resumed his call to the Massachusetts churches to separate from the Church of England. He also continued his public advocacy of the Native Americans' land rights, and soon he added another political firestorm to the mix. In May 1635, the Massachusetts General Court voted to require all male residents in the colony to take the Resident's Oath, as a way of soliciting a pledge of loyalty from the droves of new immigrants to the colony. In the seventeenth century, an oath was a customary sign of public trustworthiness and was assumed to be an essential building block of stable society, but Williams almost immediately objected to this requirement of citizenship on theological grounds. Since an oath was a promise declared in the name of God, Williams believed it was essentially a prayer, an act of worship. To require this act of all residents, then, was to enforce a religious practice that he believed could violate the consciences of both unbelievers (who may not subscribe to the implicit religious conviction in the practice) and believers (who might object to participating in an act of worship with unbelievers). From the point of view of the Massachusetts leadership, however, Williams's rejection of the public oath was an attack on the stability of the colony, just as his objection to royal charters had been.

As if being embroiled in these political controversies were not enough, Williams found himself near the center of two other disturbances emanating from Salem. He weighed in on a debate over whether women should cover their heads in church (he believed they should) and was implicated, probably without direct cause, in the case of several prominent residents of Salem who were accused of desecrating the English flag (the perpetrators cut out the red cross that was a part of the flag at the time, because they objected to its Catholic origins). To top it all, in 1635 he also began to insist publicly that civil authority had no right to govern in matters of religion and conscience, arguing that the power of the state extends only over the bodies and goods of its citizens. The increasingly worried Massachusetts General Court monitored Williams's activities in Salem through much of 1635, summoning him periodically to give an account of his teachings. They even attempted to isolate him from his Salem allies by holding up the town's request for additional land until the town disassociated itself from Williams. Chastised by the General Court and increasingly abandoned by the people of Salem, Williams refused to recant any of the public positions he had taken, so that finally in the winter of 1635 the General Court voted to banish him:

> Whereas Mr. Roger Williams, one of the elders of the church of Salem, has broached and divulged diverse new and dangerous opinions against the authority of magistrates [and has] also written letters of defamation both of the magistrates & churches here, & that before and [after] conviction yet maintains the same without retraction, it is therefore ordered that the said Mr. Williams shall depart out of this jurisdiction within six weeks now next ensuing, which if he neglect to perform, it shall be lawful for the Governor & two of the magistrates to send him to some place out of this jurisdiction, not to return any more without license from the Court.[8]

Because he was ill, Williams was granted a stay until spring, so long as he refrained from further public controversy. But Williams proved incapable of keeping his opinions to himself, and when the Court received word that he was again teaching from his home in Salem, they dispatched men to put him on a boat to England (where Archbishop Laud would certainly send him straight to the Tower of London). Some of his friends, however, alerted Williams to the Court's intention, and he set out hurriedly into the New England wilderness.[9] Famously, Williams survived the winter with the help of his Narragansett friends, and in the spring he received from them land for his own settlement south of the Bay Colony, which he called "Providence." His family and some loyalists soon joined him, to be followed by other social delinquents asked to leave Massachusetts (including Anne Hutchinson), who then established the neighboring towns of Portsmouth, Newport, and Warwick. Together these settlements would become Rhode Island and Providence Plantations, a safe haven for freedom of conscience.

The Bloody Tenent of Persecution

Once settled in Providence, Williams apparently began an exchange of correspondence with Boston minister John Cotton over the subject of his banishment. Cotton (1584–1652) had been a leader of some prominence in

---

8. Nathaniel B. Shurtleff, ed., *Records of the Governor and Company of the Massachusetts Bay in New England* (1628–1686), 5 vol. (Boston: W. White, 1853–1854), 1:160–61.

9. One of these friends may have been John Winthrop, who despite disagreeing with Williams in almost all of his theological and political controversies, maintained a warm friendship with Williams through much of his life.

England, and his move to New England was seen as a great benefit to the Puritan experiment in Massachusetts.[10] Cotton accepted the position in the Boston church that Williams had declined, which immediately made Cotton an important figure in both ecclesial and (indirectly, at least) political matters in the colony. Contrary to popular assumption, Puritan society was no theocracy; civil law was not simply torn from the pages of the Old Testament nor were clergy permitted to serve in political office.[11] Nonetheless, although ministers could not directly rule in political matters, they had considerable influence on the proceedings of the General Court through their service as advisors to the civil magistrates. It was in Cotton's role as advisor to the Court that Williams implicated Cotton in his banishment from Massachusetts.

Most of the two men's early correspondence unfortunately is lost, but in 1643 Williams returned to London to secure a charter for the four towns of Rhode Island. Both Massachusetts and Connecticut, uneasy with the presence of unorthodox misfits right outside their borders, had on different occasions conspired with residents of Rhode Island to annex property and reassert traditional Puritan discipline in the wayward colony. Williams went to London to plead his colony's case to Parliament, and while he was there one of the letters Cotton wrote to him on the subject of his banishment "mysteriously" found itself in print. In this letter, Cotton denied Williams's charge that he had masterminded the Puritan deviant's banishment from the Bay Colony. On the contrary, Cotton insisted, he had tried hard to mediate between the Court and Williams and worked to soften the Court's judgment, until he became convinced himself of Williams's stubbornness and danger to Massachusetts. Because Cotton was not a member of the Court, he could not see why Williams would think him responsible for his banishment. Instead, he insisted that Williams had banished himself by refusing to heed the correction of his clergy colleagues.

Cotton was later incensed at the violation of confidentiality he had assumed in their correspondence, but while Williams claimed ignorance concerning how the letter was published, he felt compelled to respond publicly, which he did in *Mr. Cotton's Letter, Lately Printed, Examined and Answered,* published early in 1644. Although Williams acknowledged that Cotton possessed no vote on the Court, he nonetheless insisted that Cotton's counsel to

10. For an introduction to John Cotton, see Sargent Bush, ed., *The Correspondence of John Cotton* (Durham: The University of North Carolina Press, 2001), 1–67.

11. For more on Puritan political theory and practice, see Edmund S. Morgan, ed., *Puritan Political Ideas* (Indianapolis: Bobbs-Merrill, 1965).

the magistrates was instrumental in their verdict. In fact, Williams insisted that some who had voted for his banishment later "with tears to [me] confessed, that they could not in their souls have been brought to have consented to the sentence had not Mr. Cotton in private given them advice and counsel, providing it just and warrantable to their consciences." Disagreement over *why* Williams was banished dominates the treatise, with Williams assuming (contrary to Cotton) that it was for his separatist religious views and not any civil crimes. Whether or not Williams was right to conclude that he was being punished for his religion (the General Court articulated the charges against him in almost exclusively civil terms, but Cotton later let slip that Williams had "banished himself" from the churches), the result was that as early as this treatise, Williams began to articulate his conviction that the ends of religion and the responsibilities of the state should remain separate. While most of *Mr. Cotton's Letter* amounts to an apology for separatist theology, the treatise also features glimpses of what would become Williams's characteristic defense of religious liberty.

Williams soon would have other occasions to explore this commitment to religious liberty, for during his stay in London, Parliament was preoccupied with questions of religion. In league with Scotland against King Charles I, the Calvinist-dominated Parliament in 1643 called into being the Westminster Assembly, a group of divines commissioned to recommend a thorough reform of the Church of England. As thanks for their pledge of military support, the Scots fully expected Parliament to establish Presbyterianism as the official form of liturgy and government in the Church of England, but while the Assembly was dominated by Presbyterians, it also included a small but well-connected group of Independents. The difference between Presbyterian and Independent may seem minor in retrospect, for they shared much in common theologically, including a commitment to Calvinist doctrine and a virulent suspicion of anything resembling Roman Catholicism. But in the seventeenth century no theological difference was minor, and the disagreements between Presbyterians and Independents caused civil discord for the next two decades. Presbyterians were committed to a form of church government in which individual congregations participated in, and were responsible to, higher governing bodies called synods, while Independents (or Congregationalists, as they eventually would be known in America) insisted that every Christian congregation should be an autonomous body modeled after the early Christian communities. Presbyterians thought Independents lacked a mechanism for collective discipline and thus a means for ensuring the orthodoxy of particular congregations. Independents considered Presbyterianism simply a variation of the "papist" hierarchy already at work in the Church of England. In particular, many Independents could see little difference between the persecution they suffered under Catholic and Anglican rule and the restrictions threatened by the Presbyterian majority; as Independent John Milton famously penned it, on the matter of religious establishment, the "new *Presbyter* is but old *Priest* writ large."[12]

When Presbyterianism appeared to be on the verge of becoming the official religion of England, a caucus of Independents known as the "Five Dissenting Brethren" published a public attack on the Presbyterians and an argument for the strengths of congregationalism. The Presbyterians quickly responded, and the rising hostility between Protestant factions threatened to divide the Parliamentary base and further complicate England's civil war. In response, and only weeks after the appearance of *Mr. Cotton's Letter*, Williams published a short treatise entitled *Queries of Highest Consideration*. *Queries* was a rejection of the idea of an "official religion" of either Presbyterian or Independent flavor. As a separatist, Williams argued that the best thing for the church was to remove itself from the pollution of political entanglement. Biblical authority did not sanction the creation of a politically established church; in fact the use of civil power to enforce religion flew in the face of Christ's intention for the church. As an advocate of religious liberty, Williams insisted that a collusion of church and state and the persecution of dissenters guaranteed neither ecclesial purity nor civil health. Both biblical precedent and recent English history testified to the futility of trying to maintain religious orthodoxy or civic morality through the punishment of minority religions.

In *Queries* Williams fired a single shot over the bow of religious establishment, but in the summer of 1644 he would provide a more sustained attack. A decade earlier John Cotton had received a copy of an anonymous critique of religious persecution entitled *An Humble Supplication to the King's Majesty*.[13] He thought that Williams had sent him the text, so when he prepared a de-

---

12. John Milton, "On the New Forcers of Conscience under the Long Parliament" (1647), in *John Milton: Complete Poems and Major Prose,* ed. Merritt Y. Hughes (Indianapolis: Odyssey Press [Bobbs-Merrill], 1957), 144–145.

13. The text was originally published anonymously around 1620. Williams attributed it to John Murton, a religious dissenter who was jailed in London for his appeals to liberty of conscience. Williams includes the text, renamed "Scriptures and Reasons," as a preface to *The Bloody Tenent of Persecution.* Cotton's response to the text serves as the pretense for *The Bloody Tenent,* but because Williams was not the author, "Scriptures and Reasons" is not included in this volume.

tailed rebuttal, he forwarded it to Williams. In possession of Cotton's treatise
while in London, Williams assumed that it was a public document and prepared a hurried response, published under the title *The Bloody Tenent
[Tenet] of Persecution for Cause of Conscience, discussed in a Conference between Truth and Peace, Who, in all tender Affection, present to the High Court
of Parliament (as the Result of their Discourse) these (amongst other Passages)
of highest consideration.* Mercifully known since as simply *The Bloody Tenent
of Persecution,* Williams's treatise was a point-by-point response to Cotton's
defense of the pursuit of religious uniformity in Massachusetts. Once again
Williams would infuriate Cotton by making public what he thought was a
private exchange, but the result would be one of the most significant de-
fenses of religious liberty in western history.[14]

Written as a dialogue between the figures Truth and Peace, *The Bloody
Tenent of Persecution* masterfully (if unsystematically) harnesses the "authority of holy Scriptures, the commands and declarations of the Son of
God" and the lessons learned from "the lamentable experiences of former
and present slaughters" in the name of religion in order to refute the core assumptions that lay behind the Puritan practice of enforcing religious orthodoxy with the power of the state. As the antagonist of the treatise, John
Cotton represented the conventional Puritan preference for religious uniformity. The Massachusetts Puritans had not emigrated from England in
pursuit of religious freedom for everyone, but to pursue religious freedom
for themselves or, more accurately, to meet their responsibility to establish a
social community that reflected the religious and moral standards they believed to be true. Having achieved a certain level of success in their effort to
create a "holy commonwealth," they assumed that maintaining the health of
religion was an important social objective. Religious laxity would endanger
the church and by doing so would also threaten the most important source
for moral education and social cohesion in the colony.[15] Religious deviance

14. The second half of *The Bloody Tenent of Persecution* is an equally detailed response to a document entitled "A Model of Church and Civil Power," which elaborates on the cooperative powers of
church and state to which Williams had such strong objections. Williams claimed that this document was prepared by the Bay Colony ministers and sent to the church in Salem as a chastisement
for their delinquency and their support of Williams, but Cotton denied both his role in it and that it
was ever sent to Salem.

15. For more on the Puritan defense of religious uniformity, see Timothy L. Hall, *Separating
Church and State: Roger Williams and Religious Liberty* (Urbana: University of Illinois Press, 1998),
chapter 2; Edmund S. Morgan, *Roger Williams: The Church and the State* (New York: W. W. Norton,
1967), chapters 3 and 4; Irwin H. Polishook, *Roger Williams, John Cotton, and Religious Freedom: A
Controversy in New and Old England* (Englewood Cliffs, N.J.: Prentice-Hall, 1967), 1–4, 26–30.

would invite anarchy and chaos to the commonwealth; but perhaps more worrisome for Puritans, "liberty in all matters of Worship and of Faith" could be, as Richard Baxter assumed, "the open and apparent way to set up Popery in the Land."[16] Better to clamp down hard on religious deviance, for all the talk about liberty "signifieth the Reign of Satan, and not of Christ." Therefore, as Cotton himself would write, "if a man hold forth & Professe any Errour, or false way, with a boisterous, & arrogant spirit, to the disturbance of Civill Peace, He may justly be punished according to the quality, & measure of the Disturbance caused by Him."[17]

Considering it an obvious social good that right religion be maintained, the Puritans saw little problem in commissioning the state with the authority to pursue that good. Most Puritans (and most seventeenth-century Christians) believed that the Bible entrusted responsibility for defending the faith to civil authority. Romans 13 referred to secular authorities as the ministers of God, commissioned to punish impiety and immorality. More to the point, ancient Israel provided a biblical template for how religion and secular government should coexist, with separate institutions (temple and crown) and offices (priests and kings) cooperating to ensure the good of both. Although kings were not permitted to interfere with sacerdotal functions, Old Testament law gave them license to use the sword against blasphemers and idolaters in order to protect the integrity of religious practice. Applying the precedent of Israel to the Massachusetts experiment, Cotton insisted that "the external equity of that judicial law of Moses was of moral force and binds all Princes to express that seal and indignation, both against blasphemy . . . and against seduction to idolatry."[18] As in ancient Israel, church and state were institutions with largely separate functions in Puritan society, but they cooperated in the shared goal of creating a holy commonwealth worthy of God's continued blessing.

16. Richard Baxter, *A Holy Commonwealth,* ed. William Lamont (1659; reprint, Cambridge: Cambridge University Press, 1994), 29–30.

17. Letter from John Cotton to John Hall, *The Correspondence of John Cotton,* 194. Sargent Bush identifies the recipient of this letter by Williams's version of the events surrounding Cotton's acquisition of *An Humble Supplication,* namely, Williams's contention that it was not he but a "Master Hall of Roxbury" who sent the text to Cotton for his reaction. However Cotton came to possess *An Humble Supplication,* he seems to have sent at least a copy of his response (that is, this letter) to Williams, whether or not Williams was the principal addressee.

18. John Cotton, *The Bloody Tenent, Washed and Made White in the Blood of the Lamb* (1647), in Polishook, *Roger Williams, John Cotton, and Religious Freedom,* 85.

Entrusting civil magistrates with the responsibility for maintaining right religion placed the Puritans squarely in the mainstream of the Calvinist tradition, for Calvin himself assumed that "no government can be happily established unless piety is the first concern."[19] Articulating a sentiment many Puritans would accept, Calvin taught that "civil government has as its appointed end . . . to cherish and protect the outward worship of God, to defend sound doctrine of piety and the position of the church, to adjust our life to the society of men, to form our social behavior to civil righteousness, to reconcile us with one another, and to promote general peace and tranquility."[20] While the magistrate had no authority to meddle in the internal duties of the clergy, he was responsible for promoting the overall health of religion in the commonwealth, which included the punishment of error so arrogant or disruptive as to constitute a threat to the church or the state. This responsibility was intricately intertwined with other social ends that civil government was divinely ordained to pursue, so that Calvin could easily have endorsed Cotton's assertion that "the flourishing of religion is the flourishing of the civil state, and the decay of religion is the decay and ruin of the civil state."[21]

The importance of the magistrate's responsibility to promote religion ultimately derived from the covenant the Puritans believed God had made with their civil community. The covenant was a central image in the Puritans' theology, which they employed on a variety of levels to make more comprehensible the incomprehensible Calvinist God. The Puritans believed that God had made two covenants with human beings. The covenant of works was God's promise of life to Adam upon the condition that he live in perfect obedience; when Adam broke that covenant, God established a second with fallen humanity, the covenant of grace. In the covenant of grace, God promised life and salvation to human beings through Christ, as well as the ability to accept that promise (since the Fall rendered human beings incapable of doing so on their own), requiring only faith in return.

The covenant metaphor was instrumental in the Puritans' understanding

19. John Calvin, *Institutes of the Christian Religion,* 2 vols., trans. Ford Lewis Battles and ed. John T. McNeill (Philadelphia: Westminster Press, 1960), IV.20.9, 1495.

20. Ibid., IV.20.2, 1487.

21. John Cotton, *The Bloody Tenent, Washed and Made White in the Blood of the Lamb* (1647), in Alan Heimert and Andrew Delbanco, eds., *The Puritans in America: A Narrative Anthology* (Cambridge, Mass.: Harvard University Press, 1985), 205.

of personal salvation, but they also extended it to elucidate their understanding of the institutions of church and state. A church was a group of
faithful Christians who made covenant with one another and God to live
faithfully together as "visible saints" in the pattern bequeathed to them by
Christ. Similarly, a commonwealth rested on at least an implicit covenant
between its members to honor laws held in common and to work together
for the public good, a covenant to which God was a party, too. While the Puritans were clear in their Calvinist conviction that the efficacy of the covenant of grace was not dependent upon the actions of the human participants, they were more willing to consider the success of church and social
covenants with God as being contingent on the communities' moral and religious faithfulness. In these covenants, God pledged to bless the faithful
church or "holy commonwealth" that maintained true religion within its
bounds and served its weakest members, and these faithful societies would
serve as the building blocks for Christ's kingdom when he returned to earth.
But God would abandon the society that permitted impiety and injustice to
flourish in its bounds, which is why enforcing religious uniformity was so
paramount a social goal among the Puritans. Laxity in matters of religion
would displease God and threaten the removal of God's good pleasure.

Although he was a Puritan in his theological convictions, Williams rejected most of the political implications of the Puritans' doctrines. In particular, he objected to their assignment of religious authority to civil magistrates, and he rejected the idea that religious uniformity was necessary to the
health of either church or civil society. The dark underside of a social policy
of religious uniformity, argued Williams, is the persecution of dissenters
necessary to ensure that uniformity. Persecution in the name of piety injures
the health of the church more than does the existence of religious diversity,
since persecution is "so directly contradicting the spirit and mind and practice of the Prince of Peace." In addition, intolerance is "destructive to the
civil peace and welfare of all kingdoms, countries, and commonwealths" in
the strife that it causes; thus, civil compulsion of religion also fails to ensure
the social stability for which it aims. Neither the church nor a productive society requires religious compulsion for its well-being, insisted Williams, and
in fact "true civility and Christianity may flourish in a state or kingdom,
notwithstanding the permission of diverse and contrary consciences." To
insist otherwise contradicts the testimony of human experience and the
wishes of the divine and constitutes a "bloody tenent"—"bloody to the bodies, first of the holy witnesses of Christ Jesus" and "second of the nations

and peoples slaughtering each other for their several respective religions and consciences."

Williams argued that religious authority and state power should be distinct and separate, and that the civil powers should not only respect religious liberty but protect it. In articulating these positions, first in *The Bloody Tenent* and then in several texts published during his return to London in 1652, Williams argued on three fronts: the theological, the political, and the practical. On the theological front, Williams noted that civil enforcement of religious uniformity violated the spirit of the gospel and was contrary to the intentions of Christ, who wished that faith be spread not by coercion but by persuasion. Williams insisted that a "state policy and state necessity which (for the peace of the state and preventing of rivers of civil blood) permits the consciences of men will be found to agree most punctually with the rules of the best politician that ever the world saw, the King of kings, and Lord of Lords." Not only did Williams think that using state force to further the ends of the church was contrary to the character of Christianity, he also believed it was counterproductive. Rather than helping its cause as the Massachusetts establishment assumed it would, state force imperiled the church, because assimilation of the sinful means of power politics obscured the church's true identity and proper allegiance. Williams believed that historically the church was purest when it existed as a minority religion under the shadow of an ambivalent or even antagonistic state. When Constantine elevated the church to an official institution of the Roman Empire, "Christianity fell asleep in Constantine's bosom." To Williams, the success of the church did not require assistance from the state; its success required that it distance itself from coercive politics, faithfully proclaim the gospel, and maintain its own internal discipline, without—and even in the face of—state power. "When Christianity began to be choked, it was not when Christians lodged in cold prisons, but down beds of ease, and persecuted others."

On the political front, Williams rejected the conventional Puritan assumption that religious uniformity was necessary for a good society. His arguments in this arena are especially worth noting, for many assume that Williams's preoccupation with religious liberty was solely an extension of his concern for the church. The difference between Williams and Thomas Jefferson, so the saying goes, is that the latter was trying to protect the state from the church, while the former was only interested in protecting the church from the state. This pithy analysis fails from both sides, but it does particular damage to an accurate reading of Williams, for Williams's defense of religious liberty and the separation of church and state was rooted in both ecclesial and political interests, in both a concern for the purity of the church and an appreciation for what makes a commonwealth flourish. Toward this latter end, Williams argued against religious compulsion as a requirement of the good society on the grounds that religious uniformity did not ensure social stability and peace. Appealing to the rich Christian tradition of natural law, Williams asserted that God endows all human beings with a basic capacity for morality, for peaceful coexistence and social cooperation, independent of religious convictions (or the lack of them). Holding up his Native American friends as the quintessential example, he argued that social cooperation and civility are not particular to adherents to the Christian faith: "Hence it is that so many glorious and flourishing cities of the world maintain their civil peace, yea the very Americans and wildest pagans keep the peace of their towns and cities, though neither in one nor the other can any man prove a true Church of God in those places." Williams agreed that a peaceful and productive commonwealth required the cultivation of public virtue, but he denied that unified subscription to Protestant Christianity was necessary to ensure that virtue.

In addition to questioning the necessity of religious uniformity to social morality, Williams argued that civil authority lacked the ability to ensure this uniformity. He pointed out that unless one could guarantee that only "true" Christians served as magistrates (thus establishing a religious litmus test for public service and depriving the state of the talents of gifted but unqualified citizens), the protection of orthodoxy potentially would be entrusted to religious deviants. As an important corollary to this argument, Williams also employed the Puritans' political theory of popular consent to point out that entrusting the defense of religion to the magistrates amounted to yielding the determination of true religion to the whims of popular sentiment. In rejecting the divine right of kings, the Puritans had insisted that authority to rule derives from the consent of the people governed. The logical extension of Puritan political theory on the question of church and state, however, was that by investing magistrates with the power to enforce and defend religion, Puritan commonwealths were implying that the prerogative to determine orthodoxy resides with the people, a concept that the Puritans would find repulsive (had they taken the logic that far). Competency for recognizing heterodoxy and cultivating good religion resided with the clergy, concluded Williams, and the magistrates' jurisdiction was properly limited to the bodies and goods of their citizens.

Complementing his appeals to theology and political theory, Williams observed that, practically speaking, compulsion of religion does not work. Persecution in the name of social harmony actually achieves the opposite, for it tends to create more violence and strife than it prevents. Williams insisted that if public disruption follows religious dissent, that strife usually "is not made by such doctrines but by the boisterous and violent opposers of them." In his experience, "such persons only break the cities' or kingdoms' peace who cry out for prison and swords against such who cross their judgment or practice in religion." Furthermore, persecution cannot work to create the converts it desires because faith is a matter of intellect, subject to the power of persuasion but usually impervious to brute manipulation of the will. As a result, persecution sometimes effects hypocrisy, because it encourages citizens to profess convictions contrary to their own in order to escape punishment; encouraging this lack of trustworthiness is hardly a social asset, argued Williams. But more often persecution creates martyrs, for force usually manages only to harden the convictions of its victims: "Now all these consciences walk on confidently and constantly even to the suffering of death and torments, and are more strongly confirmed in their belief and conscience, because such bloody and cruel courses of persecution are used toward them." Persecution creates hypocrites and martyrs, perhaps, but it does not regularly produce converts, for faith requires search and examination, the application of persuasive arguments, and the provision of intellectual evidence to persuade.

Many of Williams's conclusions about the impracticability of religious compulsion in *The Bloody Tenent* and other works derive from his theological understanding of the workings of conscience. The conscience in Puritan theology was understood to be an internal moral compass, the intuitive recognition of divine law, and the locus of God's judgment and direction. Conscience was the "mean between God and man," as Calvin put it;[22] and as such the Puritans recognized the moral authority of appeals to conscience and respected a limited freedom of conscience among believers. At the same time, most Puritans took for granted that the dictates of a so-called erroneous conscience were subject to correction according to the "objective" standards of the Bible. In fact many Puritans argued that because conscience was attuned to the divine law, it could not disagree with scriptural mandates; instances of apparent disagreement were really cases of a person willfully dis-

---

22. Calvin, *Institutes of the Christian Religion*, III.19.15, 848.

regarding both the teachings of the Bible and the intuitions of his or her own conscience. Willful disobedience of both internal and written revelation invited religious sanction and civil punishment, and the idea of extending liberty of conscience to those who would exercise it in this way was absurd to the Puritans.

Although Williams never offered his own systematically developed theology of conscience, his appeals for religious liberty depended upon a variation of the Calvinist understanding of the moral faculty. In *The Bloody Tenent*, Williams described conscience as "the secret checks and whisperings" that haunt all persons, regenerate or not, and which "take God's part against man's self, in smiting [and] accusing [him]." In the sequel to his greatest treatise, Williams offered an even more straightforward definition: "a persuasion fixed in the mind and heart of a man which forces him to judge (as Paul said of himself, a persecutor) and to do so and so, with respect to God [and] his worship." Metaphorically, conscience was "the candle of the Lord, searching . . . within the bosom of all mankind." This "spirit," he claimed, resides in all persons, though it may be more refined in some by education, observation, experience, or simply "finer animal spirits." But the authority of conscience derived from its status as the voice of God's judgment "searching" within a person, and Williams cautioned that persecution of those following the dictates of conscience could be tantamount to fighting against God himself.

Williams's assumption that conscience was a moral authority common to all human beings was vitally important to his arguments for religious freedom. The capacity to exercise the deliberative functions of this moral faculty may be more or less healthy in a particular person, but "this conscience is found in all mankind, more or less, in Jews, Turks, Papists, Protestants, [and] Pagans." In fact, a "conscience of good and evil" was something that even "every savage Indian in the world has," a fact that he confirmed in his substantial interactions with the Native Americans.[23] While he believed that all human beings have a conscience, however, Williams was not so naïve as to think that everyone's conscience operated properly. Some people commit social crimes because they disregard their conscience, of course, but some transgress accepted standards of good and evil at the behest of conscience—

---

23. According to his testimony in the *Key*, Williams believed that Native Americans not only valued mature moral conscience more than the English, but they also showed far more respect for variations in conscience than he observed in his own society, certainly more than he himself experienced in the Massachusetts Bay Colony. See, for instance, *Key*, 129.

in other words, a conscience could be wrong. Oddly enough, despite his occasional use of the language of "erroneous" or "blind" conscience, Cotton often implied that the conscience could not err and that in fact all social deviance was a result of sinning against what conscience taught to be right and good. Dissenters were guilty of either ignorance (misunderstanding the dictates of their own conscience) or malice (willfully disregarding it). If they were guilty of ignorance, the civil and religious authorities were obliged to offer correction, first privately and then publicly as necessary. If dissenters persisted in the claim of "conscientious objection" even after being shown the error of their ways, Cotton believed that such perpetrators were guilty of malice and should be punished by the magistrate. Such a verdict was affirmed by the conscience itself.

By contrast, Williams believed that conscience could err. As he understood the conscience to be primarily a faculty of the intellect, Williams believed that "erroneous conscience" was usually a matter of improper understanding; an erroneous conscience misunderstood the relevant moral or religious principles, or misapplied them to the situation at hand. Since conscience was not a volitional experience (that is, not subject to control of the will), force normally would not work to change it. Williams believed it absurd to suggest that persons could "will or entrust such a power to the civil magistrate to compel their souls and consciences" to conform to convention or a government mandate, for conscientious conviction is by definition an inalienable experience over which no third party can assume control. To try to change matters of conscience by force was to Williams impractical and irrational, and in fact risked abusing conscience to the point that it ceased to function properly in a person:

> The straining of men's consciences by civil power is so far from making men faithful to God or man that it is the ready way to render a man false to both. My ground is this: civil and corporal punishment do usually cause men to play the hypocrite, and dissemble in their religion, to turn and return with the tide, as all experience in the nations of the world does testify now. . . . This binding and rebinding of conscience, contrary or without its own persuasion, so weakens and defiles it that it (as all other faculties) loses its strength, and the very nature of a common honest conscience.

Conscientious conviction is subject only to the rules of understanding, which effect change on belief not by force of will but by persuasion, education, argumentation, and "Search and Examination." Williams recognized that there would be moments when public safety justified the magistrate's compulsion of behavior that might violate a citizen's conscience, but even in those instances when the pursuit of the common good permitted it, there still was no avoiding the fact that the civil authority was violating the conscience of the dissenter. And for Williams the circumstances that permitted such compulsion were much rarer than those his fellow Puritans would allow. As social policy, Williams feared that the systematic repression of conscience threatened both church and state; it risked punishing the righteous as well as abusing citizens to the point that they would learn to disregard deeply held principles and intuitions.

Arguments "from Religion, Reason, [and] Experience"

Williams's thoughts on freedom of conscience radically departed from those of many of his fellow Puritans, but they derived from fundamental Calvinist doctrine. Contrary to his reputation through much of the nineteenth and twentieth centuries, Williams was neither a rationalist nor a transcendental seeker; he was in most ways an orthodox Puritan. Indeed, he based his entire apology for religious liberty on sources of authority his Puritan counterparts would recognize and respect, even if they disagreed vehemently with his use of them. He began *The Bloody Tenent of Persecution* with his intention to present arguments from "Religion, Reason, [and] Experience," and by the end of *The Bloody Tenent Yet More Bloody* he was still "humbly confident of Grace and Conscience, Reason, and Experience" being on his side.

Williams's preferred method of biblical interpretation was thoroughly Puritan, for instance, though in his hands it traveled to places his Massachusetts colleagues were unwilling to go. Especially in reading the Old Testament, the Puritans often employed a method of interpretation called typology: figures, communities, events, and images in the Old Testament were read as foreshadows (types) of things to come in the age of Christ and his church (the "antitypes"). For instance, the story of Jonah's being swallowed by a big fish and spit out again three days later was understood to prefigure the death and resurrection of Christ. The love poems recorded in the Book of Canticles (or Song of Songs) were understood typologically as Christ's declaration of love to his church. Even Adam, the first son, was understood as a type for the "second Adam," Jesus Christ. While the Puritans did not ignore the literal meanings of these Old Testament texts, they believed their real benefit lay in how they prefigured the New Testament of Christ.

Not all passages in the Bible were to be read typologically, however, so Puritan theologians were challenged to distinguish those places in the Old Testament where the literal meaning held primary force from those whose significance was gleaned typologically. Some passages inspired disagreement, but others enjoyed more consensus. Most Puritan ministers believed that the parts of the Mosaic Law that governed Israelite rituals were best understood typologically; references to circumcision and Passover, for instance, simply foreshadowed the Christian rites of Baptism and the Lord's Supper. By contrast, they read the moral requirements of the Mosaic Law (including the Ten Commandments) literally and considered them to be as binding on the church as they were on Israel. Another part of the Old Testament that most Puritans applied literally to their own circumstances was the relationship between religion and state in ancient Israel. The Puritans explicitly eschewed a typological reading of Israel, instead adopting God's most favored nation in the Old Testament as their inspiration for constructing a Christian commonwealth in which religion and civil power were closely aligned. Just as God blessed or punished Israel in response to the piety of her kings and the purity in her religion, so Massachusetts's fortunes would depend on raising up devout leaders who looked after the good of religion in the colony with the powers of civil government.

Like his Puritan colleagues, Williams read the Bible typologically; but he believed Cotton and others erred when they read the collusion of religion and state in ancient Israel as license to recreate a similar policy in New England. The proper "antitype" for Israel was not the polis but the church, which Jesus commissioned to defend religion not with the sword, but with "spiritual weapons"—the Word, prayer, and powers of persuasion. According to Williams, in the life and death of Jesus Christ, God had radically changed the way he related to human beings. No people retained "most favored nation" status any longer; God shifted his special bond from a particular state to the church. After Jesus Christ, the language of divine covenant was misplaced in the political arena; social communities simply cohered and flourished by virtue of "covenants" among citizens themselves. But if the church was now the people of God, then the lessons gleaned from the pattern of Israel had to be adjusted accordingly. This meant spiritualizing them, or reading Israel almost completely as typology for the church. For Williams, Jesus himself embodied the difference between the types of the Old Testament and the antitypes of the New, for unlike the kings of Israel Jesus refused to resort to violence, instead spreading his message by teaching and exhortation. Williams claimed that to talk of a covenant between God and the state that justified violent enforcement of religion was to misread the Bible's typology and illicitly baptize sinful social structure. Utilizing conventional Puritan interpretative method, then, Williams turned Puritan theology on itself, undercutting much of the biblical defense of religious coercion and rooting his own apology for religious liberty in scriptural authority.

Williams's scriptural disagreements with Cotton were not all about Old Testament typology, however. Another prominent point of debate between the two men lay in their contrary readings of Jesus' parable of the wheat and tares in Matthew 13:

> Another parable put he forth unto them, saying, "The kingdom of heaven is likened unto a man which sowed good seed in his field. But while men slept, his enemy came and sowed tares among the wheat, and went his way. But when the blade was sprung up, and brought forth fruit, then appeared the tares also. So the servants of the householder came and said unto him, Sir, didst not thou sow good seed in thy field? from whence then hath it tares? He said unto them, An enemy hath done this. The servants said unto him, Wilt thou then that we go and gather them up? But he said, Nay; lest while ye gather up the tares, ye root up also the wheat with them. Let both grow together until the harvest: and in the time of harvest I will say to the reapers, Gather ye together first the tares, and bind them in bundles to burn them: but gather the wheat into my barn. . . ."

Interpreting this parable, Cotton argued that the field was the church, the good seed symbolized true Christian members of the church, and the servants were God's ministers. The tares were subtle hypocrites in the church, members of the congregation who appeared to be faithful but who may secretly hold deviant beliefs. Read this way, the parable served as a warning to ministers not to pursue excessive ecclesial discipline in separatist zeal for a pure church. More importantly, Cotton thought the parable had absolutely nothing to say about the *civil* prosecution of religious deviance.

Williams disagreed with both Cotton's interpretation and his conclusion. In Williams's reading, the field was not the church but the world, the servants were magistrates, and the tares represented not only subtle hypocrites but also more explicit dissenters and nonbelievers living in civil society. Read this way, Williams believed that Jesus was using the parable to warn

against the civil persecution of the "weeds." Permit religious deviants to coexist with the faithful in civil society, counseled Jesus, for magistrates will
not always be able to distinguish the orthodox from others. Just as importantly, in their zeal to root out the deviants, magistrates risk pulling up the
faithful with them. Religious persecution threatens the whole garden with
discord, strife, and violence; better to let the wheat and the tares coexist in
civil society until Jesus returns to sort them out himself. For Williams, this
parable was important biblical testimony that persecution violated the intentions of Jesus himself.

Like any good seventeenth-century Calvinist, then, Williams respected
the preeminent authority of the Bible and relied on that authority in his defense of religious liberty. Also consistent with his Calvinist heritage, however, Williams appealed to extra-biblical sources of authority, including reason and experience, to make his arguments. Far from the antirational
biblicists that they are sometimes portrayed to be, the Puritans made room
for reason in their conception of the moral life, insisting that there is an inherent "reasonableness" to the created and moral order and that this reasonableness projects from the rationality of God. The rational foundation of
the cosmos consisted of what the Puritans called the natural law. A concept
inherited from the catholic Christian tradition, the natural law was "said to
consist of all those divine decrees which called creation into being and by
which it moves. It is a law evident to reason, which is itself a work of God,
and this law, though transcended is by no means invalidated by grace."[24]
Calvin believed human access to this natural law to be severely damaged by
sin, though he thought that enough awareness remained to permit human
beings to cooperate in social communities (and to render them guilty when
they transgress the moral law). The Puritans tended to afford more prominence to natural law in their moral and political arguments than Calvin, invoking it famously in their fight against the extension of royal power prior
to the English civil war. In fact, they used it as a barometer for measuring the
legitimacy of civil law. As historian William Haller summarized the Puritan
position, the "law of man's making must conform to the law of nature or be
of no force."[25] While subscribing to a doctrine of total depravity in matters
of salvation (believing that human faculties alone are insufficient for know-

24. William Haller, *Liberty and Reformation in the Puritan Revolution* (New York: Columbia University Press, 1955), 77.
25. Ibid.

ing God and meriting God's grace), the Puritans at the same time assumed that reason retained its capacity for tapping into the moral framework of creation and guiding human beings in the project of social coexistence. Sin could compromise the reliability of human reason, so the Puritans believed reason was more reliable when it was educated and directed by scripture; but even the unregenerate possessed rudimentary ability to respect basic moral codes and take up the responsibilities of citizenship. The Puritans disagreed over just how optimistic to be about the moral capabilities of the unregenerate. No less of a Puritan divine than William Ames, however, claimed that the powers of reason to invent, seek truth, make laws, and participate in rational discourse are all scaled-down reflections of the rational activity of God; and the fact that these capacities have been partially retained represents the residual *imago dei* in human beings.[26]

Williams subscribed to the Puritan conception of reason and its access to a "law of nature," or "natural wisdom," that serves as "that Candle or Light" in a person and provides moral direction. With its knowledge of natural law, reason provides a moral compass that differentiates human beings from other creatures and enables them to strive for a semblance of moral community. Although Williams taught that reason could be refined by exposure to moral education, scripture, and life experience, he was confident that the law of nature by itself was a moral power common to all human beings and upon which a basic level of moral performance and coexistence could be maintained and expected. The obvious proof for his claim was in the accomplishments of the Native Americans. "The sociableness of the nature of man appears in the wildest of them, who love society; families, cohabitation, and consociation of houses and towns together," wrote Williams in the *Key*.[27] This inclination toward social cooperation, along with the "favor of civility and courtesy even amongst these wild Americans, both amongst themselves and towards strangers," testified to a natural human capacity for moral and social endeavors.[28]

Appeal to the authority of reason and natural law served as a complement to Williams's biblical arguments for religious liberty. Much of Williams's political philosophy, for example, derived from a philosophical justification of

26. William Ames, *The Marrow of Theology* (1623), ed. John Dykstra Eusden (Grand Rapids: Baker Books, 1968), 106.

27. *Key*, 47.

28. Ibid., 9–10.

popular consent as a limit on the nature and extent of governmental power. "Governments . . . have no more power, nor for no longer time, than the civil power or people consenting and agreeing shall entrust them with," wrote Williams, a statement that he admitted had no direct basis in scripture but was confirmed by reason. He also employed arguments from reason in rejecting the idea that an outside party could exercise authority over an inviolable right, such as free conscience. More directly, Williams believed that the imperative to respect freedom of conscience itself was embedded in the natural law. Citing the early church theologian Tertullian, Williams asserted that "by the natural law of equity, men are not to be compelled to any religion, but permitted to believe or not believe at all." Religious persecution deprives people of civil rights that are rooted in their natural rights, which the natural law gives no political institution authority to compromise. Finally, because the law of nature was a universal source of moral authority, Williams argued that religious liberty was a right that ought to be recognized and respected among people of different religions and cultures. Again, he saw the universal imperative to respect freedom of conscience demonstrated among the Native Americans in particular, who showed "a modest Religious persuasion not to disturb any man, either themselves, English, Dutch, or any [other], in their conscience and worship," despite there being no Christian influence among them.[29] Puritans, "Papists," Spanish "Turks," New England governors, English kings, and American sachems all could—and should—recognize the moral imperative to religious freedom, because that freedom was not solely dependent on the authority of biblical revelation but resounded with the set of moral principles that all human beings should recognize as consonant with their own.

Finally, Williams thought that the moral rightness and political value of religious freedom were confirmed not only by reason but also by human experience. Surveying both historical precedent and his contemporary landscape, Williams amassed countless examples of how religious persecution actually increased social instability and violence toward righteous Christians. He also highlighted several examples of societies in which religious tolerance brought greater peace and social benefit (his favorite example was Holland). Furthermore, he was sure that the historical record demonstrated that Christian loyalties were not necessary to make a person an effective civil

29. Ibid., 129.

leader, for "we know the many excellent gifts wherewith it has pleased God to furnish many, enabling them for public service to their countries both in peace and war (as all ages and experience testify), on whose souls he has not yet pleased to shine in the face of Jesus Christ." The net effect of these accounts to Williams was a correlation between the teachings of scripture, the dictates of reason and moral law, and the witness of human experience: religious persecution serves neither church nor state, while religious liberty benefits both. Appealing to these varied sources, Williams argued that religious persecution was theologically dubious, politically dangerous, and practically ineffective to the causes for which his Puritan opponents commended it. By contrast, religious liberty honored the natural need and right to follow one's conscience, put an end to the violence associated with religious compulsion, and opened the way for the appropriate means for spreading good religion: intellectual persuasion and personal search and examination.

Neither Cotton nor the larger Puritan culture in England and New England would be immediately persuaded by the arguments Williams made in *The Bloody Tenent,* which was burned in London within months of its appearance in the summer of 1644. By that time, Williams was headed back to Providence with his new charter, only to return to London in 1652 with Baptist and fellow Rhode Islander John Clarke, again defending the colony's right to independent existence against the incursion of the colonies around it (and traitors within). During this second stay in England, Williams would publish the sequel to *The Bloody Tenent,* a response to Cotton's response imaginatively entitled *The Bloody Tenent Yet More Bloody.* By the time this treatise was released, John Cotton was dead and Cromwell's protectorate was increasingly embarrassed by tales of New Englanders' intolerance. A spirit of religious tolerance was growing in England, but its limits were still unclear, and during his second tenure there Williams contributed to the ongoing debates over religious freedom through the publication of two anonymous tracts entitled *The Fourth Paper, Presented by Major Butler* and *The Examiner Defended.* He also published an attack on mandatory public support of clergy, *The Hireling Ministry None of Christ's.* While Clarke would remain in London for another decade, waiting for a political climate conducive to a renewed charter, Williams returned to Rhode Island in 1653 to resume his work at creating a society founded on a commitment to religious liberty.

Religious Freedom and Social Obligation

Immediately after Williams returned from his first mission to London in 1644, he was elected "chief officer" of Providence. With him thus lay the task of convincing not only his own town but also the other three Rhode Island towns to accept the charter he had procured, as well as the accompanying idea that they were now a single commonwealth. The project was difficult, for a dearth of social institutions, greed for property, political infighting, and an inordinate preference for "self-government" over public responsibility had left the towns with little sense of unity. Raising the pressure, Massachusetts and Connecticut loomed just across the borders of the fledgling colony, ever ready to conspire with disgruntled residents within and assert their jurisdiction over territory the charter had granted to Rhode Island.[30] All four towns finally ratified the charter in 1647, but not without some haggling, and Williams quickly recognized that the citizens of his young colony had "long drunk of the cup of as great liberties," an indulgence that "rendered many of us wanton and too active" in demanding personal liberty.

The occasionally painful intersection of personal liberty and social obligation intensified after Williams's second trip to England. While he was in London defending Rhode Island's charter, Williams had written to his fellow citizens to take care "that no private respects or gains or quarrels may cause you to neglect the public and common safety, peace and liberties" of the colony. When he returned, he found his fellow citizens had failed to heed his counsel, and the lack of social cooperation became particularly dangerous in light of the rising threat of violence from the native tribes that surrounded them. Wasting the goodwill Williams had established as ambassador to the Native Americans, Massachusetts and Connecticut leaders in the 1640s had foolishly manipulated rivalries between the Narragansetts and the Uncas in an attempt to squelch the power of Miantunomi, a leader of the Narragansetts and a close friend of Williams. The eventual death of Miantunomi at the hand of the Uncas, a murder the New England leadership sanctioned, raised tensions between the Narragansett and the English that would flare up again a decade later, when the United Colonies at-

---

30. The schemes of three political rivals in particular—Samuel Gorton, William Harris, and William Coddington—put the integrity of the colony at risk for much of Williams's political tenure. See Winslow, *Master Roger Williams,* especially chapters 10, 11, and 15.

tempted unsuccessfully to domesticate Ninigret, a Narragansett sachem who was accused of attacking Americans allied with the English. In response to the elevated threat, the town of Providence decided to establish a citizen militia; but some members of the colony refused to serve, and many of them (including Williams's brother, Robert) invoked a conscientious objection to compulsory military service as justification. Generally reluctant to endorse the use of violence himself, Williams nonetheless rejected this invocation of religious freedom. To his mind, the defense of the state was one of those rare circumstances in which civil authority could justifiably violate a citizen's conscience. In a note famously referred to as the "Ship of State" letter, Williams assured his fellow citizens "that ever I should speak or write a tittle that tends to such an infinite liberty of conscience" as to encourage the abdication of fundamental social responsibility "is a mistake." In matters of public safety and security, Williams insisted that appeals to freedom of conscience were often out of order, a position his critics (then and since) believed contradicted the liberties he had defended for so long.

The potential for conflict between social obligation and claims of religious freedom grew clearer with two other public disagreements late in Williams's life. Never really compensated for either of his own forays, Williams (now serving as a colony assistant) sought to have John Clarke reimbursed for the extraordinary costs he absorbed in his time in London on Rhode Island's behalf. In the fall of 1664, the General Assembly of Rhode Island levied a tax on each of the towns to cover Clarke's expenses. When the people of Warwick refused to contribute to the cause, Williams wrote them a terse letter. Appealing to the "common honesty and common justice" that dictates that people settle their debts, as well as the "common gratitude" he assumed the people of Warwick should feel for Clarke's labors, Williams implored the town to carry its end. He reminded them that the very liberty they invoked to refuse payment was bought for them by Clarke's work to secure the charter. He also reminded them that, as citizens, they had a share in the common obligations of the colony and that neglect of this social responsibility would be a "stink" that reached "the nostrils of our neighbors, yea of all the inhabitants of the world that hear of us" and soil the reputation of both the colony and the "soul liberty" for which it stood. While he ultimately did not succeed in convincing his fellow citizens to own their responsibility to Clarke (who never received adequate reimbursement for his efforts as colony ambassador), Williams continued to insist that individual freedom, so cherished by Rhode Island's residents, must be balanced with an appreciation for social obligation in order for a society to flourish.

The second major case of Williams's notions of religious freedom conflicting directly with social expectations involved his confrontation with the Quakers. Many Quakers had come to Rhode Island during the first several decades of its existence in order to escape persecution at the hands of the Massachusetts authorities, who abhorred them for both their theological beliefs and their social deviance. The Quakers elevated inner experience of the divine to a degree of importance that challenged the Puritans' deference to the authority of scripture. The Puritans accused the Quakers of antinomianism (literally, "against the law"), and the charge seemed confirmed by their resistance to civil authority as well. The Quakers were notorious for ignoring common social conventions (such as keeping one's hair cropped) and public laws of decency and order (such as clothing oneself in public). An orthodox Puritan himself in many respects, Williams shared the distaste for the Quakers, and he chafed at their increase in his colony. In 1672 his disgust reached its apex when George Fox, the leader of the Quakers, paid a visit to Rhode Island and publicly preached his theology there. Williams felt compelled to respond, but Fox left the colony before Williams could challenge him to a public debate. Williams was left to argue with his surrogates, John Burnyeat, John Stubbs, and William Edmondson, resulting in a belabored verbal contest that Williams recounted in a bloated treatise entitled *George Fox Digg'd out of His Burrowes*.[31]

George Fox is of importance mainly as a demonstration of the Calvinist orthodoxy to Williams's theology, in contrast to subsequent interpretations of him as a rationalist or transcendentalist. But his actual confrontation with the Quakers is instructive as well. On the one hand, Williams had opened Rhode Island to the Quakers at a time when the other Puritan colonies were aggressively pushing them out (or violently suppressing them when they would not leave). Despite his personal intolerance for their theology, Williams felt obligated to extend to the Quakers the same protections from state persecution that he had sought for himself, largely responding to

---

31. Interestingly, though not surprisingly, Williams's attack on Quaker theology is the only piece in his corpus that was published in Massachusetts. The title of the treatise is a play on the names of George Fox and Edward Burrough (1634–1663), a prominent spokesperson for the Quaker movement in the mid-seventeenth century. Both Fox and Burrough engaged in a famous written duel with notable English Puritan John Bunyan.

their deviant beliefs through debate, not civil force. On the other hand, while the presence of the Quakers in Rhode Island testified to the colony's (and Williams's) commitment to religious freedom, Williams occasionally indicated that he was willing to consider civil consequences for the public disruption and violation of social mores that accompanied the Quakers' religious practices. Again critics would charge Williams with contradicting his own defense of religious freedom, though he would counter that occasionally incursion upon personal liberty was necessary to ensure the common good. At any rate, his ambiguous response to the Quakers demonstrated the difficulty of balancing religious freedom and civil order.

Central to his objection to the Quakers' public behavior was Williams's expectation that all citizens adhere to at least a basic sense of common morality, which he routinely called civility. Civility represented human traits of "sociableness," which allowed human beings to live in relations "soberly and justly among their neighbors." Williams believed that there were certain public mores that all human beings should recognize as necessary for a stable society, whether they learn these mores from religion or know them intuitively through conscience and natural law. Common courtesy, a sense of justice, loyalty, honesty, and fidelity were features of common civility that Williams assumed all human beings would value. The gratitude he reminded his Warwick friends they should feel toward one who had labored on their behalf was, to his mind, a mark of civility, as was respect for authority and decorum, which he believed the Quakers violated so flagrantly. In fact, Williams virulently opposed the Quakers not primarily because of theology but because he feared that their practices threatened the cultivation of some of the important virtues of civility, and by extension the moral foundation of society.

The need for civility could justify a limit on personal freedom, suggested Williams, for participation in a particular society implies tacit consent to certain civil obligations. When the exercise of freedom compromises a basic need of the common body, it is appropriate to curtail that liberty in the name of social good. What constituted a public interest so fundamental that it could justifiably restrict the exercise of personal freedoms was and is, of course, a matter of debate. For his part, Williams was more restrained than his Massachusetts counterparts in the list of public interests he would permit to curtail personal freedom, insisting that freedom of conscience normally was vital, and not antithetical, to a stable society. But he also argued that settlement and protection under the Rhode Island charter implicitly obliged its citizens to share in the costs of that charter and its defense. And this same collective obligation made adherence to civil authority and public decency a condition of the Quakers' welcome, too. Ultimately, though, Williams assumed that no desire for social stability could justify the regular and systematic violation of conscience, a conviction that distinguished his more guarded willingness to entertain boundaries on personal liberties from Massachusetts's blatant preference for social order over individual freedom.

The human capacity for civility itself served Williams's defense of religious liberty and the separation of church and state, and he often appealed to the universality of civility in his arguments. Because Williams assumed that all human beings were capable of this kind of social virtue, even without benefit of Christian indoctrination, he argued that civility did not require the establishment of religion; Christian minorities and even non-Christians should be afforded the same rights and responsibilities of citizenship as those in the Puritan majority. To Williams, Cotton's assertion that good citizenship required Christianity was "dangerously destructive to the very roots of all civil relations, converse, and dealing; yea, and any civil being of the world itself." He wondered, for instance, "how Mr. Cotton could chain up all papists in an impossibility of yielding civil obedience" when it was empirically verifiable that Catholics had been and could be perfectly capable of civility. His time with the Native Americans likewise confirmed to him the universality of civility, as he experienced firsthand their extension of mutual care. His *Key* served as a testament to certain universal virtues of civility recognized by humans generally and on display in particular among the Native Americans. The existence of this capability across differences in culture and religion convinced Williams that the establishment of religion was not necessary for the stability of a commonwealth or the cultivation of good citizenship in its members. The teachings of Christianity "are of another sphere and nature than civility is," and in the public realm he thought only the latter was necessary.

For the entire second half of his life, Williams would struggle to cultivate civility and cohesion among the towns of Rhode Island, discovering in the process that the freedoms he championed were not always easily compatible with the sense of mutual responsibility needed to ensure the new colony's day-to-day existence. Along the way, he would serve the colony as legislator, president, and ambassador. Beyond the age of seventy, he would even serve

as a captain in the militia during King Philip's War. From the founding of
Providence to his death around 1683, Roger Williams labored for that delicate balance between social obligation and a robust respect for freedom of
conscience.

Roger Williams and Religious Liberty in America

New England history outside of Rhode Island proceeded with barely a
notice of Williams's passing. Cotton Mather remarked that Williams was at
best an overheated "windmill," a reputation that died slowly in Massachusetts and Connecticut.[32] And despite the trend toward greater toleration in
the next century, Williams was seldom remembered as a pioneer in the effort. Plagued with a reputation for anarchy and moral laxity, Rhode Island
was not regarded as a model of the success of religious liberty; if anything, it
represented to the other colonies the risk to social order that comes from in-
dulging individualism. Even Perry Miller, the twentieth-century literary historian and great friend of the Puritans, admitted that Williams's contribution to the American tradition of religious freedom was slight and symbolic,
for while Williams was its first great defender, he "exerted little or no direct
influence on theorists of the Revolution and the Constitution."[33] Even now,
Williams does not receive the kind of popular attention reserved for the ar-
chitects of the First Amendment. This neglect can be explained by a number
of factors, including the dearth of personal information about Williams
and the near rock-star status our Revolutionary War heroes enjoy in the
American consciousness. An eighteenth-century patriot exudes more glam-
our than an elusive seventeenth-century Puritan deviant, and surely the fact
that Williams wrote as a radical Calvinist and not as the American ev-
eryman renders him even less approachable to some. Certainly the inacces-
sibility of his writings has contributed to this public neglect, a problem that
this volume aims to correct. Regardless of the reasons, however, the lack of
serious attention paid to Williams obscures the important contribution he
made—and continues to offer—to the legacy of religious freedom in the
United States.

32. Edwin Gaustad discusses Mather's assessment of Williams in *Liberty of Conscience: Roger Williams in America* (Grand Rapids: Eerdmans, 1991), 199–201.
33. Perry Miller, *Roger Williams: His Contribution to the American Tradition* (Indianapolis:
Bobbs-Merrill, 1953), 254.

It is unlikely that the framers consulted *The Bloody Tenent* when debating wording for the First Amendment, but the case can be made that Williams's impact on the codification of religious liberty in the United States was more than symbolic. Eighteenth-century evangelical Baptists, themselves given insufficient credit for their role in establishing religious freedom in America, considered Williams to be their denominational forefather and their inspiration on the subject of religious liberty. (He is credited with helping to establish the first Baptist church in America, though he remained a member of the congregation only briefly.) Persecuted mercilessly by the Puritan leadership of seventeenth-century New England, the Baptists grew in the span of a century to become a formidable religious presence in the new Republic, and they used that power to mobilize popular support for liberty of conscience and a more thorough separation of the institutions of religion and state. Harnessing the energy of the First Great Awakening through their preaching and pamphleteering, the Baptists (and other evangelical denominations) were as active a force in the evolution of religious liberty as Enlightenment rationalism, representing the voice of minority religion against state establishments, tax support for clergy, and government licensing requirements that were used as a way of controlling dissenting preachers. They were influential enough to have the ear of presidents, including Thomas Jefferson, who wrote to assure the Danbury (Connecticut) Baptist Association of his commitment to religious freedom when he penned his famous "wall of separation" metaphor. But unlike their Enlightenment-indebted counterparts, the Baptists offered a tradition of theological justification for religious freedom, and for this they had Williams's influence to thank. In fact, the most prominent Baptist spokesman of the eighteenth century, Isaac Backus, appealed directly to Roger Williams in his protest of religious establishment in Massachusetts.[34] As William Lee Miller observes, "the stream of liberty does not run straight from the Protestant Reformation. . . . It does, however, run crookedly, as it were, from those sources, a tributary that grows" in part from the informal evangelical alliance in the early Republic that motivated essential popular support for passage of the

34. See Isaac Backus's *A History of New England, with Particular Reference to the Denomination of Christians Called Baptists* (1777). Edwin S. Gaustad emphasizes the importance of Backus's recovery of Williams in his book *Roger Williams* (New York: Oxford University Press, 2005), 122–124.

First Amendment.[35] Williams's influence through this evangelical tradition should not be underestimated.

Perhaps, too, we should not understate his influence on the Enlightenment theorists, though here the connection is more roundabout through John Locke, the seventeenth-century political philosopher and author of three tracts on religious toleration. Locke matured in the context of the English parliamentary debates over toleration to which Williams contributed significantly, and many arguments that Williams made on behalf of religious freedom appear almost verbatim in Locke's works. Limiting civil jurisdiction to the "bodies and goods" of its citizens, asserting the inalienable nature of religious belief, noting the incompatibility of coercion with the teachings of Jesus, and pointing out the absurdity (from both a religious and political point of view) of the idea of a "Christian commonwealth" are just some of what makes Locke's *Letter Concerning Toleration* read like a lucid Williams. Locke did not develop these ideas de novo, but considered them from within a culture indebted to the Protestant Radicals' life-and-death struggle for religious liberty at midcentury. He may have had occasion to read Williams's contributions to these debates (*The Bloody Tenent of Persecution* would have been considered a little less nefarious by Locke's time), though we cannot know for sure.[36] At the very least, Locke's historical, religious, and intellectual milieu, in which Williams was a principal player, played a formative role in Locke's philosophy of toleration, which substantially influenced the cause of American revolutionaries a century later. Locke helped inspire the Act of Toleration of 1689, through which England brought the American colonies into closer conformity with a newfound respect for religious freedom. In addition, Thomas Jefferson's philosophical indebtedness to Locke is apparent in the "Virginia Bill for Establishing Religious Freedom," while James Madison would have encountered Locke as a necessary part of his Scottish Enlightenment education at Princeton.

35. William Lee Miller, *The First Liberty*, rev. ed. (Washington, D.C.: Georgetown University Press, 2003), 129–130.

36. William Lee Miller is one scholar who insists that Locke read Williams (see *The First Liberty*, 176), though he does not present specific evidence to justify that claim. Others who have asserted Locke's direct indebtedness to Williams include David Little, "Roger Williams and the Separation of Church and State," in *Religion and the State: Essays in Honor of Leo Pfeffer*, ed. James E. Wood, Jr. (Waco: Baylor University Press, 1985), 7; and Winthrop S. Hudson, "Locke: Heir of Puritan Political Theorists," in *Calvinism and Political Order*, ed. George L. Hunt (Philadelphia: Westminster Press, 1965), 117–118.

Williams's importance to religious freedom in the United States extends beyond his anticipation of, or even influence on, the arguments of later thinkers. He is also important because of the manner in which his vision of religious liberty augments and corrects more famous proposals. For instance, as a Calvinist theologian Williams worked with a more complex understanding of religious commitment than did either Locke or Jefferson: he recognized that religious obligations usually entail both right beliefs and the manifestation of those beliefs in practice. By contrast, Locke and Jefferson normally restricted the religion they sought to protect to matters of belief or, in Jefferson's vocabulary, "opinions." Neither thinker considered the realm of religious practice to qualify for substantial protection, in part because they thought conflict between religious practices and public standards would be rare. Locke subscribed to a strict private-public distinction in drawing the bounds of religion and state, and although he held that religious beliefs were a private affair, Locke assumed that the practices associated with religious commitment were at least partially public in nature and so subject to regulation by civil authority. Locke admitted that some believers could feel compelled by conscience to engage in practices prohibited or restricted by the state, and in those cases he advised the religious person to follow his or her conscience. But since many religious practices are public acts, he also considered it appropriate for the state to take action against behavior considered deviant, and he warned believers to be prepared to be punished for the manifestation of conscientious convictions in actions that transgressed public law.[37]

Jefferson adopted Locke's private-public distinction in his assumption that guaranteed protection extends only to religious "opinions," but he also assumed that there would be few conflicts between religious practices and social standards. To Jefferson's mind, good religion was synonymous with good morality (he famously had little appetite for the "superstitious" elements in Christianity or other religions), so he assumed a fundamental

37. John Locke, *A Letter Concerning Toleration* (Buffalo, N.Y.: Prometheus, 1990), 56–61. Locke acknowledges briefly that the particular issue of morality seems to "belong therefore to the jurisdiction both of the outward and inward court" (56), thus complicating his public-private distinction between civil and religious matters. But immediately after recognizing this possible contradiction, he assumes that "if what has been already said concerning the limits of both these governments be rightly considered, it will easily remove all difficulty in this matter." To his credit, Williams realized that drawing the line between the civil government's duty to protect civil order and the unjustified restriction of religious practice was not nearly this simple in reality.

compatibility between religious practices and social order that blinded him to the possibility of serious conflict between the two. From his rationalist perspective, Jefferson believed it to be almost a contradiction in terms that a citizen would feel religiously obligated to engage in acts that violated social mores, but his commitment to Locke's private-public distinction—as well as his disdain for the "superstitious" varieties of faith that might lead one to be socially deviant—allowed him easily to support the enforcement of social standards when such conflict occurred.[38]

By contrast, Williams knew from personal experience that religious belief often dictated certain actions (including but not limited to speech) that might conflict with the standards of majority culture, and that the point where social standards and religious practice clash is where a policy of religious liberty is most important and most difficult to maintain. He recognized that it was not simply the freedom to hold religious opinions that required protection; no one since the Spanish Inquisition had attempted to persecute dissenters solely on the private subscription to minority convictions. Religious dissent became susceptible to persecution only when it manifested itself publicly in religious *speech* and *practices,* yet it is precisely the latter category of religious adherence that Locke and Jefferson were so unconcerned to protect. As is clear from his interactions with the Quakers and his response to the pacifist citizens of Providence, Williams did not regard the balance between religious liberty and social order easy to find, and he did not consider it out of the question to sacrifice personal liberty for the collective good in these kinds of stalemates. But he also worried about how easy it was for civil leaders to violate religious freedom unjustifiably in the name of public interest. As a religious practitioner and a member of a dissenting minority, Williams knowingly cautioned against careless restrictions on religious practice in the hard cases when social standards and religious obligation collide, in a way Locke and Jefferson, with their cerebral definitions of religion, found difficult to consider seriously.

As a religious dissenter, Williams represents in particular the concerns of the separatist in debates over religious freedom. For the separatist, what is at stake is not (contra Jefferson) simply the protection of a peculiar species of

---

38. For a discussion of the implicit theological premise at work in Jefferson's assumption that religious morality and social standards would only infrequently conflict, see Hall, *Separating Church and State,* 129–130.

"opinions," but the compatibility between two competing objects of fundamental allegiance, God and the state. Timothy L. Hall rightly points out that
when confronted with civil requirements that violate religious scruples, the
separatist is forced to choose between individual religious identity and op-
portunities to participate in civil society. Faced with this choice, the citizen
often will choose to withdraw from public spheres—schools, public service, or employment—in order to protect religious identity. In other words,
forced to choose between God and the state, the ultimate cost of restricted
religious freedom usually will not be to the separatist's religious convictions
but to public citizenship. The necessity of such a decision makes little sense
from the Jeffersonian perspective, but Williams makes clearer the fundamental choice at stake for members of religious minorities in moments of
conflict between conscience and civil obligation, a standoff that continues to
be tested in latter-day Supreme Court jurisprudence.[39]

Ironically, Williams's commitment to a particular religious tradition also
led him to articulate a more inclusive theory of religious freedom than
Locke's liberalism allowed. In his *Letter Concerning Toleration* (1689), Locke
argued that religious tolerance should be extended only to Protestant Christians, for he thought Catholics and Muslims incapable of maintaining their
political loyalties to the state in light of their religious ties to the pope or the
"mufti of Constantinople."[40] Similarly, Locke argued that atheists could not
be trusted as citizens because "promises, covenants, and oaths, which are the
bonds of human society, can have no hold upon an atheist."[41] By contrast,
Williams's rejection of oaths as a political tool and his Calvinist subscription
to natural morality allowed him to imagine that all persons, regardless of religious commitment (or the lack thereof), possessed the rudimentary capabilities necessary to make them trustworthy and productive citizens. The
limitations to Locke's theory of toleration might seem insignificant and easily explainable by historical context, were it not for the ease with which similar restrictions find their way into offers of toleration in all kinds of historical circumstances. Perhaps on this front Locke inadvertently illustrates the

39. Timothy Hall argues that Justice Antonin Scalia, in his opinions in *Lee* v. *Weisman* and other
First Amendment cases of the 1990s, reflects a particularly "disapproving view of Separatism" as
well as a lack of appreciation for the tough choices faced by adherents of minority religion. See ibid.,
159–166.
40. Locke, *A Letter Concerning Toleration*, 63–64.
41. Ibid., 64.

inferiority of a top-down toleration to a respect for full religious liberty, but what is certain is that Williams's theologically informed moral anthropology permitted him to be more optimistic about the stability of a religiously pluralistic society and therefore more inclusive in the freedom of conscience he could entertain.

Thus, Williams's theological approach to religious liberty provides an important conceptual complement and even corrective to the dominant Enlightenment interpretation of this American doctrine. Perhaps Williams's most significant contribution, though, is that he provides an alternative language in which to articulate a commitment to religious liberty, a theological vocabulary that may be more persuasive to some members of what remains a thoroughly religious American culture. The fact that Williams defended religious freedom as a believer makes him especially important to this particular American tradition, for it is a tradition that historically requires support from both believers and skeptics in order to work. As a theologian, Williams assures the skeptic that religious convictions, even intensely held ones, are not necessarily antithetical to the cause of religious liberty. In fact, Williams remains the quintessential example of how a religious perspective can be an ally to the cause of religious liberty, by offering theological grounds— an *internal* argument, if you will—for supporting the right of others to hold and practice their beliefs even if we disagree with them. At the same time, Williams assures the believer that respect for religious freedom does not necessarily require a relativistic respect for all accounts of truth as equally valid. Williams despised the Quakers' theology, thought the Catholic Church served the Antichrist, and assumed with his Puritan colleagues that many of the Native Americans' religious rituals were devil worship. While he considered all these religions false and his own Puritan faith true, he nonetheless defended their right to hold and practice their religion without state interference. If Williams reminds the skeptic that dogmatism is not antithetical to a respect for religious liberty, he assures the believer that supporting religious freedom need not impinge on a dogmatic commitment to one's version of the truth. More broadly, Williams provides a pattern for articulating respect for religious freedom in the language of religious commitment, an important resource for cultivating such support in a culture dominated by religious persons. As Timothy Hall has observed, "Any political discourse likely to include believers within a liberty-supporting consensus must speak to their deepest intuitions—and these, being religious, must be spoken to in religious syllables."[42]

Roger Williams may not have sat at the table on which the First Amendment was drafted, but his fingerprints are all over the tradition of religious freedom in America. He introduces us to an alternative set of voices clamoring for free conscience, those of religious dissenters who historically were just as responsible as their Enlightenment partners for the tense but successful relationship between church and state forged through more than three hundred years of American history. We do well not to underestimate the political importance of his particular insight, despite (or because of) its origins in religious zeal. Assuming that Williams has nothing to say to a pluralistic liberal democracy because his language was principally theological does as much injury to his legacy as assuming that the believers for whom he speaks are incapable of caring for civil society because of their allegiance to church, synagogue, or mosque. Williams's voice is an important one to recover precisely because he cared simultaneously about the good of the church *and* the flourishing of civil society, and he was unwilling to purchase one at the expense of the other. Williams believed religious liberty made both good theology and good public policy, which is why his words are worthy of a new reading.

42. Hall, *Separating Church and State,* 149.

CHAPTER ONE

Mr. Cotton's Letter Lately Printed, Examined, and Answered

Within a few weeks after Roger Williams left Massachusetts, he and John Cotton began an exchange of letters in which they debated the circumstances surrounding Williams's banishment. How this exchange began is not clear, but what is certain is that Williams considered Cotton to be chiefly responsible for his predicament. For his part, Cotton denied playing a meaningful role in Williams's sentence, insisting instead that Williams himself and his controversial pronouncements were the cause of his troubles. In these early letters, Cotton and Williams debated some of Williams's contrary opinions, in particular his belief that "godly Christians" must separate themselves from and renounce the pollutions of the established church in England. When Williams traveled to London in 1644, one of Cotton's letters "mysteriously" found its way into print (probably at the hands of a Williams sympathizer), and once this occurred Williams felt compelled to respond publicly. In this published response, while we see glimpses of the insistence on separation of church and state that will dominate later treatises, Williams is principally concerned to defend his separatist ecclesiology and to charge that Cotton's theological error and political conspiracy were what pushed him from the Bay Colony.

To the Impartial Reader:

This letter[1] I acknowledge to have received from Mr. Cotton, whom for his personal excellencies I truly honor and love, yet at such a time of my distressed wanderings amongst the Barbarians, being destitute of food, of clothes, [and] of time, I reserved it . . . and afterward prepared an answer to be returned. In the interim, some friends being much grieved that one publicly acknowledged to be godly and dearly beloved should yet be so exposed to the mercy of a howling wilderness in frost and snow, Mr. Cotton, to take off the edge of censure from himself, professed in both speech and writing that he was no procurer of my sorrows. Some letters then passed between us, in which I proved and expressed that if I had perished in that sorrowful winter's flight, only the blood of Jesus Christ could have washed him from the guilt of mine. His final answer was "had you perished, your blood would have been on your own head; it was your sin to procure it and your sorrow to suffer it."

Here I confess I stopped and ever since suppressed my answer, waiting [to see] if it might please the Father of mercies more to mollify and soften and render more humane and merciful the ear and heart of that otherwise excellent and worthy man. It cannot now be justly offensive that finding this letter public (by whose procurement I know not), I also present to the same public view my formerly intended answer. I rejoice in the goodness and wisdom of him who is the Father of lights and mercies, in ordering the season both [for] my own present opportunity [to] answer . . . and especially [for] such protestations and resolutions of so many fearing God, to seek what worship and worshippers are acceptable to him in Jesus Christ. . . .

If him you seek in these searching times, make him alone your white and soul's beloved, willing to follow and be like him in doing, in suffering—although you find him not in the restoration of his ordinances according to his first pattern[2]—yet shall you see him, reign with him, eternally admire him, and enjoy him, when he shortly comes in flaming fire to burn up millions of ignorant and disobedient.

Your most unworthy countryman, Roger Williams

1. Cotton's letter, to which Williams responds here, may be found in Sargent Bush, Jr., ed., *The Correspondence of John Cotton* (Chapel Hill: University of North Carolina Press, 2001), 211–225.

2. This preference for the model of the early church and the assumption that it alone provided the template for proper worship (a template the established church in England failed to follow) marked Williams's ecclesiology as "primitivist."

The Stated Reasons for Williams's Banishment

Mr. Cotton: "Beloved in Christ."[3]

Answer. Though I humbly desire to acknowledge myself unworthy to be beloved, and most of all unworthy of the name of Christ and to be beloved for his sake, yet since Mr. Cotton is pleased to use such an affectionate compellation and testimonial expression to one so afflicted and persecuted by himself and others (whom for their personal worth and godliness I also honor and love), I desire it may be seriously reviewed by him and them and all men whether the Lord Jesus be well pleased that one beloved in him should (for no other cause than shall presently appear) be denied the common air to breathe in and a civil cohabitation upon the same common earth, yea and also without mercy and humane compassion be exposed to winter miseries in a howling wilderness. . . .

Mr. Cotton: "Though I have little hope . . . that you will hearken to my voice, [you] who have not hearkened to the body of the whole church of Christ with you, [nor] the testimony and judgment of so many elders and brothers of other churches, yet I trust my labor will be accepted [by] the Lord. And who can tell but that he may bless it to you also, if (by his help) I endeavor to show you the sandiness of those grounds out of which you have banished yourself from the fellowship of all the churches in these countries."

Answer. . . . Mr. Cotton endeavors to discover the sandiness of those grounds out of which, as he says, I have banished myself. . . . But because the reader may ask both Mr. Cotton and me what were the grounds of such a sentence of banishment against me, . . . I shall relate in brief what those grounds were, some whereof he is pleased to discuss in this letter, and others of them not to mention.

After my public trial and answers at the General Court, one of the most eminent magistrates (whose name and speech may by others be remembered) stood up and spoke: "Mr. Williams . . . holds forth these four particulars: first, that we have not our land by patent from the king, but that the Natives are the true owners of it, and that we ought to repent of such a receiving it by patent; secondly, that it is not lawful to call a wicked person to

---

3. Because this treatise is a point-by-point rebuttal of Cotton's earlier letter, he regularly cites even the smallest phrase as a springboard into an extended response. Here Williams is responding to Cotton's reference to him as "beloved in Christ."

swear, to pray, as being actions of God's worship; thirdly, that it is not lawful to hear any of the ministers of the parish assemblies in England; fourthly, that the civil magistrate's power extends only to the bodies and goods [and] outward state of men."[4]

I acknowledge the particulars were rightly summed up, and I also hope that as I then maintained the rocky strength of them to my own and other consciences' satisfaction, so (through the Lord's assistance) I shall be ready for the same grounds, not only to be bound and banished, but also to die in New England, as for most holy truths of God in Christ Jesus.

Yea, but says he: upon those grounds you banished yourself from the society of the churches in these countries. I answer, if Mr. Cotton means my own voluntary withdrawing from those churches resolved to continue in those evils and persecuting the witnesses of the Lord presenting light to them, I confess it was my own voluntary act—yea, I hope the act of the Lord Jesus sounding forth in me . . . the blast which shall in his own holy season cast down the strength and confidence of those inventions of men in the worshipping of the true and living God. . . . But if by banishing myself he intends the act of *civil* banishment from their common earth and air, I then observe with grief the language of the Dragon in a lamb's lip.[5] Among other expressions of the Dragon, are not these common to the witnesses of the Lord Jesus rent and torn by his persecutions? "Go now, say you are persecuted, you are persecuted in Christ, suffer for your conscience, [but] no, it is your schism, heresy, obstinacy; the Devil has deceived you, you have justly brought this upon yourself, you have banished yourself." Instances are abundant in so many books of martyrs and the experience of all men, and therefore I spare to recite [them] in so short a treatise.

Secondly, if he means this civil act of banishing, why should he call a civil sentence from the civil state—within a few weeks execution in so sharp a time of New England's cold—why should he call this a banishment from the *churches,* except he silently confess that the frame or constitution of their churches is but implicitly national, which yet they profess against? For otherwise why was I not yet permitted to live in the world or commonwealth, except for this reason: that the commonwealth and church is yet but one,

---

4. For a discussion of Williams's position on each of these fronts, see the introduction to this volume.

5. For biblical reference to Satan as the "dragon," see Revelation 12–13.

and he that is banished from the one must necessarily be banished from the other also.

Cotton's Role in the Sentence

Mr. Cotton: "Let not any prejudice against my person, I beseech you, forestall either your affection or judgment, as if I had hasted forward the sentence of your civil banishment; for what was done by the magistrates in that kind was done neither by my counsel nor [with my] consent."

Answer. Although I desire to hear the voice of God from a stranger, an equal, an inferior, yea an enemy, yet I observe how this excellent man cannot but confess how hard it is for any man to do good [or] to speak effectually to the soul or conscience of any whose body he afflicts and persecutes, and that only for their soul and conscience sake. . . . Now to the ground from whence my prejudice might arise, he professes my banishment proceeded not with his counsel or consent. I answer, I doubt not but that what Mr. Cotton and others did in procuring my sorrows was not without some regret and reluctance of conscience and affection. . . . Yet to the particular that Mr. Cotton consented not, what need he, being not one of the civil court? But that he counseled it (and so consented), beside what other proof I might produce and what [he] himself here expresses, I shall produce a double and unanswerable testimony.

First, he publicly taught and teaches (except lately Christ Jesus has taught him better) that body-killing, soul-killing, and state-killing doctrine of not permitting, but persecuting, all other consciences and ways of worship but his own in the civil state—and so consequently in the whole world, if the power of empire thereof were in his hand! Secondly, as at that sentence diverse worthy gentlemen dared not concur with the rest in such a course, so some that did consent have solemnly testified, and with tears to [me] confessed, that they could not in their souls have been brought to have consented to the sentence had not Mr. Cotton in private given them advice and counsel, providing it just and warrantable to their consciences. I desire to be as charitable as charity would have me, and therefore would hope that either his memory failed him or else he meant that in the very time of sentence passing he neither counseled nor consented (as he has since said, that he withdrew himself and went out from the rest, probably out of that reluctance which before I mentioned). [But even] so, I cannot reconcile his own expression. . . .

At this point in his rebuttal, Williams moves to Cotton's assertion that it was Williams's separatist views that precipitated and justified his banishment from the colony. Cotton had invoked Proverbs 11:26—"He that withholdeth corn, the people shall curse him: but blessing shall be upon the head of him that selleth it"—to metaphorically make the point that separatism deprives persons from a saving encounter with the Gospel. In his own belabored exegesis of this passage from Proverbs, Williams counters with what will become three familiar arguments in his repertoire: first, that separatism rightly protects the integrity of the church's worship and preaching; second, that Cotton himself endorses separatism (at least implicitly) through his own removal to and practice in New England; and third, that regardless of the rightness or wrongness of separatism, religious dissent should not be punished with civil penalty. Perhaps anticipating the objection to a religious justification for a civil sentence, Cotton qualified his answer, suggesting that perhaps it was not separatism itself that brought about the banishment but instead the danger of Williams's beliefs to both church and civil society. Williams leaps upon Cotton's apparent waffling.

Mr. Cotton [writes]: "And yet it may be [that] they passed that sentence against you not upon that ground,[6] but (for ought I [to] know) for your other corrupt doctrines, which tend to the disturbance of both civil and holy peace, as may appear by that answer which was sent to the [elders] of the church of Salem and yourself."

I answer, it is no wonder that so many, having been demanded the cause of my sufferings, have answered that they could not tell for what, since Mr. Cotton himself knows not distinctly what cause to assign, but says it *may* be they passed not that sentence on that ground. O, where was the waking care of so excellent and worthy a man, to see his brother and beloved in Christ so afflicted [and] he knows not distinctly for what! He alleges a Scripture to prove the sentence righteous, and yet concludes it may be it was not for that but for other corrupt doctrines which he names not (nor any Scripture to prove them corrupt, or the sentence righteous for that cause). O, that it may

6. That is, the charge of separatism.

please the Father of lights to awaken both him and others of my honored countrymen, to see how though their hearts [are] awake [with] respect [to] personal grace and [the] life of Jesus, yet they sleep, insensitive [to] much concerning the purity of the Lord's worship or the sorrows of such whom they style[7] brothers and beloved in Christ, [though] afflicted by them.

But though he names not these corrupt doctrines, a little before I have, as they were publicly summed up and charged upon me, and yet none of them tending to the breach of holy or civil peace, of which I have ever desired to be unfeignedly[8] tender, acknowledging the ordinance of magistracy to be properly and adequately fitted by God to preserve the civil state in civil peace and order. [Just] as [God] has also appointed a spiritual government and governors in matters pertaining to his worship and the consciences of men, both which governments, governors, laws, offenses, [and] punishments are essentially distinct, and the confounding of them brings all the world into combustion.

Persecutors Would Appreciate Tolerance More if They Were the Ones Persecuted

Mr. Cotton [adds]: "And to speak freely what I think, were my soul in your soul's stead, I should think it a work of mercy of God to banish me from the civil society of such a commonwealth where I could not enjoy holy fellowship with any church of God amongst them without sin. What should the daughter of Zion do in Babel; why should she not hasten to flee from there?"[9]

Answer. Love bids me hope that Mr. Cotton here intended me a cordial,[10] to revive me in my sorrows. Yet if the ingredients [of his statement] be examined, there will appear no less than dishonor to the name of God, danger to every civil state, a miserable comfort to myself, and contradiction with itself. . . . It is a dangerous doctrine to affirm it a misery to live in that state where a Christian cannot enjoy the fellowship of the public churches of God

---

7. "Call" or "refer to as."

8. Genuinely.

9. Perhaps sarcastically, Cotton argued that if Williams held such unsatisfied standards for church purity, he should consider it a good thing to be ushered out of a community that fails so consistently to meet those expectations.

10. Meaning "an encouragement."

without sin. Do we not know many famous states wherein is known no church of Jesus Christ? Did not God command his people to pray for the peace of the material city of Babel (Jeremiah 27) and to seek the peace of it, though [there be] no church of God in Babel . . . ?

. . . For myself, I acknowledge it a blessed gift of God to be enabled to suffer, and so to be banished for his Name's sake. And yet I doubt not to affirm that Mr. Cotton himself would have counted it a mercy if he might have practiced in Old England what now he does in New, with enjoyment of the civil peace, safety, and protection of the state. Or should he dissent from the New England churches and join in worship with some other (as some few years since he was upon the point [of doing], in a separation from the churches there as [being too] legal),[11] would he count it a mercy to be plucked up by the roots, him and his, and to endure the losses, distractions, [and] miseries that do attend such a condition? . . . And might it please God to persuade the mother[12] to permit the inhabitants of New England her daughter to enjoy their conscience of God after a particular congregational way, and to persuade the daughter to permit the inhabitants of the mother Old England to walk there after their conscience of a parishional way (which yet neither mother nor daughter is persuaded to permit), I conceive Mr. Cotton himself, were he seated in Old England again, would not count it a mercy to be banished from the civil state.

And therefore (lastly) as he casts dishonor upon the name of God to make him the author of such cruel mercy, so had his soul been in my soul's

---

11. Here Williams is referring to Cotton's role in the antinomian controversy of the late 1630s. Anne Hutchinson, heavily influenced by Cotton's preaching, began holding meetings in her home, during which she taught a radical form of the Calvinist doctrine of the sufficiency of grace. She argued that any emphasis on good works and morals (as characterized much of Puritan preaching in New England) distracted from the priority God's grace serves in personal salvation. This position led her opponents to charge her with teaching that the moral law held no force for believers (hence the disparaging term "antinomian"). Increasingly, Hutchinson took her complaints public, charging that nearly all of the ministers of the Bay Colony (excepting her beloved teacher, John Cotton) were guilty of preaching "legalism" and "works righteousness." Such charges, not to mention the very idea of a woman teaching publicly, brought the full weight of the General Court down on Hutchinson, and the controversy threatened for a while to implicate Cotton as well. Cotton successfully (if not admirably) distanced himself from Hutchinson, whom the Court exiled in 1638. She temporarily joined Williams in Rhode Island and later moved to New York, where she was killed in an Indian raid. For more on the antinomian controversy, see David D. Hall, *The Antinomian Controversy, 1636–1638: A Documentary History* (Middletown, Conn.: Wesleyan University Press, 1968). Incidentally, no evidence exists that Cotton ever seriously considered separation over the issue of "legalism," as Williams suggests here.

12. That is, Old England.

case—exposed to the miseries, poverties, necessities, wants, debts, hardships
of sea and land, in a banished condition—he would, I presume, reach forth
a more merciful cordial to the afflicted. But he that is despised and afflicted
is like a lamp despised in the eyes of him that is at ease. . . .

Williams's Separatist Principle

*Williams proceeds to Cotton's suggestion that the counsel of colony leaders, the
trial and sentence, and even the serious illness Williams suffered at the time of
his banishment were all means to God's chastisement and correction. To the
contrary, Williams responds, his tribulations have been like the suffering that
saints and martyrs commonly endure for righteous cause. Next Williams turns
to Cotton's charge that there is an inherent contradiction to his separatism, in
that Williams agrees that members of the visible church may be considered
godly yet simultaneously asserts that they are unfit to constitute a true church.
In responding to Cotton, Williams lays out some of the basic assumptions of his
separatist ecclesiology, while redounding the charge of contradiction back to his
antagonist.*

Mr. Cotton: "Two stumbling blocks I perceive have turned you off from
fellowship from us: first, the want of fit matter of our church; second, disre-
spect of the separating churches in England under affliction, ourselves practicing separation in peace. For the first, you acknowledge . . . that godly persons are the visible members of these churches, but yet you see not that
godly persons are matter fitted to constitute a church, no more than trees or
quarries are fit matter proportioned to the building. This exception seems to
me to imply a contradiction to itself, for if the matter of the churches be,
as you say, godly persons, they are not then as trees unfelled and stones
unhewed. Godliness cuts men down from the former root and hews them
out of the pit of corrupt nature and fits them for fellowship with Christ and
with his people.[13]

"You object [that there is] a necessity lying upon men before they can be
fit matter for church fellowship, [namely] to see, bewail, repent, and come

---

13. In other words, to Cotton's mind either these persons are true saints and thus (by definition)
members of the church or they are unregenerate and unworthy to be called the church. To Cotton,
Williams seemed to be saying both at the same time.

out of the false churches. . . . And this is to be done not by a local removal or contrary practice, but by a deliverance of the soul, understanding, will, judgment and affection. [To answer], first we grant that it is not local removal from former pollution, nor contrary practice, that fits us for fellowship with Christ and his church, but that it is necessary also that we repent of such former pollutions wherewith we have been defiled and enthralled. . . . But this we profess to you, that wherein we have reformed our practice, therein have we endeavored unfeignedly to humble our souls for our former contrary walking. If any through hypocrisy are wanting herein, the hidden hypocrisy of some will not prejudice the sincerity and faithfulness of others, nor the church estate of all."

Answer. That which requires answer in this passage is a charge of seeming contradiction, namely that persons may be godly and yet not fitted for church estate. . . . For the clearing of which let the word of truth be rightly divided and a right distinction of things applied, [and] there will appear nothing contradictory, but clear and satisfactory to each man's conscience.

First then I distinguish a godly person thus: In some acts of sin which a godly person may fall into, during those acts, although before the all-searching and tender eye of God (and also in the eyes of such as are godly) such a person remains still godly, yet to the eye of the world externally such a person seems ungodly and a sinner. Thus Noah in his drunkenness, thus Abraham, Lot, Samson, Job, David, [and] Peter in their lying whoredom, cursing, murder, denying and forswearing of Christ Jesus, although they lost not their inward sap and root of life, yet suffered they a decay and fall of leaf, and the show of bad and evil trees. In such a case, Mr. Cotton will not deny that a godly person falling into drunkenness, whoredom, deliberate murder, [or] denying and forswearing of Christ, the church of Christ cannot receive such persons into church fellowship before [seeing] humble bewailing and confessing of such evils, notwithstanding that love may conceive there is a root of godliness within.

Secondly, God's children, notwithstanding a principle of spiritual life in their souls, yet are lulled into a long continued sleep in the matters of God's worship. . . . The heart is awake in spiritual life and grace as concerning personal union to the Lord Jesus and conscionable endeavors to please him in what the heart is convinced. Yet [it is] asleep [with] respect [to] abundant ignorance and negligence, and consequently gross abominations and pollutions, of worship, in which the choicest servants of God and most

faithful witnesses of many truths have lived, more or less, yea in main and
fundamental points, ever since the Apostasy.[14]

Not to instance in all, but in some particulars which Mr. Cotton has in
New England reformed, I earnestly beseech him (and all) to ponder well
how far he himself now professes to see and practice that which so many
thousands of godly persons of high note in all ages (since the Apostasy)
saw not: As first, concerning the nature of a particular church, to consist
only of holy and godly persons; secondly, of a true ministry called by that
church; thirdly, a true worship free from ceremonies [and] common prayer;
fourthly, a true [church] government in the hands only of such governors
and elders as are appointed by the Lord Jesus. Hence God's people, not seeing their captivity in these points, must first necessarily be enlightened and
called out from such captivity before they can be next fitted and prepared
for the true church, worship, [and] ministry.

Secondly, this will be more clear if we consider God's people and church
of old, the Jews: captivated in material Babel, they could not possibly build
God's altar and temple at Jerusalem until the yoke and bonds of their captivity were broken and they [were] set free to return with vessels of the
Lord's house to set up his worship in Jerusalem, as we see in the Books of
Ezra, Nehemiah, Daniel, [and] Haggai. Hence in the antitype,[15] God's people (the spiritual and mystical Jews) cannot possibly erect the altar of the
Lord's true worship and build the temple of his true church without true
sight of their spiritual bondage [with] respect [to] God's worship, and a
power and strength from Jesus Christ to bring them out and carry them
through all difficulties in so mighty a work. And as the being of God's people in material Babel and [the] necessity of their coming forth before they
could build the temple did not in the least deny them to be God's people, no

14. Williams does not specify exactly what he means by his reference to the Apostasy, but two interpretations are possible. First, traditional Calvinists of the seventeenth century tended to see the
Roman Church's capitulation to apostasy as an evolution over time, beginning perhaps in the fourth
or fifth century but definitely culminating in the Council of Trent's reaffirmation of papal hierarchy
and Roman liturgy and its rejection of many Protestant reforms. Alternatively, many Anabaptist traditions located the beginning of the Apostasy more precisely in Emperor Constantine's protection
of Christianity in the Edict of Milan, the effective end of Christianity's persecuted status and the beginning of "Christendom." Elsewhere Williams endorses the Anabaptists' rejection of Constantinian
Christianity, arguing that with political protection came theological and ecclesiastical corruption.
Thus, the more plausible reading here is that by the Apostasy Williams is referring to the beginning
of Constantinian Christianity.

15. That is, the church after the death and resurrection of Christ.

more now does God's people being in mystical Babel (Rev. 18) nor the necessity of their coming forth hinder or deny the godliness of their persons, or spiritual life within them.

Thirdly, how many famous servants of God and witnesses of Jesus lived and died and were burnt for other truths of Jesus, not seeing the evil of their Antichristian calling of bishops, [for instance]. How did famous Luther himself continue a monk, set forth the German Mass, acknowledge the pope, and hold other gross abominations concerning God's worship, notwithstanding the life of Christ Jesus in him, and wrought in thousands by his means.

Fourthly, Mr. Cotton must be requested to remember his own practice (as before), how he refuses to receive persons eminent for personal grace and godliness to the Lord's Supper and other privileges of Christians . . . until they be convinced of the necessity of making and entering into a church covenant with them, with a confession of faith. And if any cannot be persuaded of such a covenant and confession, notwithstanding their godliness, yet are they not admitted.

Lastly, how famous is that passage of that solemn question put to Mr. Cotton and the rest of the New England elders by diverse ministers of Old England (eminent for personal godliness, as Mr. Cotton acknowledges): whether they might be permitted in New England to enjoy their consciences in a church estate different from the New English.[16] To which Mr. Cotton and the New England elders returned a plain negative (in effect thus much); with the acknowledgment of their worth and godliness above their own, and their hopes of agreement, yet . . . if they agree not (which they are not like to do) and submit to that way of church fellowship and worship which in New

16. Samuel Caldwell, editor of the Narragansett edition of *The Bloody Tenent,* identified the document to which Williams refers as "Church-Government and Church-Covenant discussed, In an Answer of the Elders of the several Churches in New-England to two and thirty Questions, sent over to them by divers Ministers in England, to declare their judgements therein." According to Caldwell, Richard Mather was the principal author of the New England clergy's response to a query "whether would you permit any Companie of Ministers and People (being otherwise in some measure approvable) to sit downe by you, and set up and practice another forme of Discipline, enjoying like libertie with yourselves in the Commonwealth, and accepted as a sister church by the rest of your Churches?" The New England ministers' answer was negative, based in the belief that "if that Discipline which we here practise be (as we are perswaded of it) the same which Christ hath appointed, and therefore unalterable, we see not how another can be lawful; and therefore if a company of people shall come hither, and here set up and practise another, we pray you think not much, if we cannot promise to approve of them in so doing, especially untill we see how approvable the men may be, and what Discipline it is they would set up."

England is set up, they not only cannot enjoy church fellowship together, but [they cannot] permit them to live and breathe in the same air and commonwealth together—which was my case, although it pleased Mr. Cotton and others most incensed to give [me] a testimony of godliness.

And this is the reason why, although I confess with joy the case of the New England churches that no person be received to fellowship with them in whom they cannot first discern true regeneration and the life of Jesus, yet I said and still affirm that godly and regenerate persons . . . are not fitted to constitute the true Christian church until it has pleased God to convince their souls of the evil of the false church, ministry, [and] worship. And although I confess that godly persons are not dead but living trees, not dead but living stones, and need no new regeneration (and so in that respect need no felling nor digging out), yet need they a mighty work of God's Spirit to humble and shame them, and to cause them to loath themselves for their abominations (or stink in God's nostrils, as it pleases God's Spirit to speak of false worships: hence Ezek. 43:11). God's people are not fit for God's house until holy shame be wrought in them for what they have done. . . . Hence it is that I have known some previous godly hearts confess that the plucking of their souls out from the abominations of false worship has been a second kind of regeneration. . . .

A Distinction between Personal Godliness and Purity in Practice

Now whereas Mr. Cotton adds that godly persons are not so enthralled to Antichrist as to separate them from Christ (else they could not be godly persons), I answer [that] this comes not near our question, which [does] not [concern] personal godliness . . . but the godliness . . . of worship.[17] Hence the Scripture holds forth Christ Jesus first personally as that God-Man, that one Mediator between God and man . . . whom all God's people by faith receive, and in receiving become sons of God, . . . although they yet see not the particular ways of his worship. . . . Second, the Scripture holds forth Christ

---

17. Throughout this discussion, Williams has the pope in mind when he uses the term "Antichrist." One of Williams's chief objections to the national church in England is that it retained the liturgical dressings of Roman Catholicism (for instance, in requiring the wearing of vestments and the use of the Book of Common Prayer) and thus remained "enthralled" in the grasp of "Antichristianity."

as Head of his church, formed into a body of worshippers, in which respect the church is called Christ. . . .

Now in the former respect, Antichrist can never so enthrall God's people as to separate them from Christ, that is from the life and grace of Christ, although [he may] enthrall them into ever so gross abominations concerning worship. . . . Yet in the second respect, as Christ is taken for the church, I conceive that Antichrist may separate God's people from Christ, that is, from Christ's true visible church and worship.[18] This Mr. Cotton himself will not deny if he remembers how little a while it is since the falsehood of a national, provincial, diocesan, and parishional church—and the truth of a particular congregation consisting only of holy persons—appeared to him.

The papists' question to the Protestant—"where was your church before Luther?"—is thus well answered: that since the Apostasy, truth and the holy city . . . have been trodden under foot, and the whole earth has wandered after the Beast,[19] yet God has stirred up witnesses to prophesy in sackcloth against the Beast. . . . Yet those witnesses have in their times more or less submitted to Antichrist, and his church, worship, and ministry, and so consequently have been ignorant of the true Christ, that is, Christ taken from the church in the true profession of that holy way of worship which he himself first appointed. . . .

I ask whether it be not absolutely necessary to his uniting with the true church, that is, with Christ in true Christian worship, that [a godly person] see and bewail and absolutely come out of from that former false church or Christ and his ministry [and] worship . . . ? The Jews come out of Babel before they build the temple in Jerusalem; the husband of a woman [must] die or be legally divorced before she can lawfully be married to another; the graft [must be] cut off from one before it can be grafted into another stock; the Kingdom of Christ (that is, the Kingdom of the saints) is cut out of the

---

18. This is really a debate over the Calvinist doctrine of the perseverance of the saints. Cotton charged that if Williams thought so-called godly persons not fitted to constitute the church, he must be arguing that they had "lost" their status as the gracefully elected of God. But to believe such a loss of election possible would be to contradict the Calvinist claim that God's power and grace, and not human striving, are sufficient for salvation. (In his own theology, Cotton gave such priority to divine grace over a human contribution to salvation that he left himself open to antinomian interpretation—see note 13 above.) Williams responds with the equally Calvinist distinction between justification and sanctification, agreeing with Cotton that the elected status of "godly persons" is assured by grace, but recognizing that perfection in practice among the saints is not guaranteed. Even the worship of true believers was susceptible to error, especially since the Apostasy.

19. Revelation 13:4.

mountain of the Roman monarchy. Thus the Corinthians, uniting with Christ Jesus, were washed from their idolatry, as well as other sins. Thus the Thessalonians turned from their idols before they could serve the living and true God—and as in paganism, so in Antichristianity, which separates as certainly (though more subtly) from Christ Jesus. . . .

The national church of the Jews, with all the shadowy typical ordinances of kings, priests, prophets, temples, [and] sacrifices, was as a silver candlestick, on which the light of the knowledge of God and of the Lord Jesus in the type and shadow was set up shined. That silver candlestick it pleased the Most Holy and Only Wise to take away, and instead thereof to set up the golden candlesticks of particular churches (Rev. 1) by the hand of the Son of God himself. Now the first was silver (the pure will and mind of God, but intended only for a season), the second of a more precious lasting nature. . . .

Again, is there such a time allowed to any man, uniting or adding himself to the true church now, to observe the unholy holy days of feasting and fasting invented by Antichrist, yea, and (as Paul did circumcision) to practice the popish sacraments? I doubt not but if any member of a true church or assembly of worshippers shall fall to any pagan or popish practice, he must be instructed and convinced, before excommunication. But the question is whether still observing and so practicing, a person may be received to the true Christian church, as the Jews were, although they yet practiced Moses' ceremonies. These things duly pondered in the fear and presence of God, it will appear how vain the allegation is, from that tender and honorable respect to God's ordinances now vanishing from the Jews (and their weak consciences about the same) to prove the same tenderness to Satan's inventions and the consciences of men in the renouncing of pagan, Turkish, Antichristian, yea, and I add Judaical worships now, when once the time of their full vanishing was come. . . . I believe it absolutely necessary to see and bewail so much as may amount to cut off the soul from the false church, whether national, parishional, or any other falsely constituted church. . . .

"Local" Separation Not Enough—Godly Christians Must Renounce False Worship

The Scriptures or writings of truth are those heavenly righteous scales wherein all our controversies must be tried, and that blessed star that leads to Jesus all those souls that seek him. But Mr. Cotton says [that] two of those

Scriptures alleged by me (Isa. 52:11; Rev. 18:4, which I brought to a necessity of leaving the false before joining to the true church) speak of *local* separation, which he says, "[you] yourself know we have made."

For that local and typical separation from Babylon (Isa. 52) I could not well have believed that Mr. Cotton or any would make that coming forth of Babel in the antitype (Rev. 18:4) to be local and material also. What civil state, nation, or country in the world, in the antitype, must now be called Babel? Certainly, if any, then Babel itself properly so called, but there we find (as before) a true church of Jesus Christ (1 Pet. 5). Secondly, if Babel be local now, whence God's people are called, then must there be a local Judea, a Land of Canaan also, into which they are called; and where shall both that Babel and Canaan be found in all the comings forth that have been made from the church of Rome in these last times? But Mr. Cotton, having made a local departure from Old England in Europe to New England in America, can he satisfy his own soul, or the souls of other men, that he has obeyed that voice: come out of Babel my people, partake not of her sins? Does he count the very land of England literally Babel and so consequently Egypt and Sodom (Rev. 2:8), and the land of New England Judea [and] Canaan?[20]

The Lord Jesus (John 4) clearly breaks down all difference of places and (Acts 10) all difference of persons, and for myself, I acknowledge the land of England, the civil laws, government, and people of England, not to be inferior to any under heaven. Only two things I shall humbly suggest to my dear countrymen (whether more high and honorable at the helm of government, or more inferior, who labor and sail in this famous ship of England's commonwealth) as the greatest causes, fountains, and top roots of all the indignation of the Most High against the state and country. First, that the whole

---

20. Isaiah 52:11—"Depart ye, depart ye, go ye out from thence, touch no unclean thing; go ye out of the midst of her; be ye clean, that bear the vessels of the LORD;" Rev. 18:4—"And I heard another voice from heaven, saying, Come out of her, my people, that ye be not partakers of her sins, and that ye receive not of her plagues." In a previous letter, Williams apparently had cited these two passages (among others) as evidence that the Bible mandates complete separation from the context of false worship, including the public repudiation of that idolatry. Cotton countered that the passages in question refer only to physical removal from such a context, which Cotton reminds Williams that the Puritans had done by relocating to Massachusetts. Williams's response is to draw out the typological implications he sees in Cotton's reading of these texts. If, says Williams, we read the mandate of these texts to be physical separation, then the context from which we are called to separate must itself be physical and political. This would equate England itself with the despised Babel in the texts, however, as well as force the implication that New England was some kind of Promised Land (as Canaan served in the biblical texts). Williams thought this assignment was simultaneously too damning to England and gave New England too much eschatological credit. Many Puritans, of course, were comfortable with associating New England with the Promised Land.

nation and generations of men have been forced (though unregenerate and unrepentant) to pretend and assume the name of Christ Jesus, which only belongs (according to the institution of the Lord Jesus) to truly regenerate and repenting souls. Secondly, that all others dissenting from them, whether Jews or Gentiles, their countrymen especially (for strangers have a liberty), have not been permitted civil cohabitation in this world with them, but have been distressed and persecuted by them. . . .

The truth is, I acknowledge their[21] witness against ceremonies and bishops, but that yet they see not the evil of a national church (notwithstanding they constitute only particular and independent) let their constant practice speak, in still joining with such churches and ministers in the ordinances of the Word and prayer, and their persecuting of myself for my humble and faithful and constant admonishing of them of such unclean walking between a particular church (which they profess to be Christ's only) and a national, which Mr. Cotton professes to separate from. . . .

What more have I spoken than Mr. Cotton himself has uttered . . . ? As first, that godly persons may become defiled and unclean by hypocrisy and worldliness; secondly, while they lie in such a condition of uncleanness, all their offerings, persons, and labors are unclean in the sight of God, and have neither acceptance nor blessing from him . . . ; thirdly, the church of Christ cannot be constituted of such godly persons when defiled with such worldliness; [and] fourthly, the church consisting of such worldly persons (though otherwise godly and Christian), the people of God must separate from them. . . .

Cotton's Position of "Moderation" Amounts to Hypocrisy

Mr. Cotton proceeds: ". . . You conceive us to walk between Christ and Antichrist: first in practicing separation here and not repenting of our preaching and printing against it in out own country; secondly, in reproaching [you] and others at Salem for separation; thirdly, in particular, that [I] have conceived and spoken that separation is a way that God has not prospered, yet you say the truth of the church's way depends not upon the countenance of men or upon outward peace and liberty." To this he answers that they halt not, but walk in the midst of two extremes, the one of being defiled with the pollution of other churches, the other of renouncing the churches

---

21. That is, Williams's nonseparating Puritan antagonists in Massachusetts, including Cotton.

for the remnant of pollutions.[22] This moderation he (with ingenuous moderation) professes he sees no cause to repent of.

Answer. With the Lord's gracious assistance, we shall prove this middle walking to be no less than halting, for which we shall show cause of repentance. . . . First, Mr. Cotton himself confesses that no national, provincial, diocesan, or parish church (wherein some truly godly are not) are true churches. Secondly, he practices no church estate but such as is constituted only of godly persons, nor admits any unregenerate or ungodly person. Thirdly, he confesses [that] a church of Christ cannot be constituted of such godly persons who are in bondage to the inordinate love of the world. Fourthly, if a church consists of such, God's people ought to separate from them.

Upon these his own confessions, I earnestly beseech Mr. Cotton and all that fear God to ponder how he can say he walks with an even foot between two extremes when according to his own confession, national churches, parish churches, yea a church constituted of godly persons given to inordinate love of the world, are false and to be separated from. And yet he will not have the parish church to be separated from for the remnant of pollution (I conceive he means ceremonies and bishops), notwithstanding that he also acknowledges that the generality of every parish in England consists of unregenerate persons and thousands in bondage not only to worldliness, but also ignorance, superstition, scoffing, swearing, cursing, whoredom, drunkenness, theft, [and] lying. What are two or three or more regenerate and godly persons in such communions but as two or three roses or lilies in a wilderness, a few grains of good corn in a heap of chaff, a few sheep among herds of wolves or swine (or, if more civil, flocks of goats), a little good dough swallowed up with a whole bushel of leaven, or a little precious gold confounded and mingled with a whole heap of dross? The searcher of all hearts knows I write this not to reproach any, knowing that [I] myself am by nature a child of wrath, and that the Father of mercies shows mercy to whom and when he will. But for the name of Christ Jesus, in loving faithfulness to my countrymen's souls and [in] defense of truth, I remember[23] my

---

22. Under Cotton's leadership, Massachusetts had sought a moderate approach to the relationship between its congregational church polity and the mother church. Through the adoption of the "congregational way," the Bay Colony had at least implicitly disowned the episcopy, but its leaders were also careful (for the most part) not to reject the English church's legitimacy altogether, for both theological and political reasons.

23. Remind.

worthy adversary of that state and condition from which his confessions say
he must separate. His practice in gathering of churches seems to say he does
separate,[24] and yet he professes [that] there are but some remnants of pollution amongst them from which he dares not separate.

Mr. Cotton: ". . . I know no man that reproaches Salem for their separation, nor do I believe that they do separate.[25] However, if any do reproach
them for it, I think it a sin meet[26] to be censured, but not with so deep a censure as to excommunicate all the churches, or to separate from them before
it appears that they tolerate their members in such causeless reproaches. We
confess [that] the errors of men are to be contended against not with reproaches but [with] the sword of the Spirit. But on the other side, the failings of the churches are not forthwith to be healed by separation. It is not
surgery but butchery to heal every sore in a member with no other [remedy]
but abscission from the body."

Answer. The church of Salem was known to profess separation, was generally and publicly reproached, and I could mention a case wherein she was
punished for it implicitly.[27] Mr. Cotton here confesses these two things,
which I leave to him to reconcile with his former profession here and elsewhere against separation. First, he says that if any reproach them for separation, it is a sin meet to be censured. Secondly, the churches themselves
may be separated from who tolerate their members in such causeless reproaches.[28] In these later passages he seems (as in [others of] his confessions

24. This is possibly a reference both to the Puritans' own zeal for keeping church membership as
pure as possible and to the de facto separation from Anglicanism that a move across the Atlantic afforded. For more on the similarities between the New England Puritans' implicit and the separatists'
principled separation, see Edmund S. Morgan, *Visible Saints: The History of a Puritan Idea* (Ithaca:
Cornell University Press, 1963).

25. Cotton denied that the Salem congregation itself was ever accused of separatism, evidently
drawing a distinction between a congregation's error in supporting a separatist (Williams, of
course) and espousing the view themselves. In Cotton's view, Salem was reprimanded for their support of Williams, not for their own separatist leanings. The evidence suggests, however, that Salem
historically had leaned more toward the separatism of the Plymouth Colony than the nonconfor-
mity of its sister churches in Massachusetts, which is why Williams felt at home there for a time.

26. Deserving.

27. Williams is, of course, referring to his own case.

28. According to Williams, Cotton justified withdrawal from fellowship with churches that
condoned baseless charges of separation at other congregations. To Williams, this "withdrawal"
amounted to nothing less than separation, a hypocritical invocation of separatism as a strategy for
congregational discipline while principled ecclesiological separatism was condemned. In reality,
however, Cotton never made the statement in support of withdrawal that Williams attributes to
him, at least not in the letter to which Williams is presently responding (See Bush, *The Correspondence of John Cotton*, 211–225), so this argument stands as an example of the "creative" license Williams often employed in interpreting his opponent's arguments to make his own stronger.

and practices mentioned) to be for it,[29] sensible of shame, disgrace, or reproach to be cast on it.

I grant with him the failings of the churches are not forthwith to be healed by separation, yet [he] himself within a few lines confesses there is a lawful separation from churches that do tolerate their members in causeless reproaches. I confess also that it is not surgery but butchery to heal every sore with no other medicine but with abscission from the body. Yet [he] himself confesses before that even churches of godly persons must be separated from for immoderate worldliness. And again here he confesses they may be separated from when they tolerate their members in such their causeless reproaches. Beside, it is not every sore or infirmity or ignorance, but an ulcer or gangrene of obstinacy for which I maintained that a person ought to be cut off, or a church separated from. But if he call that butchery, conscientiously and peaceably to separate from [the] spiritual communion of a church or society, what shall it be called by the second Adam the Lord Jesus . . . to cut off persons, them and theirs, branch and root, from any civil being [in] their territories (and consequently from the whole world, were their territories so large), because their consciences dare not bow down to any worship but what they believe the Lord Jesus appointed, and being also otherwise subject to the civil state and laws thereof. . . .

Separatism Is an Extension of Puritan Principles

Again, I believe that there hardly has ever been a conscientious Separatist who was not first a Puritan, for . . . the grounds and principles of the Puritans against bishops and ceremonies and [the profanity] of people professing Christ and the [needs] of Christ's flock [for] discipline must necessarily, if truly followed, lead on to and enforce a separation from such ways, worships, and worshippers, to seek out the true way of God's worship according to Christ Jesus. But what should be the reason, since the separation witnesses against the root of the church constitution itself, that yet he should find (as Mr. Cotton says) more favor than the Puritan or Nonconformist?[30]

---

29. That is, separation.

30. In response to Williams's charge that the New England Puritans were secretly practicing de facto separatism while hurting the cause of the separatists in old England with their diatribes against it, Cotton observed that the separatists actually enjoyed more pleasant political circumstances than the nonseparatist Puritans in England. Here Williams suggests a couple of reasons why that might be the case.

Doubtless the reasons are evident: First, most of God's servants who out of sight of the ignorance, unbelief, and profanity of the body of the national church, have separated and [dare] not have longer fellowship with it—I say most of them have been poor and low, and not such gainful customers to the bishops, their courts, and officers. . . . Secondly, it is a principle in nature to prefer a professed enemy before a pretended friend. Such as have separated have been looked at by the bishops and theirs as known and professed enemies, whereas the Puritans professed subjection and have submitted to the bishops, their courts, their officers, their common prayer and worships, and yet (as the bishops have well known) with no greater affection than the Israelites bore their cruel Egyptian taskmasters. . . .

Whether New England Christians Should Worship in the English Parishes

Lastly [Mr. Cotton] adds that such as erring through simplicity and tenderness have grown in grace, [they] have grown also to discern their lawful liberty in the hearing of the Word from English preachers.[31]

Answer. I will not question the uprightness of some who have gone back from many truths of God which they have professed. Yet my own experience of four sorts who have backslidden I shall report for a warning to all into whose hands these may come. . . . First, I have known no small number of such torn to absolute familism, and under their pretenses of great raptures of love deny all obedience to or seeking after the pure ordinances and appointments of the Lord Jesus.[32] Second, others have laid the reigns upon the

---

31. In the letter to which Williams is responding, Cotton observed that "separation is not a way that God hath prospered," by which he referred not to material or political fortune but to the fact that "he [God] hath not blessed it either with peace among themselves, or with growth of grace." By contrast, he points to the maturation of other Puritan sects who "erring through simplicitie and tendernesse of conscience have growne in grace" and as a result "have growne also to discerne their lawfull liberty to returne to the hearing of the word from English Preachers" (Bush, *The Correspondence of John Cotton,* 220). Cotton's point, then, is that separatism is a sign of spiritual immaturity; but Williams critiques the New Englanders' habit of visiting Anglican services while in the mother country as a sign of "backsliding."

32. The familists, or The Family of Love, were a sect that followed the teachings of the sixteenth-century Dutch mystic Hendrik Niclaes. Their emphasis on an immanent experience of Christ and heightened spiritual illumination, sometimes at the expense of external authorities like scripture, terrified the Puritans as much as the Quakers and other "antinomians" did. For more on familism, see Christopher W. Marsh, *The Family of Love in English Society, 1550–1630* (Cambridge: Cambridge University Press, 1994) and Christopher Hill, *The World Turned Upside Down: Radical Ideas during the English Revolution* (London: Penguin Books, 1984), 22–29.

necks of their consciences, and like the dog licked up their vomit of former looseness and profanations of lip and life, and have been so far from growing in grace that they have turned the grace of God into wantonness. Third, others backsliding have lost the beauty and shining of a tender conscience toward God and of a merciful compassion toward men, becoming most fierce persecutors of their own formerly fellow witnesses, and of any others who have differed in conscience from them. Lastly, others, although preserved from familism, profanations, and persecuting of others, yet the leaf of their Christian course has withered, the later beauty and favor of their holiness has not been like their former, and they . . . wish they were at liberty in their former freedom. . . .

Yes, says he, they have grown to discern their lawful liberty to return to the hearing of the Word from English preachers. Here I might engage myself in a controversy which . . . this treatise will [not] permit. . . . For such excellent and worthy persons whom Mr. Cotton here intends by the name English preachers, I acknowledge myself unworthy to hold the candle to them. Yet I shall humbly present what Mr. Cotton himself professes in three particulars: first, concerning this title "English preachers"; secondly, hearing the Word from such English preachers; thirdly, the lawful calling of such to the ministry or service, according to Christ Jesus.

For the first, he acknowledges that the ordinary ministers of the Gospel are pastors, teachers, bishops, overseers, [and] elders, and that their proper work is to feed and govern a truly converted, holy, and godly people, gathered into a flock or church estate. [It is] not properly [for] preachers to convert, beget, or make disciples, which the apostles and evangelists professedly were. Now then, that man that professes himself a minister, and professes to feed a flock or church with the ordinances of Word and prayer, he must acknowledge that his proper work is not to preach for conversion, which is most preposterous among a converted Christian people fed up with ordinances in church estate. So that according to Mr. Cotton's confession, English preachers are not pastors, teachers, bishops, or elders, but preachers of glad news (evangelists), men sent to convert and gather churches (apostles), ambassadors, trumpeters with proclamation from the King of Kings, to convert, subdue, and bring in rebellious unconverted, unbelieving, unchristian souls to the obedience and subjection of the Lord Jesus.

I readily confess that at the pastor's . . . feeding of his flock and the prophet's prophecy in the church, an unbeliever coming in [may be] convinced, fall on his face, and acknowledge God to be there. Yet this is accidental that any unbelievers should come in, and the pastor's work is to feed his flock (Acts 20). Prophecy is not for unbelievers but for them that believe, to edify, exhort, and comfort the church. . . .[33]

This passage I present for two reasons: first, because so many excellent and worthy persons mainly preach for conversion, as conceiving . . . the body of the people in England to be in a natural and unregenerate estate, and yet account they themselves fixed and constant officers and ministers to particular parishes or congregations, to whom they also administer the holy things of God, though sometimes few and sometimes none regenerate or new-born have been found among them. . . . Secondly, that in these great earthquakes wherein it pleases God to shake foundations civil and spiritual, such a ministry of Christ Jesus may be sought after whose proper work is preaching for converting and gathering of true penitents to the fellowship of the Son of God.

The second thing which Mr. Cotton himself has professed concerning English preachers is that . . . the Word [but] not the seals[34] may be received from them, because (says he) there is not communion in hearing and the Word is to be preached to all, but the seals he conceives (and that rightly) are profaned in being dispensed to the ungodly.

Answer. Mr. Cotton himself maintains that the dispensing of the Word in a church estate is Christ's feeding of his flock (Cant. 1:8), Christ's kissing of his spouse or wife (Cant. 1:2), Christ's embracing of his spouse in the marriage bed (Cant. 1:16), Christ's nursing of his children at his wife's breast (Cant. 4). And is there no communion between the shepherd and his sheep, the husband and his wife in chaste kisses and embraces, and the mother and her child at the breast? Besides, he confesses, that fellowship in the Gospel is

---

33. Here Williams is drawing on his distinction between "evangelists" or "apostles," with whom resided the authority to seek the conversion of nonbelievers and gather new churches, and "pastors," who were charged simply with caring for the spiritual needs of the believers entrusted to them. Williams argued that the Puritans erred by confusing the two offices; the lineage of properly commissioned apostles died out with the Constantinian compromise, and now pastors of congregations should not be in the business of actively trying to convert unbelievers to the faith. His use of this distinction undercut a major Puritan justification for compulsory church attendance, namely that it placed the reprobate in a context conducive to spiritual rebirth. For more on this aspect of Williams's ecclesiology and its implications for his arguments for religious liberty, see W. Clark Gilpin, *The Millenarian Piety of Roger Williams* (Chicago: University of Chicago Press, 1979); and James Calvin Davis, *The Moral Theology of Roger Williams* (Louisville, Ky.: Westminster John Knox Press, 2004), especially chapter 2.

34. Sacraments.

a fellowship or communion in the Apostles' doctrine, community, breaking of bread, and prayer, in which the first church continued (Acts 2:46)—all [of] which overthrows that doctrine of a lawful participation of the Word and prayer in a church estate, where it is not lawful to communicate in the breaking of bread or seals.

Thirdly, concerning the lawful communion or calling of English preachers: Mr. Cotton himself and others most eminent in New England have freely confessed that, notwithstanding their former profession of ministry in Old England, yet in New England until they received a calling from a particular church, they were but private Christians. Secondly, that Christ Jesus has appointed no other calling to the ministry but such as they practice in New England, and therefore consequently that all others which are not from a particular congregation of godly persons are none of Christ's—[for instance], a calling or commission received from a bishop, [or] from a parish of natural and unregenerate persons, [or] from some few godly persons yet remaining in a church fellowship after the parish way. . . .[35]

Conclusion

The close of this letter is an answer to a passage of mine which he repeats in an objection thus: "but this you fear is to condemn the witness of Jesus (the separate churches in London and elsewhere), and our jealous God will visit us for such arrears . . . because we come not forth to help Jehovah against the mighty; we pray not for them, we come not at them (but at parishes frequently), yea, we reproach and censure them." To which he answers . . . that they fear not the angels' curse, because it is not to help Jehovah but Satan to withdraw people from the parishes where they have found

---

35. Again, Williams is using Cotton's own theology against him to point out inconsistencies between what Cotton has taught and what he is practicing. Cotton, like most of the Puritan divines, believed that a true church was nothing more than a gathering of godly Christians who agreed by covenant to be a community of faithful worship and scriptural discipline. Consistent with this congregational vision of the church, ministers were commissioned by local churches and received their authority from this local calling. All of this was in contrast with the theology of apostolic succession under which the Church of England still operated; there bishops received their authority not from individual congregations, but from the hierarchy of the larger church. Williams cites this crucial theological difference to remind Cotton and his fellow Puritans of the illegitimacy of Anglican bishops in their own theology. Given this illegitimacy, Williams cannot understand how Cotton and his colleagues can justify sending their parishioners to worship under their leadership.

more preference of Christ and evidence of his Spirit than in separated churches. . . .[36]

However Mr. Cotton believes and writes of this point, yet he has not duly considered the following particulars:

First, the faithful labors of many witnesses of Jesus Christ, extant to the world, abundantly prove that the church of the Jews under the Old Testament in the type, and the church of the Christians under the New Testament in the antitype, were both separate from the world, and that when they opened a gap in the hedge or wall of separation between the Garden of the church and the wilderness of the world, God broke down the wall itself, removed the candlestick, and made his garden a wilderness, as at this day. And therefore if he will ever please to restore his garden and Paradise again, it must of necessity be walled in peculiarly to himself from the world, and all that shall be saved out of the world are to be transplanted out of the wilderness of [the] world and added to his church or garden.

Second, that all the grounds and principles leading to oppose bishops, ceremonies, common prayer, [and] prostitution of the ordinances of Christ to the ungodly and to the true practice of Christ's own ordinances, do necessarily . . . conclude a separation of holy from unholy, penitent from impenitent, godly from ungodly. . . .

Thirdly, the multitudes of holy and faithful men and women since Queen Mary's days have witnessed this truth by writing [and] disputing, and in suffering loss of goods and friends in imprisonments, banishments, [and] death. I confess [that] the Nonconformists[37] have suffered also, but they that have suffered for this cause have far exceeded in not only witnessing to those

36. In an earlier exchange, Williams had charged that the practices of the New England Puritans, in particular their frequenting of parish churches while in England and their disparaging public sentiments on separatism, were hurting the separatist cause in England, and that their abandonment of the struggling separatist movement was a failure "to help Jehovah against the mighty." Cotton responded that "it is not to helpe Jehovah, but Satan against him, to withdraw the people of God from hearing the voice of Christ which is preached in the evidence, and simplicity, and power of his Spirit in sundry Congregations (though they be Parishes) in our native Country." In fact, Cotton asserted, many New Englanders found more evidence of the Holy Spirit in parish churches than among the separatist congregations. Finally, Cotton admitted that "we doe not pray for the separate Churches by name . . . because we cannot pray in faith for a blessing upon their separation, which we see not to be of God not to be led to him" (Bush, *The Correspondence of John Cotton*, 221).

37. That is, the nonseparatist Puritans like Cotton.

grounds of the Nonconformists but to those truths also [which are] the un-
avoidable conclusions of the Nonconformists' principles.

Fourthly, what is that which Mr. Cotton and so many hundreds fearing
God in New England walk in, but a way of separation? Of what matter do
they profess to constitute their churches, but of true godly persons? In what
form do they cast this matter, but by a voluntary uniting or adding of such
godly persons whom they carefully examine and cause to make a public
confession of sin and profession of their knowledge and grace in Christ?
Nay, when other English have attempted to set up a congregation after the
parishional way, have they not been suppressed? Yea, have they not professedly and lately answered many worthy persons, whom they account
godly ministers and people, that they could not permit them to live in the
same commonwealth together with them, if they set up any other church
and worship then what themselves practice? Let their own souls, and the
souls of others, seriously ponder in the fear of God what should be the reason why themselves so practicing, [they] should persecute others for not
leaving open a gap of liberty to escape persecution and the cross of Christ by
frequenting the parishes in Old England, which parishes [they] themselves
persecute in New England, and will not permit to breathe in the common
air amongst them. . . .[38]

Upon these considerations how can Mr. Cotton be offended that I should
help (as he calls them) any zealous souls, not against the mighty ordinances
of the Lord Jesus, but to seek after the Lord Jesus without halting? Yea, why
should Mr. Cotton, or any desirous to practice reformation, kindle a fire of
persecution against such zealous souls, especially considering that [they]
themselves, had they so inveighed against bishops, common prayer, [and the
like] in the days of Edward VI, [would have] been accounted as great heretics in those reforming times as any now can be in these? Yet would it have
been then, and since has it been, great oppression and tyranny to persecute
their consciences, and still will it be for them to persecute the consciences of
others in Old or New England.

How can I better end than Mr. Cotton does, by warning that all that will

38. In other words, Williams asks why he and others are persecuted when they refuse to grant
spiritual clemency to those who frequent parish churches when in England, when those very same
churches are suppressed when they are introduced in New England.

not kiss the Son (that is, hear and embrace the words of his mouth) shall perish in their way (Ps. 2:12)? And I desire Mr. Cotton, and every soul to whom these lines may come, seriously to consider in this controversy: if the Lord Jesus were himself in person in Old or New England, what church, what ministry, what worship, what government would he set up, and what persecution would [he] practice toward them that would not receive Him?

CHAPTER TWO

Queries of Highest Consideration

Proposed to Mr. Thomas Goodwin, Mr. Phillip Nye, Mr. William Bridges,
Mr. Jeremiah Burroughs, Mr. Sidrach Simpson and
to the Commissioners from the General Assembly (so called)
of the Church of Scotland
upon occasion of their late printed apologies
for themselves and their churches.
In all humble reverence presented to the view of the
Right Honorable House of the High Court of Parliament.

In 1643, the year before Roger Williams's first return to England, the House of Commons officially requested that Charles I call a general synod to pursue ecclesiastical reform. Recognizing that an attack on the prelacy was an assault on the authority of the throne itself, Charles refused. With this final breach between king and Parliament, the English Civil War began. Parliament soon entered into political league with Scotland, a covenant that ensured the defeat of the royalists but included the stipulation that Parliament would push England toward an embrace of Presbyterianism, the form of government practiced in the Church of Scotland. Later that year, Parliament commissioned the Westminster Assembly with the expectation that it would pursue just these kinds of reform.

Among the Westminster divines, however, was a small but politically well-connected group of Independents, led by the so-called "Five Dissenting Brethren"—Thomas Goodwin, Phillip Nye, William Bridges, Sidrach Simpson, and Jeremiah Burroughs. When Presbyterianism appeared set to prevail in the Assembly, the Five Dissenting Brethren issued a public letter of protest, entitled "An Apologetical Narration," in which they defended the superiority of congregational church polity and rejected the idea of established Presbyterianism. Prominent Scottish participants in the Assembly publicly fired back, and the intractable hostility between Independents and Presbyterians threatened to divide the Parliamentary forces. In England during these controversies, Williams in 1644 published the following "queries" as an anonymous challenge to both

*factions in the debate. On display in this treatise are his dual principles of sepa-
ratism and religious freedom, culled in the New England wilderness and now
applied to similar controversies in the mother country.*

To the Right Honorable Both Houses of the High Court of Parliament

Right Honorable:

It is a woeful privilege attending all great states and personages that they seldom hear any other music but what is known will please them. Though our music sounds not sweet but harsh, yet please you first to know it is not fitted to your ears, but to your hearts, and the bleeding heart of this afflicted nation. It is true [that] we have been humbly bold to presume, as Esther into Ahaserus's presence, against your Order, for who can pass the many locks and bars of any the several licensers appointed by you with such a message?[1] By such circumscribing and immuring of yourselves by such a guard (their persons we honor and esteem), it is rarely possible that any other light but what their hemisphere affords shall ever shine on your honors' souls, though never so sweet, so necessary, and though it come from God, from Heaven.

These worthy and much esteemed persons to whom we query we have heard to be men of conscience, of abilities, and [they] are in this worthy of double honor, that (according to their consciences) they appear in the front and present their molds and patterns of church government from Holland[2] [and] from Scotland[3] to our inquiring England. Their mutual just excep-tions which they have already or may further express against each others' tenets we leave to themselves (though we might express them to our advan-tage), [but] we shall be humbly bold in the name of the Lord Jesus, and the many thousand precious souls for whom he has paid so dear a ransom, to present such queries to your honors' views. . . .

Most renowned patriots, you sit at [the] helm in as great a storm as ever poor England's commonwealth was lost in. Yet be you pleased to remember that (excepting the affairs of heaven, of religion, of souls, of eternity) all

---

1. The advisors to whom Williams refers are presumably the combatant divines associated with the Westminster Assembly.

2. Most of the Independents had ties to Holland, where a policy of religious tolerance allowed them to set up their churches in the congregational form they preferred. Because of the tolerant cli-mate in Holland, many Puritans sought refuge there during royalist campaigns against them, in-cluding the prominent Puritan theologian William Ames and some who eventually made their way to New England.

3. Scotland, of course, was the primary source of the influx of Presbyterianism in this contest.

your consultations, conclusions, executions, are not of the quantity or the value of one poor drop of water, or the little dust of the balance, if Isaiah were a true prophet (Isaiah 40:15).[4] Yet concerning souls, we will not (as most do) charge you with the loads of all the souls in England, Scotland, [and] Ireland. We shall humbly affirm and (by the help of Christ) maintain that the bodies and goods of the subject [are] your charge. Their souls (and yours) are set on account to those that profess to be the lights and guides, the messengers and ambassadors sent from heaven to them.[5]

You will please to say: we are constantly told, and we believe, that religion is our first care, and reformation of that our greatest task. Right honorable, your wisdoms know the fatal miscarriages of England's parliaments in this point, what setting up, pulling down, what formings, reformings, and again deformings, to admiration. . . . We shall in all humble reverence suggest our fears, that for the very laws and statutes of England's parliaments concerning religion (and happily for some not yet suspected), the Lord Jesus has drawn this sword that's daily drunk with English blood.

It shall never be your honor to this or future ages to be confined to the patterns of either French, Dutch, Scotch, or New England churches. We humbly conceive some higher act concerning religion attends and becomes your consultations. If he whose name is Wonderful Counselor be consulted and obeyed according to his last will and testament (as you may please in the Queries to view), we are confident you shall exceed the acts and patterns of all neighbor nations, highly exalt the name of the Son of God, provide for the peace of this distressed state, engage the souls of all that fear God to give thanks and supplicate for you, further the salvation of thousands, and leave the sweet perfume of your names precious to all succeeding generations.

Queries Propounded to the Five Holland Ministers, and the Scottish Commissioners

Worthy Sirs, in serious examination of your late apologies, we shall in all due respect and tenderness humbly query:

4. "Behold, the nations are as a drop of a bucket, and are counted as the small dust of the balance. . ." (Isaiah 40:15).
5. Presumably Williams is referring to ministers, evangelists, and other religious leaders. In contrast to many representatives of his Calvinist tradition (including Calvin himself), Williams did not believe that magistrates had any divinely ordained responsibility to defend the faith with civil power.

Query I: Neither the name nor the function of the assembly of divines is biblically justified

First, what precept or pattern has the Lord Jesus left you in his last will and testament for your synod or assembly of divines, by virtue of which you may expect his presence and assistance? If you say (as all popish synods and councils do) the pattern is plain, Acts 15, we ask if two or three brethren of one particular congregation at Antioch sent to that first mother church at Jerusalem, where the Apostles were—who being (immediately) inspired from God, could say, "It seems good to the Holy Spirit and us to lay upon you no greater burden," [and] who also had power to make decrees for all churches (Acts 16)—we ask whether this be a pattern for a nation or kingdom . . . to send their several priests and deacons . . . to reform or form a religion?

We pray you to consider if the golden image be not a type and figure of the several national and state religions, which all nations set up and ours has done, for which the wrath of God is now upon us?

We pray you also to answer in what part of Christ's testament is found that title "the assembly of divines," and whether it be not in English "the church of godly ones"? And as we queried your ground for such a church so have we also cause to pray you to tell us where Christ Jesus has given you power to assume and appropriate such a title to yourselves, which seems in Scripture to be common to all the children of God? Some express it in print and pulpit, "the assembly of godly divines." We derogate not from the worth or godliness of any of them, yet you know the assembly of saints or godly divines is no other in English than the assembly or church of saints. . . . We presume you will grant others to be saints and godly too in that sense. . . .

Query II: Both Presbyterians and Independents err in seeking a state-established church polity

Whereas you both agree (though with some difference) that the civil magistrate must reform the church, establish religion, and so consequently must first judge and judicially determine which is true [and] which is false, or else must implicitly believe as the Assembly believes and take it upon trust, so consequently is [the magistrate] the Head, Root, and Fountain of the Supremacy of all spiritual power and has the power of the Keys of opening and shutting heaven's gates.[6] Of which power King Henry, upon a grudge (as 'tis said) about his wife, despoiled the pope and with consent and act of Parliament sat down himself in the pope's chair in England, as since his successors have done? We now query, since the Parliament (being the representative [of the] commonwealth) has no other power but what the commonwealth derives to and trusts it with, whether it not evidently follow that the commonwealth, the nation, the kingdom, and (if it were in Augustus his time) the whole world must rule and govern the church, and Christ himself as the church is called (1 Cor. 12:12).

Furthermore, if the Honorable Houses (the representative [of the] commonwealth) shall erect a spiritual court for the judging of spiritual men and spiritual causes (although a new name be put on it), yet [we ask] whether or no such a Court is not in the true nature and kind of it a High Commission?[7] And is not this a reviving of Moses, and the sanctifying of a new Land of Canaan, of which we hear nothing in the Testament of Christ Jesus, nor of any other holy nation but the particular Church of Christ (I Peter 2:9)?

Is not this to subject this holy nation, this heavenly Jerusalem, the wife and spouse of Jesus, the pillar and ground of truth, to the vain uncertain and changeable mutations of this present evil world? Who knows not in how few years the commonwealth of England has set up and pulled down? The fathers made the children heretics, and the children the fathers. How does the Parliament in Henry VIII's days condemn the absolute popery in

6. "And Simon Peter answered and said, Thou art the Christ, the Son of the living God. And Jesus answered and said unto him, Blessed art thou, Simon Barjona: for flesh and blood hath not revealed it unto thee, but my Father which is in heaven. And I say also unto thee, That thou art Peter, and upon this rock I will build my church; and the gates of hell shall not prevail against it. And I will give unto thee the keys of the kingdom of heaven: and whatsoever thou shalt bind on earth shall be bound in heaven: and whatsoever thou shalt loose on earth shall be loosed in heaven" (Matthew 16:16–19). The "power of the keys" historically was interpreted by the Roman Catholic Church as Jesus' conferral of all ecclesiastical authority on Peter and his successors in the papacy. In rejecting the pope's authority, Protestants tended to interpret the "power of the keys" as the authority of the church as a body to forgive sins, to welcome and excommunicate members, and in general to represent the will of Christ on earth. By arguing that state-supported religion effectively transfers the power of the keys to the civil magistrate, Williams is arguing that Presbyterians and Independents have replaced the pope with Parliament, an especially biting indictment in anti-Catholic England.

7. The Court of High Commission was the highest ecclesiastical court in post-Reformation England and served essentially as an arm of enforcement for the crown. Charged with defending the monarch's prerogatives as Supreme Head of the Church of England and squelching religious dissent, the High Commission in the seventeenth century devoted much of its time to rooting out especially troubling Puritans. One of the first acts of the Puritan-heavy Parliament in its revolt against King Charles I was the dissolution of the High Commission in 1641.

Henry VII? How, in the time of Edward VI, [is] the Parliament of Henry VIII condemned for their half popery half Protestantism? How soon does Queen Mary's Parliament condemn Edward for his absolute Protestantism? And Elizabeth's Parliament as soon condemn Queen Mary's for their absolute popery? 'Tis true, Queen Elizabeth made laws against popery and papists, but the government of bishops, the common prayer, [and] the ceremonies were then so high in that queen's and Parliament's eye that the members of this present and ever renowned Parliament would have then been counted little less than heretics. And oh, since the commonwealth cannot without a spiritual rape force the consciences of all to one worship, oh that it may never commit that rape, in forcing the consciences of all men to one worship, which a stronger arm and sword may soon (as formerly) arise to alter. . . .

Query VII: The idea of a "national covenant" challenged by scripture and experience

Since the Law was given by Moses but grace and truth came by Jesus Christ, by whom . . . he has now revealed his counsel in these last times (Heb. 1), we query where now you find one footstep, print, or pattern in this doctrine of the Son of God for a national holy covenant, and so consequently . . . a national church? Where find you evidence of a whole nation, country, or kingdom converted to the faith, and of Christ's appointing a whole nation or kingdom to walk in one way of religion? If you repair to Moses, consult with Moses and the old covenant or Testament, we ask are you Moses' or Christ's followers? Or do you expect the coming of the Son of God to set up the Christian Israel, the holy nation, the particular congregation of Christian worshippers in all parts of the world (1 Peter 2, Heb. 12)?

We further query whether a national covenant leads not . . . unavoidably to a holy covenant of many nations, and yet to a holy league or covenant . . . of the whole world, which should then turn the Darling and Spouse of God between whom and it there is such enmity (that is, "if any man love the world, the love of the Father is not in him" [1 John 2])? . . .

Again, we ask whether the constitution of a national church can possibly be framed without a racking and tormenting of the souls, as well as of the bodies, of persons. For it seems not possible to fit it to every conscience; sooner shall one suit of apparel fit every body, one law [preside over] every case, or one size . . . every foot! Lastly, [we ask] whether it be not the cause of a world of hypocrites, the soothing up of people in a formal state of worship, to the ruin of their souls, the ground of persecution to Christ Jesus in his members, and sooner or later, the kindling of the devouring flames of civil wars, as all ages justify!

Query VIII: Christ does not endorse violent defense of religion

Although (as is expressed) the godly in the three kingdoms desire a reformation, yet since the Lamb of God and Prince of Peace has not in his Testament given us a pattern, precept, or promise for the undertaking of a civil war for his sake, we query how with comfort to your souls you may encourage the English treasure to be exhausted and the English blood to be spilled for the cause of Christ? We readily grant the civil magistrate armed by God with a civil sword (Rom. 13) to execute vengeance against robbers, murderers, and tyrants. Yet where it merely concerns Christ, we find when his disciples desire vengeance upon offenders (Luke 9), he meekly answers, "You know not what spirit you are of; I came not to destroy men's lives but to save them." If ever there was cause for the servants of Christ Jesus to fight, it was when . . . his most holy person was in danger (Matt. 26). Yet then that Lamb of God checks Peter beginning to fight for him, telling him "that all who take sword shall perish by the sword." For with one request from his Father, he could have been rescued by more than twelve legions of angels. He renders the reason [for] his unwillingness to have fighting for his sake, which was his Father's good pleasure in the fulfilling of the Scripture. To which also may be added John 18:36—"My kingdom is not of this world; if my kingdom were of this world, then would my servants fight that I should not be delivered."

If it be said his kingdom then was not of this world but now it is or shall be, then was the hour of his suffering but now of his servants reigning—[if this be said, then] we query . . . what means that general rule of the Lord Jesus [in] Luke 9: "If any man will follow me, let him take up his cross . . . ," and that of Paul: "all that will live godly in Christ Jesus must suffer persecution" (2 Timothy 4)?[8]

We query (if security may be taken by the wisdom of the state, for civil subjection) why even the papists themselves and their consciences may not be permitted in the world? For otherwise, if England's government were the government of the whole world, not only they but a world of idolaters of all

---

8. In other words, Williams contends that suffering, not political power, is the response to persecution that Christ expected his church to adopt.

sorts . . . must be driven out of the world! We query whether the common body of Protestants, impenitent and unregenerate, be not further off salvation and lie not under a greater guilt . . . than does the body of ignorant papists? And we humbly desire it may be deeply pondered what [kindled] the jealousy of God to pour forth the blood of so many thousands of Protestants by the bloody hands of the papists—whether or not the laws enacted and violence offered even to the consciences of papists themselves have not kindled these devouring flames?[9]

'Tis true, the prophecies are great concerning Christ and Antichrist throughout the prophets and the Revelation, but can you sufficiently demonstrate these to the consciences of men? . . . Can you clear up the mysteries of Daniel's 2300 days (Dan. 8), Daniel's seven weeks and three score and two weeks, his one week, and his half week (Dan. 9)? . . . Can you unlock those mystical numbers of John's 42 months, 1260 days, the three days and a half (Rev. 11:12), . . . with diverse others which may establish the judgments and consciences of men, and give them warrant whereon to venture their souls and shed their blood for the present destruction of pope and popery, not by the breath of Christ's mouth and the sword of the Spirit, but by the breath of murdering cannons and a flaming sword of steel?[10] Otherwise we query whether the blood of so many hundreds of thousands of Protestants, mingled with the blood of so many hundreds of thousands of papists—as was spilled some hundred years since in the Waldensian wars,[11] when all the

9. Williams's point here, that Roman Catholics should be permitted religious and political tolerance (and that failure to do so puts Protestants throughout Europe in jeopardy), is remarkably radical for seventeenth-century England. English Protestants, for both political and religious reasons, deeply distrusted Catholics.

10. Seventeenth-century Protestants often took license for their violence toward Catholics from biblical prophecy. The pope was widely regarded as the Antichrist whose rule was predicted in scripture, so that his defeat was understood to be a necessary step toward ushering in the return of Christ. By contrast, Williams recommends theological humility in reading these prophecies; even if the Roman pope is the Antichrist (a conviction Williams shared with his fellow Puritans), it is a mistake to interpret biblical prophecy as encouraging anything more than *spiritual* battle against the influence of Catholicism.

11. The war to which Williams is referring is likely (given his reference to "some hundred years since") the persecution of the Waldensians in France, persecution that resulted in the virtual elimination of the sect in the Provence area by the middle of the sixteenth century. The Waldensians were a Christian community originating in the twelfth century and emphasizing voluntary poverty and itinerant preaching. At the time of the persecution to which Williams refers, the sect was closely allied with other French Protestant communities. The Catholic Church considered the Waldensians to be heretics and pursued their destruction periodically throughout Europe from their initial appearance through the seventeenth century.

Protestant party that took the sword perished with it—be not a warning to us their offspring?

It is true, John tells us of Christ's great battles against the kings of the earth, against the Beast and the false prophet, against Gog and Magog,[12] but where speaks he of other ammunition and artillery used by the saints [except for] what we find in Paul's Christian magazine, Ephesians 6?[13] Where read we of any horse and arms but those all white (Rev. 19)? And yet the Lamb shall have the victory over the Beast, the false prophet, and over Gog and Magog in the appointed season. . . .

Query X: Success in suppressing heresy is not proof of a commonwealth's godliness

Since you report your opposing and suppressing of heresies [as] glorious successes, we query whether that be a demonstrative argument from the Scriptures, . . . since even the Church of Rome may boast of the same against many schisms and heresies, and does triumph with wonderful success, even against the truth (and witnesses of it), according to Daniel's and John's prophecies (Dan. 11, Rev. 13)? Thus it pleased God in his providence to turn the scales of victory . . . to the idolatrous Israelites and Edomites against the Moabites (2 Kings 3) and miraculously to deliver idolatrous apostate Israel from the mighty armies of the Syrians (2 Kings 7). Thus he also awarded hypocritical Jehu for his temporal service in destroying Ahab's house with a temporal honor to the fourth generation, though [he] and his continued in the schism, apostasy, and idolatry of the house of Israel. . . . Thus the Lord Jesus heard the prayers of the devils themselves [in]

---

12. "And when the thousand years are expired, Satan shall be loosed out of his prison, and shall go out to deceive the nations which are in the four quarters of the earth, Gog and Magog, to gather them together to battle: the number of whom is as the sand of the sea. And they went up on the breadth of the earth, and compassed the camp of the saints about, and the beloved city: and fire came down from God out of heaven, and devoured them" (Revelation 20:7–9).

13. "Finally, my brethren, be strong in the Lord, and in the power of his might. Put on the whole armour of God, that ye may be able to stand against the wiles of the devil. For we wrestle not against flesh and blood, but against principalities, against powers, against the rulers of the darkness of this world, against spiritual wickedness in high places. Wherefore take unto you the whole armour of God, that ye may be able to withstand in the evil day, and having done all, to stand. Stand therefore, having your loins girt about with truth, and having on the breastplate of righteousness; And your feet shod with the preparation of the gospel of peace; Above all, taking the shield of faith, wherewith ye shall be able to quench all the fiery darts of the wicked. And take the helmet of salvation, and the sword of the Spirit, which is the word of God . . ." (Ephesians 6:10–17).

Luke 8.[14] Upon the cry of the idolatrous mariners, God mercifully provided to answer their prayers and cease the storm by the casting out of Jonah. Thus upon the external legal humiliation of Nineveh, [the city] was reprieved and spared a season. . . .

We query whether all these instances amount to more than evidence of the infinite mercies, goodness, and patience of God, but are not proofs of their worshipping of God according to his ordinance, that their institutions were from him and their reformations according to his appointment? Yes, we further query whether the power of godliness shining forth in persons may evidence their state and worship good? You both[15] confess the great profession of the power of godliness in England, yet we believe one of you acknowledges [the idea of] the Church of England as a national church [to be] not true,[16] and both confess the [current church] government, governors, and the common prayer . . . to be abominable. Yet it is confessed that England's false national church with her bishops, common prayer, and ceremonies had more evidence of the power of godliness in her children than was to be found among the Scotch, French, or Dutch, who pretend a purer reformation. It seems therefore evident that neither opposing heresies nor success in victories . . . nor power of godliness in some persons can evidence and prove their state and worship to be right and pleasing to God, according to his ordinance in Christ Jesus. . . .

Query XII: Religious persecution is inconsistent with Christ's way and a desire for civil peace

Since you both profess to want more light, and that a greater light is yet to be expected, yea, that the Church of Scotland may yet have need of a greater reformation: we query how you can profess and swear to persecute all others

---

14. "And when he went forth to land, there met him out of the city a certain man, which had devils long time, and ware no clothes, neither abode in any house, but in the tombs. When he saw Jesus, he cried out, and fell down before him, and with a loud voice said, What have I to do with thee, Jesus, thou Son of God most high? I beseech thee, torment me not. . . . And Jesus asked him, saying, What is thy name? And he said, Legion: because many devils were entered into him. And they besought him that he would not command them to go out into the deep. And there was there an herd of many swine feeding on the mountain: and they besought him that he would suffer them to enter into them. And he suffered them. Then went the devils out of the man, and entered into the swine: and the herd ran violently down a steep place into the lake, and were choked" (Luke 8:27–33).

15. Again, referring to both Independents and Presbyterians.

16. The Independents rejected the idea of a single national church, while the Presbyterians retained it.

as schismatics and heretics that believe they see a further light and dare not join with either of your churches? Whether the Lamb's wife[17] has received any such commission or disposition from the Lamb her husband so to practice?[18] Whether (as King James once wrote upon Rev. 20) it be not a true mark and character of a *false* church to persecute, it being the nature only of a wolf to hunt the lambs and sheep but impossible for a lamb or sheep or a thousand flocks of sheep to persecute one wolf? (We speak of spiritual sheep and spiritual wolves; for other wolves against the civil state we profess it to be the duty of the civil state to persecute and suppress them.)

And lastly, whether the states of Holland who tolerate, though not own (as you say), the several sects amongst them which differ from them and are of another conscience and worship—whether or not they come not nearer the holy pattern and command of the Lord Jesus, to permit the tares to have a civil being in the field of the world, until the harvest the end of it (Mat. 13)? Whether those tares can possibly be taken for hypocrites in the church or scandalous persons in the commonwealth, but are most properly [interpreted as] false worshippers . . . ?[19] Whether for this very truth which those states profess, it has not pleased the Lord to prosper the state above any other state in the world, beyond either England or Scotland, for the time since their wise permission?

Whether there can possibly be expected the least look of peace in these fatal distractions and tempests raised but by taking counsel of the great and wisest politician that ever was, the Lord Jesus Christ, in this particular? We know the allegations against this counsel: the head of all is that from Moses . . . , his pattern in the typical land of Canaan, the kings of Israel and Judah. We humbly desire it may be searched into, and we believe it will be found [that civil compulsion of religion is] but one of Moses' shadows [that] vanished at the coming of the Lord Jesus. Such a shadow is directly opposite to the very testament and coming of the Lord Jesus; opposite to the very nature of a Christian church, the only holy nation and Israel of God; opposite to the very tender bowels of humanity (how much more of Christianity!), abhorring to pour out the blood of men merely for their souls' belief and worship; opposite to the very essentials and fundamentals of the na-

17. That is, the church.
18. That is, persecution.
19. For more on Williams's interpretation of this favorite biblical parable, see the introduction to this volume.

ture of a civil magistrate, a civil commonwealth or combination of men, which can respect only civil things; opposite to the Jews' conversion to Christ, by not permitting them a civil life or being; opposite to the civil peace and the lives of millions slaughtered on this ground, in mutual persecution [of] each others' consciences (especially the Protestant and the papist); opposite to the souls of all men, who by persecutions are ravished into a dissembled worship which their hearts embrace not; opposite to the best of God's servants, who in all popish and Protestant states have been commonly esteemed and persecuted as . . . schismatics [and] heretics; opposite to that light of Scripture which is expected yet to shine, which must by that doctrine [of persecution] be suppressed as a new or old heresy or novelty. All this in all ages experience testifies, which never saw any long-lived fruit of peace or righteousness to grow upon that fatal tree.

CHAPTER THREE

The Bloody Tenent of Persecution
for Cause of Conscience

discussed in a Conference between TRUTH and PEACE,
Who, in all tender Affection, present to the High
Court of Parliament (as the Result of their Discourse)
these (amongst other Passages) of highest consideration.

While in London trying to secure a charter for his fledgling colony, Williams published The Bloody Tenent *in 1644. Written as an extended dialogue between Truth and Peace, this treatise represents Williams's most famous commendation of religious toleration. The circumstances in which Williams wrote appear to have been less than ideal, for evidence abounds in the text that he prepared it hurriedly and without the benefit of editorial review. The occasion for its appearance was also a matter of dispute. Several years before, John Cotton had received an excerpt from an anonymous attack on religious persecution entitled* An Humble Supplication to the King's Majesty *(which Williams included as a preface to* The Bloody Tenent *under the title "Scriptures and Reasons"). Cotton claimed that Williams had sent him the tract (though Williams denied it), so when he prepared a response he sent it to Williams (Williams also denied being sent Cotton's response). Cotton's response to* An Humble Supplication *serves as the backbone of* The Bloody Tenent, *with Truth (at Peace's urging) providing a point-by-point rebuttal of Cotton's defense of religious uniformity in New England. With the publishing of* The Bloody Tenent, *Cotton was incensed that Williams had violated a presumption of privacy in their correspondence, but since Williams denied having anything directly to do with both sending the tract to Cotton and receiving his rebuttal, he felt he could assume Cotton's position to be a matter of public record. In* The Bloody Tenent, *Williams presents many of his most important arguments against religious per-*

secution, insisting that persecution is not only contrary to Christian charity and the spirit of Christ, but also ineffective in promoting conversion, unnecessary and in fact counterproductive to the cause of civil stability, and unfair in light of the liberties the Puritans longed for when they were the minority in England.

The Treatise's Arguments

First, that the blood of so many hundred thousand souls of Protestants and Papists, spilled in the wars of present and former ages for their respective consciences, is not required nor accepted by Jesus Christ, the Prince of Peace.

Second, pregnant Scriptures and arguments are throughout the work proposed against the doctrine of persecution for cause of conscience.

Third, satisfactory answers are given to Scriptures and objections produced by Mr. Calvin, Mr. Beza, Mr. Cotton, and the ministers of the New England Churches and others former and later, tending to prove the doctrine of persecution for cause of conscience.

Fourth, the doctrine of persecution for cause of conscience is proved guilty of all the blood of the souls crying for vengeance under the altar.[1]

Fifth, all civil states, with their officers of justice in their respective constitutions and administrations, are proved essentially civil, and therefore not judges, governors, or defenders of the spiritual or Christian state and worship.

Sixth, it is the will and command of God that (since the coming of his Son the Lord Jesus) a permission of the most pagan, Jewish, Turkish, or Antichristian consciences and worships be granted to all men in all nations and countries, and they are only to be fought against with that sword which is only (in soul matters) able to conquer, [that is], the sword of God's Spirit, the Word of God.

Seventh, the state of the Land of Israel, the kings and people thereof in peace and war, is proved figurative and ceremonial, and no pattern nor precedent for any kingdom or civil state in the world to follow.

---

1. "And when he had opened the fifth seal, I saw under the altar the souls of them that were slain for the word of God, and for the testimony which they held. And they cried with a loud voice, saying, How long, O Lord, holy and true, dost thou not judge and avenge our blood on them that dwell on the earth?" (Revelation 6:9–10).

Eighth, God requires not uniformity of religion to be enacted and enforced in any civil state. Such enforced uniformity sooner or later is the greatest occasion of civil war, of the ravishing of conscience, of the persecution of Christ Jesus in his servants, and of the hypocrisy and destruction of millions of souls.

Ninth, in holding an enforced uniformity of religion in a civil state, we must necessarily disclaim our desires and hopes of the Jews' conversion to Christ.

Tenth, an enforced uniformity of religion throughout a nation or civil state confounds the civil and religious, denies the principles of Christianity and civility, and denies that Jesus Christ is come in the flesh.

Eleventh, the permission of consciences and worships other than that which a state professes can only (according to God) procure a firm and lasting peace (good assurance being taken according to the wisdom of the civil state for uniformity of civil obedience from all sorts).

Twelfth and last, true civility and Christianity may both flourish in a state or kingdom, notwithstanding the permission of diverse and contrary consciences, either of Jew or Gentile.

To the Right Honorable, Both Houses of the High Court of Parliament

Right Honorable and Renowned Patriots:

Next to the saving of your own souls (in the lamentable shipwreck of mankind), your task as *Christians* is to save the souls, but as *magistrates* the bodies and goods, of others. Many excellent discourses have been presented to your fathers' hands and yours in former and present parliaments. I shall be humbly bold to say that in what concerns your duties as magistrates towards others, a more necessary and seasonable debate was never yet presented. . . .

Your Honors have been famous to the end of the world for your unparalleled wisdom, courage, justice, and mercy in vindicating your civil laws and liberties. Yet let it not be grievous to your Honors' thoughts to ponder a little why all the prayers and tears and fastings in this nation have not pierced the heavens and quenched these flames, which yet who knows how far they'll spread, and when they'll out! Your Honors have broken the jaws of the oppressor and taken the prey out of their teeth (Job 29), for which act I believe it has pleased the Most High God to set a guard, not only of trained men but of mighty angels, to secure your sitting and the city.[2]

But I fear we are not pardoned, though reprieved: O that there may be a lengthening of London's tranquility, of the Parliament's safety, by mercy to the poor (Dan. 4)! Right Honorable, soul yokes, soul oppression, plunderings, and ravishings are of a crimson and deepest dye, and I believe the chief of England's sins, unstopping the vials of England's present sorrows. This glass[3] presents your Honors with arguments from *Religion, Reason,* [and] *Experience,* all proving that the greatest yokes yet lying upon English necks (the peoples' and your own) are of a spiritual and soul nature.

All former parliaments have changed these yokes according to their consciences, popish or Protestant. 'Tis now your Honors' turn at the helm, and as it is your task, so I hope it is your resolution, not to *change* (for that is but to turn the wheel, which another parliament and the very next may turn again) but to *ease* the subjects and yourselves from a yoke . . . which neither you nor your fathers were ever able to bear. Most noble senators, your fathers (whose seats you fill) are . . . moldering their brains, their tongues to ashes in the pit of rottenness; they and you must shortly (together with two worlds of men) appear at the great bar. It shall then be no grief of heart that you have now attended to the cries of souls, thousands oppressed, millions ravished by the acts and statutes concerning souls not yet repealed, of bodies impoverished and imprisoned for their souls' belief, yea slaughtered on heaps for religion's controversies in the wars of present and former ages. . . .

It cannot be denied to be a pious and prudential act for Your Honors (according to your conscience) to call for the advice of faithful counselors in the high debates concerning your own and the souls of others. Yet let it not be imputed as a crime for any supplicant to the God of heaven for you, in the humble sense of what their souls believe, to pour forth (amongst others) these three requests at the throne of grace. First, that neither your Honors nor those excellent and worthy persons whose advice you seek limit the Holy One of Israel to their apprehensions, debates, and conclusions, rejecting or neglecting the humble and faithful suggestions of any (though as base as spittle and clay) with which sometimes Christ Jesus opens the eyes of

---

2. This is a reference to Parliament's victory over King Charles (who had fled London by the time this treatise was published), Archbishop Laud (who was in prison), and their royalist supporters.

3. That is, the current text.

them that are born blind. Second, that the present and future generations of the sons of men may never have cause to say that such a Parliament . . . should model the worship of the living, eternal, and invisible God after the bias of any earthly interest. . . . Third, whatever way of worshipping God your own consciences are persuaded to walk in, yet . . . may it never be told, at Rome nor at Oxford, that the Parliament of England has committed a greater rape than if they had forced or ravished the bodies of all the women in the world—nor that England's Parliament (so famous throughout all Europe and the world) should at last turn Papists, Prelatists, Presbyterians, Independents, Socinians, Familists, and Antinomians by confirming all these sorts of consciences by civil force and violence to their consciences.[4]

Here The Bloody Tenent *includes (1) a preface ("To Every Courteous Reader"), which outlines some of the arguments to appear in the treatise; (2) an unhelpfully detailed table of contents; (3) "Scriptures and Reasons," an excerpt from the anonymous tract originally entitled* An Humble Supplication, *which makes the case for religious toleration by citing biblical texts as well as notables from church tradition; and (4) John Cotton's response to* An Humble Supplication, *the arguments of which form the pretext for* The Bloody Tenent.

A Reply to the aforesaid Answer of Mr. Cotton, in a Conference between TRUTH and PEACE

Truth. In what dark corner of the world, sweet Peace, are we two met? How has this present evil world banished me from all its coasts and quarters? And how has the righteous God in judgment taken you from the earth (Rev. 6:4)?

Peace. 'Tis lamentably true, blessed Truth, that the foundations of the world have long been out of course. The gates of earth and hell have conspired together to intercept our joyful meeting and our holy kisses. With

---

4. The identity of the "Papists," "Presbyterians," and "Independents" is clear enough; the term "Prelatist" referred to Anglicans who were loyal to the church of England and its hierarchy of bishops. Socinians, Familists, and Antinomians were Protestant sects persecuted by just about everyone in seventeenth-century England for the mystery surrounding their communal arrangements and their seeming rejection of external authority, including scripture. For more on these and other radical Protestant sects during the Puritan Revolution, see Christopher Hill, *The World Turned Upside Down: Radical Ideas during the English Revolution* (London: Penguin Books, 1984).

what a wearied, tired wing have I flown over nations and kingdoms, cities and towns, to find out precious Truth!

Truth. Like inquiries in my flights and travels have I made for Peace, and still I am told that she has left the earth and fled to heaven.

Peace. Dear Truth, what is the earth but a dungeon of darkness, where Truth is not?

Truth. And what's the peace thereof but a fleeting dream, thine ape[5] and counterfeit?

Peace. O where's the promise of the God of heaven, that righteousness and peace shall kiss each other?

Truth. Patience, sweet Peace; these heavens and earth are growing old, and shall be changed like a garment (Ps. 102). They shall melt away and be burnt up with all the works that are therein, and the Most High Eternal Creator shall gloriously create new heavens and new earth, wherein dwells righteousness (2 Pet. 3). Our kisses then shall have their endless date of pure and sweetest joys. Until then both you and I must hope and wait, and bear the fury of the dragon's wrath, whose monstrous lies and furies shall with himself be cast into the lake of fire, the second death (Rev. 20).

Peace. Most precious Truth, you know we are both pursued and laid [in wait][6] for. My heart is full of sighs, my eyes with tears—where can I better vent my full oppressed bosom than into yours, whose faithful lips may for these few hours revive my drooping wandering spirits and here begin to wipe tears from my eyes and the eyes of my dearest children?

Truth. Sweet daughter of the God of peace, begin: pour out your sorrows, vent your complaints. How joyful am I to improve these precious minutes to revive our hearts, both yours and mine and the hearts of all that love the Truth and Peace (Zach. 8).

Peace. Dear Truth, I know your birth, your nature, your delight. They that know you will prize you far above themselves and their lives and sell themselves to buy you. Well spoke that famous Elizabeth to her famous attorney, Sir Edward Coke: "Mr. Attorney, go on as thou hast begun, and still plead, not *pro Domina Regina,* but *pro Domina Veritate.*"

Truth. It is true, my crown is high, my scepter's strong to break down strongest holds, to throw down highest crowns of all that plead (though but

---

5. That is, an imitation.

6. An addition supplied by both Samuel Caldwell and Edward Underhill in their respective editions.

in thought) against me. Some few there are, but oh, how few are valiant for
the Truth, and dare to plead my cause as my witnesses in sack-cloth (Rev.
11), while all men's tongues are bent like bows to shoot out lying words
against me!

Peace. O how I could spend eternal days and endless dates at your holy
feet, in listening to the precious oracles of your mouth! All the words of your
mouth are Truth, and there is no iniquity in them; your lips drip as the honeycomb. But oh, since we must part anon, let us (as you have said) improve
our minutes and (according as you promised) revive me with your words,
which are sweeter then the honey and the honeycomb.

Peace's "Sad Complaint": Violence in the Name of Religion

Dear Truth, I have two sad complaints: first, the most sober of your witnesses that dare to plead your cause, how are they charged to be my enemies,
contentious, turbulent, and seditious? Second, your enemies, though they
speak and rail against you, though they outrageously pursue, imprison, banish, and kill your faithful witnesses, yet how is all vermilioned[7] over for justice against the heretics? Yea, if they kindle coals and blow the flames of devouring wars that leave neither spiritual nor civil state, but burned up
branch and root, yet how do all pretend that this is a holy war? He that kills
and he that's killed, they both cry out that it is for God and for their conscience. It is true, neither one nor other seldom dare to plead the mighty
Prince Christ Jesus for their author, yet both Protestant and Papist pretend
they have spoken with Moses and the prophets, who all (say they) before
Christ came allowed such holy persecutions, holy wars against the enemies
of holy church.

Truth. Dear Peace, to ease your first complaint: it is true that your dearest
sons, most like their mother, peace-keeping, peace-making sons of God,
have borne and still must bear the blurs of troublers of Israel and turners of
the world upside down. And it is true again what Solomon once spoke: The
beginning of strife is as when one lets out water, therefore (says he) leave off
contention before it is meddled with. This caveat should keep the banks and
sluices[8] firm and strong, that strife, like a breach of waters, break not in
upon the sons of men.

---

7. That is, colored red.
8. A channel for redirecting surplus water.

Yet strife must be distinguished: It is necessary or unnecessary, godly or ungodly, Christian or unchristian. It is unnecessary, unlawful, dishonorable, ungodly, and unchristian in most cases in the world, for there is a possibility of keeping sweet peace in most cases, and if it be possible it is the express command of God that peace be kept (Rom. 13). Again, it is necessary, honorable, and godly with civil and earthly weapons to defend the innocent and to rescue the oppressed from the violent paws and jaws of oppressing persecuting Nimrods (Ps. 73, Job 29). It is as necessary, yea more honorable, godly, and Christian, to fight the fight of faith, with religious and spiritual artillery, and to contend earnestly for the faith of Jesus . . . against all opposers, and the gates of earth and hell, men or devils, yea against Paul himself, or an angel from heaven, if he bring any other faith or doctrine (Jude 4, Gal. 1:8).

Peace. With the clashing of such arms am I never awakened. Speak once again, dear Truth, to my second complaint of bloody persecution and devouring wars, marching under the colors of upright justice, and holy zeal.

Truth. My ears have long been filled with a threefold doleful outcry:

First, of 144,000 virgins (Rev. 14) forced and ravished by emperors, kings, and governors to their beds of worship and religion, set up on high in their several states and countries.

Second, the cry of those precious souls under the altar (Rev. 6), the souls of such as have been persecuted and slain for the testimony and witness of Jesus, whose blood has been spilled like water upon the earth, and that because they have held fast [to] the truth and witness of Jesus against the worship of the states and times compelling to a uniformity of state religion. These cries of murdered virgins who can sit still and hear? Who can but run with zeal enflamed to prevent the deflowering of chaste souls, and spilling of the blood of the innocent? Humanity stirs up and prompts the sons of men to draw material swords for a virgin's chastity and life, against a ravishing murderer. And piety and Christianity must awaken the sons of God to draw the spiritual sword (the Word of God) to preserve the chastity and life of spiritual virgins, who abhor the spiritual defilements of false worship (Rev. 14).

Third, the cry of the whole earth, made drunk with the blood of its inhabitants, slaughtering each other in their blind zeal for conscience, for religion, against the Catholics, against the Lutherans, etc. What fearful cries within these twenty years of hundreds of thousands of men, women, children, fathers, mothers, husbands, wives, brothers, sisters, old and young, high and low, plundered, ravished, slaughtered, murdered, famished! And hence these cries, that man fling away the spiritual sword and spiritual artillery (in spiritual and religious causes) and rather trust for the suppressing of each other's God, conscience, and religion (as they suppose) to an arm of flesh and sword of steel!

The Bloody Tenent of Persecution

Truth. Sweet Peace, what have you there?

Peace. Arguments against persecution for cause of conscience.[9]

Truth. And what there?

Peace. An answer to such arguments, contrarily maintaining such persecution for cause of conscience.[10]

Truth. These arguments against such persecution, and the answer pleading for it, written (as Love hopes) from godly intentions, hearts, and hands, yet in a marvelously different style and manner. The arguments against persecution in milk, the answer for it (as I may say) in blood. The author of these arguments against persecution (as I have been informed) being committed by some then in power close prisoner to Newgate for the witness of some truths of Jesus, and having not the use of pen and ink, wrote these arguments in milk, on sheets of paper brought to him by the woman his keeper from a friend in London, as the stopples of his milk bottle. On such paper written with milk nothing will appear, but the way of reading it by fire being known to this friend who received the papers, although the author himself could neither correct nor view what he himself had written. It was in milk, tending to soul nourishment, even for babes and sucklings in Christ. It was in milk, spiritually white, pure and innocent, like those white horses of the word of truth and meekness, and the white linen or armor of righteousness in the army of Jesus (Rev. 6, 19). It was in milk, soft, meek, peaceable and gentle, tending both to the peace of souls and the peace of states and kingdoms.

9. Peace presumably is holding a copy of the anonymous tract for toleration that Williams attached to the beginning of *The Bloody Tenent* and identified as "Scriptures and Reasons Written Long Since by a Witness of Jesus Christ, Close Prisoner in Newgate, Against Persecution in Cause of Conscience, and Sent Some While Since to Mr. Cotton."

10. The reference here is to John Cotton's reply to *An Humble Supplication,* which Williams claimed he received from a friend but which Cotton insisted he sent to Williams directly (and presumably privately), in response to Williams's sending him a copy of *An Humble Supplication.*

Peace. The answer (though I hope out of milky pure intentions) is returned in blood: bloody and slaughterous conclusions, bloody to the souls of all men forced to the religion and worship which every civil state or commonwealth agrees on and compels all subjects to in a dissembled uniformity. Bloody to the bodies, first of the holy witnesses of Christ Jesus, who testify against such invented worships, second of the nations and peoples slaughtering each other for their several respective religions and consciences.

Enforcing Conformity Is as Much Persecution as Not Permitting Different Practices

Truth. In the answer Mr. Cotton first lays down several distinctions and conclusions of his own, tending to prove persecution.[11] Second, Mr. Cotton offers answers to the Scriptures and arguments proposed against persecution.

Peace. The first distinction is this: By persecution for cause of conscience, "I conceive you mean either for professing some point of doctrine which you believe in conscience to be the truth, or for practicing some work which you believe in conscience to be a religious duty."

Truth. I acknowledge that to molest any person, Jew or Gentile, for either professing doctrine or practicing worship merely religious or spiritual is to persecute him, and such a person (whatever his doctrine or practice be, true or false) suffers persecution for conscience. But with all I desire it may be well observed that this distinction is not full and complete. For beside this, a man may be persecuted because he holds or practices what he believes in conscience to be a truth. . . . I say besides this a man may also be persecuted because he dares not be constrained to yield obedience to such doctrines and worships as are by men invented and appointed. So the three famous Jews were cast into the fiery furnace for refusing to fall down (in a non-conformity to the whole conforming world) before the golden Image (Dan. 3:21). So thousands of Christ's witnesses (and of late those bloody Marian days) have rather chosen to yield their bodies to all sorts of torments than to

11. The "distinctions" to which Truth refers were Cotton's way of carefully parsing the arguments of *An Humble Supplication,* in his attempt simultaneously to agree that persecution of conscience is wrong and to insist that what the Massachusetts authorities were doing did not constitute persecution.

subscribe to doctrines or practice worships to which the states and times . . . have compelled and urged them.

A chaste wife will not only abhor to be restrained from her husband's bed as adulterous and polluted, but also abhor (if not much more) to be constrained to the bed of a stranger. And what is abominable in corporal is much more loathsome in spiritual whoredom and defilement. The spouse of Christ Jesus who could not find her soul's beloved in the ways of his worship and ministry (Cant. 1:3, 5) abhorred to turn aside to other flocks and worships and to embrace the bosom of a false Christ (Cant. 1:8).

Persecution Not Justified by the Distinction of "Fundamental" Doctrines

Peace. [Mr. Cotton's] second distinction is this: In points of doctrine, some are fundamental, without right belief whereof a man cannot be saved. Others are circumstantial and less principal, wherein a man may differ in judgment without prejudice of salvation on either part.

Truth. To this distinction I dare not subscribe, for then I should everlastingly condemn thousands and ten thousands, yea the whole generation of the righteous, who since the falling away from the first primitive Christian state or worship have and do err fundamentally concerning the true matter, constitution, gathering, and governing of the church. And yet far be it [for] any pious breast to imagine that they are not saved, and that their souls are not bound up in the bundle of eternal life. . . .[12] If Mr. Cotton maintains the true church of Christ to consist of the true matter of holy persons called out from the world, and the true form of union in a church-covenant, and that also neither national, provincial, nor diocesan churches are of Christ's institution, then how many thousands of God's people of all sorts . . . will they find, both in former and later times, captivated in such national, provincial, and diocesan churches? Yea, and so far from living in . . . any such churches . . . as they conceive now only to be true, that until of late years, how few of

12. Williams is referring to his ecclesiological differences with Cotton and other nonseparatist Puritans (see the introduction to this volume for a discussion of those differences). Williams considered the corruptions in Anglican worship and the New England Puritan majority's failure to separate from the established church to be "fundamental" error. But by Cotton's logic, the presence of this error would mean that the majority of English Protestants (and, by extension, the majority of Christians for centuries, since Williams thought the errors in English worship were rooted in the historical corruption of Constantinian Christendom) were destined for eternal damnation, a pronouncement Williams was charitably unwilling to make.

God's people knew any other church than the parish church of dead stones or timber, it being a late marvelous light revealed by Christ Jesus the Sun of Righteousness, that his people are a company or church of living stones (1 Pet. 2:9)?

And however his own soul and the souls of many others precious to God are persuaded to separate from national, provincial, and diocesan churches, and to assemble into particular churches, yet since there are no parish churches in England but what are made up of the parish bounds within such and such a compass of houses, and that such churches have been and are in constant dependence on and subordination to the national church, how can the New England particular churches join with the Old English parish churches in so many ordinances of word, prayer, singing, [and] contribution but they must confess that as yet their souls are far from the knowledge of the foundation of a true Christian church. . . .[13]

Peace. . . . I shall now present you with Mr. Cotton's third distinction: In point of practice, says he, some concern the weightier duties of the Law—as what God we worship and with what kind of worship—whether such as if it be right, fellowship with God is held, if false, fellowship with God is lost.

Truth. It is worth the inquiry, what kind of worship he intends, for worship is of various signification—whether in general acceptation he means the rightness or corruptness of the church, or the ministry of the church, or the ministrations of the word, prayer, and seals. And because it pleases the Spirit of God to make the ministry one of the foundations of the Christian religion (Heb. 6:12), and also to make the ministry of the word and prayer in the church to be two special works (even of the Apostles themselves, Acts 6:2), I shall desire it may be well considered in the fear of God.

First, concerning the ministry of the Word: The New England ministers, when they were newly elected and ordained ministers in New England, must undeniably grant that at that time they were not ministers, notwithstanding their profession of standing so long in a true ministry in Old England, whether received from the bishops (which some have maintained true) or from the people (which Mr. Cotton and others better liked), and which ministry was always accounted perpetual and indelible. I apply and ask, will

13. Williams was profoundly bothered by some Puritans' habit of worshipping in Anglican parishes upon their return to the mother country. To him such practice violated any claim to ecclesial purity the New England churches might possess.

it not follow that if their new ministry and ordination be true, the former was false? And if false, then in the exercise of it (notwithstanding abilities, graces, intentions, labors, and—by God's gracious, unpromised, and extraordinary blessing—some success) . . . will it not, according to this distinction, follow that according to visible rule, fellowship with God was lost? Second, concerning prayer: the New England ministers have disclaimed and written against that worshiping of God by the common or set forms of prayer, which yet they themselves practiced in England, notwithstanding that they knew that many servants of God in great sufferings witnessed against such a ministry of the Word and such a ministry of prayer.

Peace. I could name the persons, time, and place when some of them were faithfully admonished for using the [Book of] Common Prayer, and the arguments presented to them then seeming weak, but now acknowledged sound. Yet at that time they satisfied their hearts with the practice of the author of the Council of Trent, who used to read only some of the choicest selected prayers in the Mass-book (which I confess was also their own practice in their using of the Common Prayer). But now according to this distinction, I ask whether or not fellowship with God in such prayers was lost.

Truth. . . . I observe that God's people may live and die in such [erroneous] kinds of worship, notwithstanding that light from God publicly and privately has been presented to them. . . , contrary to a conclusion afterward expressed [by Cotton], that fundamentals are so clear that a man cannot but be convinced in conscience, and therefore that such a person, not being convinced, is condemned of himself, and may be persecuted for sinning against his conscience. [Furthermore], I observe that in maintaining a clearness of fundamentals or weightier points, and upon that ground persecuting men because they sin against their consciences, Mr. Cotton measures that to others which he, when he lived in such practices, would not have had measured to himself: first, that it might have been affirmed of him that in such practices he did sin against his conscience, having sufficient light shining about him, and second, that he should or might lawfully have been cut off by death or banishment as a heretic, sinning against his own conscience. . . .

Civil Peace Not Threatened by the "Arrogance" of Religious Dissent

Peace. The next distinction concerns the manner of persons holding forth the aforesaid practices (that is, not only the weightier duties of the Law but also points of doctrine and worship less principal): some, says he, hold them forth in a meek and peaceable way, some with such arrogance and impetuousness [that] itself tends to the disturbance of civil peace.

Truth. In the examination of this distinction we shall discuss, first, what is civil peace (wherein we shall vindicate your name the better), and second, what it is to hold forth a doctrine or practice in this impetuousness or arrogance.

First, for civil peace, what is it but *pax civitatis,* the peace of the city, whether an English city, Scotch, or Irish city, or further abroad, French, Spanish, or Turkish city. . . . The peace of the city or kingdom is a far different peace from the peace of the religion or spiritual worship maintained and professed [by] the citizens. This peace of their worship (which worship also in some cities being various) being a false peace, God's people were and ought to be nonconformists, not daring either to be restrained from the true or constrained to false worship, and yet without breach of the civil or city-peace, properly so called.

Peace. Hence it is that so many glorious and flourishing cities of the world maintain their civil peace, yea the very Americans and wildest pagans keep the peace of their towns or cities, though neither in one nor the other can any man prove a true church of God in those places, and consequently no spiritual and heavenly peace. The peace spiritual (whether true or false) is of a higher and far different nature from the peace of the place or people, being merely and essentially civil and humane.

Truth. O how lost are the sons of men on this point? To illustrate this: The church or company of worshippers (whether true or false) is like a body or college of physicians in a city, like a corporation, society, or company of East India or Turkish merchants, or any other society or company in London. These companies may hold their courts, keep their records, hold disputations, and in matters concerning their society may dissent, divide, break into schisms and factions, sue and implead each other at the law, yea wholly break up and dissolve into pieces and [become] nothing, and yet the peace of the city not be in the least measure impaired or disturbed—because the essence or being of the city (and so the well-being and peace thereof) is essentially distinct from those particular societies, the city-courts, city-laws, city-punishments distinct from theirs. The city was before them and stands absolute and entire when such a corporation or society is taken down. . . .

Peace. Now to the second query: what it is to hold forth doctrine or practice in an arrogant or impetuous way?

Truth. Although it has not pleased Mr. Cotton to declare what is this arrogant or impetuous holding forth of doctrine or practice tending to disturbance of civil peace, I cannot but express my sad and sorrowful observation: how it pleases God to leave him, [that he would] take up the common reproachful accusation of the accuser of God's children—[that is], that they are arrogant and impetuous—with which charge (together with that of obstinacy, pertinacity, pride, troublers of the city) Satan commonly loads the meekest of the saints and witnesses of Jesus. To wipe off therefore these foul blurs and aspersions from the fair and beautiful face of the Spouse of Jesus, I shall select and propose five or six cases for which God's witnesses in all ages and generations of men have been charged with arrogance and impetuousness. Yet the God of heaven and Judge of all men has graciously discharged them from such crimes, and maintained and avowed them for his faithful and peaceable servants.

First, God's people have proclaimed, taught, and disputed for diverse months together a new religion and worship, contrary to the worship projected in the town, city, or state where they have lived (or where they have traveled), as did the Lord Jesus Himself over all Galilee, and the Apostles after him in all places, both in the synagogues and marketplaces (as appears Acts 17:2, 17; Acts 18:4–8). Yet this no arrogance nor impetuousness.

Second, God's servants have been zealous for their Lord and Master, even to the very faces of the highest and concerning the persons of the highest, so far as they have opposed the truth of God. So Elijah to the face of Ahab: "It is not I, but thou, and your Father's house that troublest Israel."[14] So the Lord Jesus concerning Herod: "Go tell that fox. . . ."[15] So Paul: "God delivered me from the mouth of the Lion," and to Ananias: "Thou whited wall."[16] And yet in all this no arrogance, nor impetuousness.

Third, God's people have been immoveable, constant, and resolved to the death in refusing to submit to false worships and in preaching and professing the true worship, contrary to express command of public authority. So the three famous worthies against the command of Nebuchadnezzar and the uniform conformity of all nations agreeing upon a false worship (Dan. 3). So the Apostles (Acts 4 and 5) and so the witnesses of Jesus in all

14. 1 Kings 18:18.
15. Luke 13:32.
16. 2 Timothy 4; Acts 23.

ages who loved not their lives to the death (Rev. 12), not regarding sweet life nor bitter death, and yet not arrogant nor impetuous.

Fourth, God's people since the coming of the King of Israel, the Lord Jesus, have openly and constantly professed that no civil magistrate, no king nor Caesar, has any power over the souls or consciences of their subjects in the matters of God and the crown of Jesus, but the civil magistrates themselves, yea kings and kaisers, are bound to subject their own souls to the ministry and church, the power and government of this Lord Jesus, the King of kings. Hence was the charge against the Apostles (false in civil, but true in spirituals) that they affirmed that there was another King, one Jesus (Acts 17:7). And indeed this was the great charge against the Lord Jesus himself, which the Jews laid against him, and for which he suffered death, as appears by the accusation written over his head upon the gallows (John 19:9): *Jesus of Nazareth, King of the Jews.* This was and is the sum of all true preaching of the Gospel . . . that God anointed Jesus to be the sole king and governor of all the Israel of God in spiritual and soul causes (Ps. 2:6; Acts 2:36). Yet this kingly power of his he resolved not to manage in his own person, but ministerially in the hands of such messengers which he sent forth to preach and baptize, and to such as believed that word they preached (John 17). And yet here neither arrogance nor impetuousness.

Fifth, God's people, in delivering the mind and will of God concerning the kingdoms and civil states where they have lived, have seemed in all show of common sense and rational policy (if men look not higher with the eye of faith) to endanger and overthrow the very civil state, as appears by all Jeremiah's preaching and counsel to King Zedekiah, . . . insomuch that the charge of the princes against Jeremiah was that he discouraged the army from fighting against the Babylonians and weakened the land from its own defense. This charge, in the eye of reason, seemed not to be unreasonable or unrighteous (Jer. 37–38), and yet in Jeremiah no arrogance nor impetuousness.

Lastly, God's people by their preaching and disputing have been (though not the cause, yet accidentally) the occasion of great contentions and divisions, yea tumults and uproars in towns and cities where they have lived and come, and yet neither their doctrine nor themselves arrogant nor impetuous, however so charged. . . .

Peace. It will be said, dear Truth, that what the Lord Jesus and his messengers taught was truth, but the question is about error.

Truth. I answer that this distinction now in discussion concerns not truth or error, but the manner of holding forth or divulging [beliefs]. I acknowledge that such may be the way and manner of holding forth—either with railing or reviling, daring or challenging speeches, or with force of arms, swords, guns, or prisons—that it may not only *tend* to break, but may *actually* break, the civil peace. . . . Yet . . . it is possible and common for persons of soft and gentle nature and spirits to hold out falsehood with more seeming meekness and peaceableness than the Lord Jesus or his servants did (or do) hold forth the true and everlasting Gospel. So that the Answerer would be requested to explain what he means by this arrogant and impetuous holding forth of any doctrine, which very manner of holding forth tends to break civil peace and [therefore] comes under the cognizance and correction of the civil magistrate. . . .

Peace. It will here be said, whence then arise civil dissentions and uproars about matters of religion?

Truth. I answer: When a kingdom or state, town or family, lies and lives in the guilt of a false God, false Christ, false worship, it is no wonder if sore eyes be troubled at the appearance of the light, be it never so sweet. No wonder if a body full of corrupt humors be troubled at strong (though wholesome) physic;[17] no wonder if persons sleepy and loving to sleep be troubled at the noise of shrill (though silver) alarms; no wonder if Adonijah and all his company be amazed and troubled at the sound of the right heir King Solomon (1 Kings 1); if the husbandmen were troubled when the lord of the vineyard sent servant after servant, and at last his only son, and they beat and wounded and even killed the son himself, because they meant themselves to seize upon the inheritance, to which they had no right (Matt. 21:38). Hence all those tumults about the Apostles in the Acts whereas good eyes are not so troubled at light, vigilant and watchful persons loyal and faithful are not so troubled at the true, nor at a false religion of Jew or Gentile.

Second, breach of civil peace may arise when false and idolatrous practices are held forth, and yet no breach of civil peace from the doctrine or practice or the manner of holding forth, but from that wrong and preposterous way of suppressing, preventing, and extinguishing such doctrines or practices by weapons of wrath and blood—whips, stocks, imprisonment, banishment, death—by which men commonly are persuaded to convert

---

17. The term refers to a medicinal product.

heretics and to cast out unclean spirits, which only the finger of God can do, that is, the mighty power of the Spirit in the Word. Hence the town is in an uproar, and the country takes the alarm to expel that fog or mist of error, heresy, blasphemy (as is supposed) with swords and guns. Whereas it is light alone, even light from the bright shining sun of righteousness, which is able in the souls and consciences of men to dispel and scatter such fog and darkness. Hence, the sons of men . . . disquiet themselves in vain, and unmercifully disquiet others, as (by the help of the Lord) in the sequel [to] this discourse shall more appear.

Cotton: An Erroneous Conscience May Be Persecuted

Peace. Now the last distinction is this: persecution for conscience is either for a rightly informed conscience or a blind and erroneous conscience.

Truth. Indeed both these consciences are persecuted, but lamentably blind and erroneous will these consciences shortly appear to be, which out of zeal for God (as is pretended) have persecuted either. And heavy is the doom of those blind guides and idle shepherds (whose right eye God's finger of jealousy has put out) who, flattering the ten horns or worldly powers, persuade them what excellent and faithful service they perform to God in persecuting both these consciences.[18] They either hang up a rightly informed conscience, and therein the Lord Jesus himself between two malefactors, or else they kill the erroneous and the blind, like Saul (out of zeal to the Israel of God) did to the poor Gibeonites whom it pleased God to permit to live. And yet that hostility and cruelty used against them (as the repeated judgment year after year upon the whole land after told them) could not be pardoned, until the death of the persecutor Saul [and] his sons had appeased the Lord's displeasure (2 Sam. 21).

Peace. After explication in these distinctions, it pleases the Answerer to give his resolution to the question in four particulars. First, that he holds it not lawful to persecute any for conscience sake rightly informed, for in per-

---

18. "And the ten horns which thou sawest are ten kings, which have received no kingdom as yet; but receive power as kings one hour with the beast. These have one mind, and shall give their power and strength unto the beast. These shall make war with the Lamb, and the Lamb shall overcome them: for he is Lord of lords, and King of kings: and they that are with him are called, and chosen, and faithful" (Revelation 17:12–14).

secuting such (says he) Christ himself is persecuted (for which reason, truly rendered, he quotes Acts 9:4: *Saul, Saul, why persecutest thou me?*).

Truth. He that shall read this conclusion over a thousand times shall as soon find darkness in the bright beams of the sun as in this so clear and shining a beam of truth, that Christ Jesus in his truth must not be persecuted. Yet this I must ask. . . : search all Scriptures, histories, records, monuments, consult with all experiences—did ever Pharaoh, Saul, Ahab, Jezebel, Scribes and Pharisees, the Jews, Herod, the bloody Neros, Gardiners, Bonners, the pope or the Devil himself profess to persecute the Son of God, Jesus as Jesus, Christ as Christ, without a mask or covering? No, Pharaoh said, the Israelites are idle, and therefore speak they of sacrificing. David is risen up in a conspiracy against Saul, therefore persecute him. Naboth has blasphemed God and the king, therefore stone him. Christ is a seducer of the people, a blasphemer against God and traitor against Caesar, therefore hang him. Christians are schismatic, factious, [and] heretical, therefore persecute them. The Devil has deluded John Hus, therefore crown him with a paper of devils and burn him.

Peace. One thing I see apparently in the Lord's over-ruling the pen of this worthy Answerer (a secret whispering from heaven to him), that although his soul aims at Christ and has wrought much for Christ in many sincere intentions. . . , yet he has never left the tents of such who think they do God good service in killing the Lord Jesus in his servants. And yet they say, if we had been in the days of our fathers, in Queen Mary's days, we would never have consented to such persecution. And therefore when they persecute Christ Jesus in his truths or servants, they say, do not say you are persecuted for the Word for Christ's sake, for we hold it not lawful to persecute Jesus Christ. Let me also add a second: so far as he has been a guide by preaching for persecution, I say, wherein he has been a guide and leader by misinterpreting and applying the Writings of Truth, so far I say his own mouth and hands shall judge (I hope not his persons, but) his actions, for the Lord Jesus has suffered by him (Acts 9:3), and if the Lord Jesus himself were present, he should suffer that in his own person which his servants witnessing his truth do suffer for his sake.

In the next several chapters of his treatise, Williams takes up Cotton's interpretation of Titus 3:10–11: "A man that is an heretick after the first and second admonition reject; knowing that he that is such is subverted, and sinneth, being condemned of himself." While Cotton cited these verses as biblical permission to punish those who (after repeated counsel and in the face of clear evidence from the Word of God) refuse to give up their erroneous views on "fundamental" matters of doctrine, Williams counters that Cotton and others have misinterpreted this scripture in order to justify their persecution of conscience. First, Williams notes the contradiction in Cotton's subtle shift from talking about an "erroneous conscience" to referring to those who "sin against conscience." More importantly, the rejection commended in Titus 3 is "not a cutting off by heading, hanging, burning, or an expelling [from] the country and coasts, neither of which (nor any lesser civil punishment) Titus nor the church at Crete had any power to exercise." Titus was not a magistrate but a church leader, Williams points out, so the punishment for heresy spoken of here clearly is meant to be taken as ecclesiastical only, the "dreadful cutting off from that visible Head and Body, Christ Jesus and his church." Finally, embedded in the excerpt that follows is a basic definition of conscience, upon which much of his defense of religious liberty depends.

Peace. Now in the second place, what is this self-condemnation?

Truth. The Apostle seems to make this a ground of the rejecting of such a person, because he is subverted and sins, being condemned of himself. It will appear upon due search that this self-condemnation is not here intended to be in heretics . . . in fundamentals only, but as it is meant here, in men obstinate in the lesser questions, [too].

First, he is subverted or turned crooked, . . . a word opposite to straightness or rightness—so that the scope is, I conceive, upon true and faithful admonition once or twice, the pride of heart, or heat of wrath, draws a veil over the eyes and heart, so that the soul is turned and loosed from the checks of truth. Second, he sins, . . . that is, being subverted or turned aside. He sins or wanders from the path of truth and is condemned by himself. . . , that is, by the secret checks and whisperings of his own conscience, which will take God's part against man's self, in smiting [and] accusing [him]. [These] checks of conscience we find even in God's own dear people, as is most admirably opened in Canticles 5, in those sad, drowned, and unkind passages of the spouse in her answer to the knocks and calls of the Lord Jesus. God's people in all their awakening acknowledge how slightly they have listened to the checks of their own consciences. This the Answerer pleases to call sinning against his conscience, for which he may lawfully be persecuted—that is, for sinning against his conscience—which conclusion (though painted over with the vermillion of mistaken Scripture. . .) I hope by the assistance of the Lord Jesus to manifest to be the overturning and rooting up [of] the very foundation and roots of all true Christianity, and absolutely denying the Lord Jesus the Great Anointed to be yet come in the flesh.

Toleration Gives God Time to Bring an Erroneous Conscience to Faith

Peace. Mr. Cotton's third conclusion is that in points of lesser moment, there ought to be a toleration. Though I acknowledge his point to be the truth of God, yet three things are very observable in the manner of laying it down, for Satan uses excellent arrows to bad marks, sometimes beyond the intent and hidden from the eye of the archer. First (says he) such a person is to be tolerated until God may be pleased to reveal his truth to him.

Truth. This is well observed by you, for indeed this is the very ground why the Apostle calls for meekness and gentleness toward *all* men, and toward such as oppose themselves (2 Tim. 2), because . . . it may be that God may give them repentance, that God that has shown mercy to one may show mercy to another. It may be that [the] eye-salve that anointed one man's eye who was blind and opposite may anoint another as blind and opposite. He that has given repentance to the husband may give it to his wife.

Hence that soul that is lively and sensible of mercy received to itself in former blindness, opposition, and enmity against God cannot but be patient and gentle toward the Jews, who yet deny the Lord Jesus to be come and justify their forefathers in a murdering of him; toward the Turks, who acknowledge Christ a great prophet yet affirm [him] less than Muhammad; yea to all the several sorts of Antichristians who set up many a false Christ instead of him; and lastly to the pagans and wildest sorts of the sons of men, who have not yet heard of the Father nor the Son. And to all these sorts—Jews, Turks, Antichristians, pagans—when they oppose the light presented to them, in sense of its own former opposition and that God peradventure[19] may at last give repentance, I add [that] such a soul will not only be patient, but earnestly and constantly pray for all sorts of men, that out of them God's elect may be called to the fellowship of Christ Jesus. And lastly, not only pray, but

19. That is, "perhaps" or "by chance."

also endeavor (to its utmost ability) their participation of the same grace and mercy. . . .

And this is the more carefully to be minded, because whenever a toleration of others' religion and conscience is pleaded for, such as are (I hope in truth) zealous for God readily produce plenty of Scriptures written to the church both before and since Christ's coming, all commanding and pressing and putting forth of the unclean, the cutting off the obstinate, the purging out the leaven, and the rejecting of heretics. As if because briars, thorns, and thistles may not be in the *Garden* of the *church,* therefore they must all be plucked up out of the *Wilderness.*[20] Whereas he that is a briar—that is, a Jew, a Turk, a pagan, or an Antichristian—today, may be (when the Word of the Lord runs freely) a member of Jesus Christ tomorrow cut out of the wild olive, and planted into the true. . . .

Civil Peace Not Threatened by Religious Dissenters, but by Their Persecutors

Peace. I shall now trouble you, dear Truth, but with one conclusion more, which is this: if a man hold forth error with a boisterous and arrogant spirit, to the disturbance of the civil peace, he ought to be punished.

Truth. To this I have spoken, too, confessing that if any man commit any of those things which Paul was accused of (Acts 25:2), he ought not to be spared, yea he ought not (as Paul says) in such cases refuse to die.[21] But if the matter be of another nature, a spiritual and divine nature, I have written before in many cases, and might in many more, that the worship which a state professes may be contradicted and preached against and yet no breach of civil peace. And if a breach follow, it is not made by such doctrines but by the boisterous and violent opposers of them. Such persons only break the cities' or kingdoms' peace who cry out for prison and swords against such who cross their judgment or practice in religion. For as Joseph's mistress ac-

20. "Wilderness" here stands for the civil realm. The distinction between the "wilderness" of the profane world and the "garden" of the church was important symbolism for Williams's separatist ecclesiology. For more on his use of this imagery, see the discussion of Williams's typology in the introduction to this volume. For an important look at the relationship between church and state in American history through the lens of this garden-wilderness dichotomy, see Mark DeWolfe Howe's *The Garden and the Wilderness: Religion and Government in American Constitutional History* (Chicago: University of Chicago Press, 1965).

21. Paul was accused of inciting violence and sedition against the Roman state.

cused Joseph of uncleanness, and called out for civil violence against him, when Joseph was chaste and she herself guilty, so commonly the meek and peaceable of the earth are traduced[22] as rebels, factious, [and] peace-breakers, although they deal not with the state or state-matters, but matters of divine and spiritual nature, when their traducers are the only unpeaceable and guilty of breach of civil peace.

The Parable of the Wheat and the Tares

Peace. We are now come to the second part of the Answer, which is a particular examination of such grounds as are brought against such persecution. The first sort of grounds are from the Scriptures:

First, Matthew 13:30–38, because Christ commands to let alone the tares to grow up together with the wheat, until the harvest. To which [Cotton] answers that tares are not briars and thorns, but partial hypocrites, like the godly but indeed carnal (as the tares are like the wheat, but are not wheat), or partly such corrupt doctrines or practices as are indeed unfounded but yet such as come very near the truth . . . and so near that good men may be taken with them. And so the person in whom they grow cannot be rooted out, but good wheat will be rooted out with them. In such a case, says he, Christ calls for peaceable toleration and not for penal prosecution, according to the third conclusion.

Truth. . . . For answer here I confess that not only those worthy witnesses . . . Calvin, Beza, etc., but of later times many conjoin with this worthy Answerer, to satisfy themselves and others with such an interpretation. But alas, how dark is the soul left that desires to walk with God in holy fear and trembling, when in such a weighty and mighty point as this is—that in matters of conscience concerns the spilling of the blood of thousands and the civil peace of the world in the taking up arms to suppress all false religions!—when, I say, no evidence or demonstration of the Spirit is brought to prove such an interpretation. . . .

Peace. The place then being of such great importance as concerning the truth of God, the blood of thousands, yea the blood of saints and of the Lord Jesus in them, I shall request your more diligent search (by the Lord's holy assistance) into this Scripture.

22. Meaning "defamed."

Truth. I shall make it evident, that by these tares in this parable are meant persons in respect of their religion and way of worship, open and visible professors, as bad as briars and thorns, not only suspected foxes but as bad as those wolves which Paul speaks of (Acts 20) who with perverse and evil doctrines labor spiritually to devour the flock and to draw away disciples after them, whose mouths must be stopped, and yet no carnal force or weapons to be used against them, but their mischief to be resisted with those mighty weapons of the holy armory of the Lord Jesus. . . .

At this point, Williams embarks on a detailed discussion of each character in the parable and its translation. For Williams, the proper identity of the characters in this parable is vital to determining whether or not this passage justifies the persecution of conscience that he experienced firsthand in New England. Cotton interpreted the "field" in the parable as the church, and the "tares" that were sown in it as subtle hypocrites within the church. Assigning the characters this way, Cotton read the parable to prohibit witch hunts aimed at rooting out minor errors in doctrine or practice, but he in no way believed that this parable proscribed the restraint (religious or civil) of those who "arrogantly" held heretical, blasphemous, or radically deviant doctrines or practices. By contrast, Williams interpreted the "field" as the world and the parable as an injunction against violently "tearing up" those (the "tares") who espoused beliefs or engaged in practices that were perceived to violate true Christianity, no matter how obnoxiously or publicly they held those beliefs or practices. Clearly, Williams and Cotton read the parable in almost opposite ways; Williams believed the parable was a warning against persecution of conscience, while Cotton believed it largely irrelevant to the civil restraint of fundamental religious deviance.

The world lies in wickedness [and] is like a wilderness or a sea of wild beasts innumerable . . . with whom God's people may converse and cohabit in cities and towns (else must they not live in the world, but go out of it[!]). In which world, as soon as ever the Lord Jesus had sown the good seed (that is, the children of the Kingdom, true Christianity, or the true church), the enemy Satan presently in the night of security, ignorance, and error (while men slept) sowed also these tares, which are Antichristians or false Christians. These strange professors of the name of Jesus the ministers and prophets of God beholding, they are ready to run to heaven to fetch fiery judgments . . . to consume these strange Christians and to pluck them by the roots out of the world. But the Son of Man, the meek Lamb of God, for the elect's sake . . . commands a permission of them in the world, until the time of the end of the world when the goats and sheep, the tares and wheat, shall be eternally separated from each other.

. . . In [the] civil state, from the beginning of the world, God has armed fathers, masters, and magistrates to punish evildoers, that is, . . . fathers, masters, and magistrates are to judge and accordingly to punish such sinners as transgress against the good and peace of their civil state (that is, families, towns, cities, or kingdoms). Their states, governments, governors, laws, punishments, and weapons are all of a civil nature. Therefore neither disobedience to parents or magistrates, nor murder nor quarrelling, uncleanness nor lasciviousness, stealing nor extortion—none of that kind ought to be let alone, either in lesser or greater families, towns, cities, kingdoms (Rom. 13), but seasonably to be suppressed as may best conduce to the public safety.

. . . [But] I conclude that [there] are sinners of another nature, idolaters, false-worshippers, Antichristians, who without discouragement to true Christians must be let alone and permitted in the world to grow and fill up the measure of their sins, after the image of him that has sown them, until the great harvest shall make the difference.

. . . As the civil state keeps itself with a civil guard, in case these tares shall attempt ought against the peace and welfare of it, let such civil offenses be punished, and yet as tares opposite to Christ's Kingdom, let their worship and consciences be tolerated.

. . . The Lord Jesus here in this parable lays down two reasons . . . to bear patiently this their contradiction and Antichristianity and to permit or let them alone. First, lest the good wheat be plucked up and rooted up also out of this field of the world. If such combustions and fighting were to pluck up all the false professors of the name of Christ, the good wheat also would enjoy little peace, but be in danger to be plucked up and torn out of this world by such bloody storms and tempests. And therefore . . . so contrary to the opinion and practice of most. . . , to let the tares alone will prove the only means to preserve their civil peace. . . .

The second reason noted in the parable which may satisfy any man from wondering at the patience of God is this: when the world is ripe in sin. . . , then those holy and mighty officers and executioners, the angels with their sharp and cutting sickles of eternal vengeance, shall down with them and bundle them up for the everlasting burnings.

Peace. You have been larger in vindicating this Scripture from the violence offered to it, because as I said before it is of such great consequence, as also because so many excellent hands have not rightly divided it, to the great misguiding of many precious feet which otherwise might have been turned onto the paths of more peaceableness in themselves and towards others.

Truth. I shall be briefer in the Scriptures following.

Peace. Yet before you depart from this, I must crave your patience to satisfy one objection: that these servants to whom the householder answers seem to be the ministers or messengers of the Gospel, not the magistrates of the civil state, and [that] therefore this charge of the Lord Jesus is not given to magistrates to let alone false worshippers and idolaters. . . .[23]

Truth. . . . I acknowledge this command was expressly spoken to the messengers or ministers of the Gospel who have no civil power or authority in their hand, and therefore not to the civil magistrate, king, or governor to whom it pleased not the Lord Jesus by himself or by his Apostles to give particular rules or directions concerning their behavior and carriage in civil magistracy (as they have done expressly concerning the duty of fathers, mothers, children, masters, servants, yea and of subjects towards magistrates, Eph. 5, 6; Col. 3, 4). I conceive not the reason [for] this to be (as some weakly have done) because the Lord Jesus would not have any followers of his to hold the place of civil magistracy, but rather that he foresaw . . . how few magistrates, either in the first persecuted or [subsequent] apostate state of Christianity, would embrace his yoke. In the persecuted state, magistrates hated the very name of Christ or Christianity; in the state apostate, some few magistrates (in their persons holy and precious, yet) as concerning their places, as they have professed to [have been governors or heads of the church], have been to many false heads and have constituted so many false

---

23. Williams here anticipates the objection that the intended audience for this command to let the tares alone—symbolized in the parable by the householder's servants—is the church, meaning that the passage does not explicitly preclude *civil* officers from attempting to "uproot" heretics and blasphemers by violent means. Williams acknowledges that the passage does not speak directly to Christian magistrates, because (he suspects) Jesus and early church fathers never anticipated that true Christians would regularly ascend to positions of civil power. But to those few civil leaders who consider themselves Christian, Williams advises that the parable's command to let the tares alone applies to them, too.

visible Christs. I conceive this charge of the Lord Jesus to his messengers, the preachers and proclaimers of his mind, is a sufficient declaration of the mind of the Lord Jesus, if any civil magistrate should question what was his duty concerning spiritual things.

The Apostles, and in them all that succeed them, being commanded not to pluck up the tares but let them alone, received from the Lord Jesus a threefold charge. First, to let them alone, and not to pluck them up by prayer to God for their present temporal destruction . . . Second, God's messengers are herein commanded not to prophesy or denounce a present destruction or extirpation of all false professors of the name of Christ, which are whole towns, cities, and kingdoms full. . . . Such denunciations of present temporal judgments are not [of] the messengers of the Lord Jesus to pour forth. 'Tis true, many sore and fearful plagues are poured forth upon the Roman emperors and Roman popes in the Revelation, yet not to their utter extirpation or plucking up until the harvest.

Third, I conceive God's messengers are charged to let them alone and not pluck them up by exciting and stirring up civil magistrates, kings, emperors, governors, parliaments, or General Courts or Assemblies to punish and persecute all such persons out of their dominions and territories as worship not the true God according to the revealed will of God in Christ Jesus. 'Tis true, Elijah thus stirred up Ahab to kill all the priests and prophets of Baal, but that was in that figurative state of the Land of Canaan. . . ,[24] not to be matched or paralleled by any other state but the spiritual state or church of Christ in all the world, putting the false prophets and idolaters spiritually to death by the two-edged sword and power of the Lord Jesus, as that church of Israel did corporally. . . .[25]

Peace. It may be said: some sorts of sinners are there mentioned (as drunkards, railers, extortionists) who are to be punished by the civil sword, so why not idolaters also? For although the subject may lawfully converse, buy and sell, and live with such, yet the civil magistrate shall nevertheless be justly blamed in suffering of them.

Truth. I answer, the Apostle in this Scripture speaks not of permission of either, but expressly shows the difference between the church and the world,

---

24. 1 Kings 18.
25. Here Williams reveals a glimpse of his typological reading of the Old Testament, an approach he will lay out more fully later in the treatise.

and the lawfulness of conversation with such persons in civil things with whom it is not lawful to have converse in spirituals, . . . that magistrates and people, whole states and kingdoms should be idolatrous and Antichristian, yet with whom notwithstanding the saints and churches of God might lawfully cohabit and hold civil converse and conversation. . . .

Peace. O how contrary to this command of the Lord Jesus have such as have conceived themselves the true messengers of the Lord Jesus, in all ages, not let such professors and prophets alone, whom they have judged tares, but have provoked kings and kingdoms (and some out of good intentions and zeal to God) to prosecute and persecute such even to death! Amongst whom God's people (and good wheat) have also been plucked up, as all ages and histories testify, and too, too often the world laid upon bloody heaps in civil and intestine desolations on this occasion. All which would be prevented, and the greatest breaches made up in the peace of our own or other countries, were this command of the Lord Jesus obeyed: let them alone until the harvest.

Upon concluding his extended exegesis of the parable of wheat and tares, Williams offers briefer expositions of Matthew 15:14 and Luke 9:54–55, two other passages that he feels demonstrate Christ's disposition for tolerating heretics and blasphemers instead of punishing them with violence.

Civil Weapons Ineffective Punishment for Spiritual Sin

Peace. But what is there in this Scripture of Timothy[26] alleged concerning the civil magistracy?

Truth. I argue from this place of Timothy in particular, thus: First, if the civil magistrates be Christians or members of the church, able to prophesy in the church of Christ, then I say as before that they are bound by this command of Christ to suffer opposition to their doctrine with meekness and gentleness, and to be so far from striving to subdue their opposites with the civil sword that they are bound with patience and meekness to wait if God peradventure will please to grant repentance to their opposites. So also it

26. "And the servant of the Lord must not strive; but be gentle unto all men, apt to teach, patient, in meekness instructing those that oppose themselves; if God peradventure will give them repentance to the acknowledging of the truth; and that they may recover themselves out of the snare of the devil, who are taken captive by him at his will" (2 Timothy 2:24–26).

pleases the Answerer to acknowledge in these words: It becomes not the spirit of the Gospel to convert aliens to the faith (such as the Samaritans, and the unconverted Christians in Crete) with fire and brimstone.[27]

Second, be [there] oppositions within, and church members (as the Answerer speaks) become scandalous in doctrine (I speak not of scandals against the civil state, which the civil magistrate ought to punish), it is the Lord only (as this Scripture to Timothy implies) who is able to give them repentance and recover them out of Satan's snare. To which end also he has appointed those holy and dreadful censures in his church or kingdom. True it is, the sword may make (as once the Lord complained, Isa. 10) a whole nation of hypocrites. But to recover a soul from Satan by repentance, and to bring them from Antichristian doctrine or worship to Christian doctrine or worship, in the least true internal or external submission, that only works the all-powerful God, by the sword of the Spirit in the hand of his spiritual officers.

What a most woeful proof hereof have the nations of the earth given in all ages? And to seek no further than our native soil within a few scores of years, how many wonderful changes in religion has the whole kingdom made, according to the change of the governors thereof, in the several religions which they themselves embraced! Henry VII finds and leaves the kingdom absolutely popish. Henry VIII casts it into a mold half popish, half Protestant. Edward VI brings forth an edition all Protestant. Queen Mary within a few years defaces Edward's work and renders the kingdom (after her grandfather Henry VII's pattern) all popish. Mary's short life and religion end together, and Elizabeth revived her brother Edward's model, all Protestant.[28] And some eminent witnesses of God's truth against Antichrist have inclined to believe that before the downfall of that Beast,[29] England must once again bow down her fair neck to his proud usurping yoke and foot.

Peace. It has been England's sinful shame to fashion and to change their garments and religions with wondrous ease and lightness, as a higher power or a stronger sword has prevailed, after the ancient pattern of

27. Cotton debated Williams's characterization of his position on this point in his rebuttal to *The Bloody Tenent*, entitled *The Bloody Tenent, Washed and Made White in the Blood of the Lamb*.

28. For a brief discussion of the Tudor legacy in English religious affairs of the sixteenth and seventeenth centuries, see the introduction to this volume.

29. Like most of his Puritan colleagues, Williams assigns this biblical character (from the Book of Revelation) to the church in Rome.

Nebuchadnezzar's bowing the whole world in one most solemn uniformity of worship to his golden image (Dan. 3). But it has been thought or said, shall oppositions against the truth escape unpunished? Will they not prove mischievous?

Truth. I answer, the magistrates (and all men that by the mercy of God to themselves discern the misery of such opposites) have cause to lament and bewail that fearful condition wherein such are entangled. . . . A carnal weapon or sword of steel may produce a carnal repentance, a show, an outside . . . uniformity through a state or kingdom. But it has pleased the Father to exalt the Lord Jesus only to be a prince armed with power and means sufficient to give repentance to Israel (Acts 5:31). Accordingly, an unbelieving soul, being dead in sin (although he be changed from one worship to another, like a dead man shifted into several changes of apparel), cannot please God (Heb. 2), and consequently whatever such an unbelieving and unregenerate person acts in worship or religion, it is but sin (Rom. 14). . . . But faith is that gift which proceeds alone from the Father of Lights (Phil. 1:29), and until he pleases to make his light arise and open the eyes of blind sinners, their souls shall lie fast asleep in the dungeons of spiritual darkness and Satan's slavery, and the faster in that a sword of steel compels them to worship in hypocrisy.[30]

Peace. I add, that a civil sword (as woeful experience in all ages has proved) is so far from bringing or helping forward an opposite in religion to repentance, that magistrates sin grievously against the work of God and blood of souls by such proceedings. Because [just] as commonly the sufferings of false and Antichristian teachers harden their followers, who being blind . . . tumble into the ditch of hell after their blind leaders with more enflamed zeal of lying confidence. So second, violence and a sword of steel begets such an impression in the sufferers that certainly they conclude . . . [that] that religion cannot be true which needs such instruments of violence to uphold it, [and] that [their] persecutors are far from soft and gentle commiseration of the blindness of others. . . .

---

30. For clarity I have altered the order of Williams's original sentence, which reads "But faith it is that gift which proceeds alone from the Father of Lights, Phil. 1.29, and till he please to make his light arise and open the eyes of blind sinners, their souls shall lie fast asleep (and the faster, in that a sword of steel compels them to a worship in hypocrisy) in the dungeons of spiritual darkness and Satan's slavery."

Williams continues his assault with biblical evidence from Isaiah 2:4, Micah 4:3, Acts 20:29, and Titus 1:9. Next he turns to important passages in 2 Corinthians 10 and Romans 13.

Truth. I acknowledge that herein the Spirit of God denies not civil weapons of justice to the civil magistrate. . . . I hence observe that there being held forth in this Scripture [2 Corinthians 10:4—"For the weapons of our warfare are not carnal, but mighty through God to the pulling down of strong holds"] a two-fold state, a civil state and a spiritual—[with] civil officers and spiritual, civil weapons and spiritual weapons, civil vengeance and punishment and a spiritual vengeance and punishment (although the Spirit speaks not here expressly of civil magistrates and their civil weapons)—yet these states being of different natures and considerations, as far differing as spirit from flesh, I first observe that civil weapons are most improper and unfitting in matters of the spiritual state and kingdom, though in the civil state most proper and suitable.

For . . . to batter down a stronghold, high wall, fort, tower or castle, men bring not a first and second admonition and after obstinacy excommunication, which are spiritual weapons concerning them that be in the church; nor exhortation to repent and be baptized, to believe in the Lord Jesus, which are proper weapons to them that be without. But to take a stronghold, men bring cannons, culverins, saker,[31] bullets, powder, muskets, swords, pikes, and these to this end are weapons effectual and proportional.

On the other side, to batter down idolatry, false worship, heresy, schism, blindness, or hardness, out of the soul and spirit, it is vain, improper, and unsuitable to bring those weapons which are used by persecutors—stocks, whips, prisons, swords, gibbets, stakes. Against these spiritual strongholds in the souls of men, spiritual artillery and weapons are proper, which are mighty through God to subdue and bring under the very thought to obedience, or else to bind fast the soul with chains of darkness and lock it up in the prison or unbelief and hardness to eternity. I observe that as civil weapons are improper in this business and never able to affect anything in the soul, so . . . they are unnecessary, for . . . as the Spirit here says (and the Answerer grants), spiritual weapons in the hand of church officers are able and

---

31. A saker is a type of falcon, but the term here might also refer to a kind of artillery, a reading that better fits the context.

ready to take vengeance on all disobedience, that is able and mighty, sufficient and ready for the Lord's work. . . .

Two Tables, Two Swords, Two Ministries

Peace. Now in the second place, concerning that Scripture Romans 13[32] which it pleases the Answerer to quote, and he and so many excellent servants of God have insisted upon to prove such persecution of conscience. How have both he and they wrested this Scripture . . . to their own and others' temporal destruction by civil wars and combustions in the world! My humble request, therefore, is to the Father of Lights to send out the bright beams of the Sun of Righteousness and to scatter the mist which . . . Satan has raised about this holy Scripture. And my request to you, dear Truth, is for your care and pains to enlighten and clear this Scripture.

Truth. First, then, upon the serious examination of this whole Scripture it will appear that from the ninth verse of chapter twelve to the end of this whole thirteenth chapter, the Spirit handles the duties of the saints in the careful observation of the second Table, in their civil conversation or walking towards men, and speaks not at all of any point or matter of the first Table concerning the Kingdom of the Lord Jesus. . . .[33]

Peace. . . . I pray you to set down the words of one or two, not unbelievers, but excellent and precious servants and witnesses of God in their times whose names are sweet and precious to all who fear God, who although their judgment ran in the common stream (that is, that magistrates were keepers of the two Tables, defenders of the faith against heretics) . . . yet the light of truth evidently shined upon their souls in this Scripture, that they absolutely denied [Rom. 13] to concern any matter of the first Table.

Truth. First, I shall produce that excellent servant of God, Calvin, who upon this 13th [chapter in the Letter] to the Romans writes . . . "this whole discourse concerns civil magistrates, and therefore in vain do they who exer-

---

32. "Let every soul be subject unto the higher powers. For there is no power but of God: the powers that be are ordained of God. Whosoever therefore resisteth the power, resisteth the ordinance of God: and they that resist shall receive to themselves damnation" (Romans 13:1–2).

33. By the two "Tables" of the law Williams is referring to the Ten Commandments. Christian theologians historically recognized a distinction between the first commandments (the "First Table"), which address obligations to God—such as avoiding idolatry—and the latter commandments (the "Second Table"), which govern interpersonal acts, such as killing and stealing.

cise power over consciences go about from this place to establish their sacrilegious tyranny."[34]

Peace. I know how far most men . . . will disclaim the dealing of all with men's consciences. Yet if the acts and statutes which are made by them concerning the worship of God be attended to, their profession . . . to suffer no other religion nor worship in their territories but one, their profession and practice to defend their faith from reproach and blasphemy of heretics by civil weapons, and all that from this very 13th [chapter] of Romans—I say, if these particulars and others be with fear and trembling in the presence of the Most High be examined, the wonderful deceit of their own hearts shall appear to them, and how guilty they will appear to be of wresting this Scripture before the tribunal of the Most High.

Williams continues his discussion of Calvin's commentary on Romans and then moves to a consideration of Theodore Beza's comments on Romans 13 in order to defend his position that this biblical passage does not justify the persecution of conscience, because it limits its discussion of civil authority to those responsibilities that fall under the second table of the law.

Peace. I now proceed to the second argument from this Scripture against the use of civil weapons in matters of religion and spiritual worship.

Truth. The Spirit of God here commands subjection and obedience to higher powers, even to the Roman emperor and all subordinate magistrates. And yet the emperors and governors under them were strangers from the life of God in Christ, yea . . . cruel and bloody persecutors of the name and followers of Jesus. And yet to these is this subjection and obedience commanded. Now true it is, that as the civil magistrate is apt not to content himself with the majesty of an earthly throne, . . . but to seat himself in the throne of David (in the church), so God's people. . . , considering their high and glorious preferment and privileges by Jesus Christ, were apt to be much

---

34. The quote, which Williams renders in Latin before translating to English, is from Calvin's commentary on Paul's Epistle to the Romans, specifically from his discussion of Romans 13:5. Despite Williams's use of Calvin in his attack on religious persecution, Calvin generally accepted that civil government had a divinely ordained responsibility to defend good religion. Besides Calvin's commentary on Romans, see his *Institutes of the Christian Religion,* Book 4, chapter 20 for evidence of a position that looks more like Cotton's than Williams's. By invoking Calvin as he does here, Williams is knowingly using Calvin to refute not only Cotton but also Calvin himself.

tempted to despise civil governors, especially such as were ignorant of the Son of God and persecuted him in his servants.

Now then, I argue [that] if the Apostle [Paul] should have commanded this subjection to the Roman emperor and Roman magistrates in spiritual causes, as to defend the truth which they were in no way able to discern (but persecuted!) . . . I say if Paul should have . . . put this work upon these Roman governors, and commanded the churches of Christ to have yielded subjection in any such matters, he must (in the judgment of all men) have put out the eye of faith and reason and sense at once!

Williams goes on to address another objection: if the state has no power in spiritual matters, then why did the Apostle Paul himself appeal to Rome in his own trial (Acts 25)? Williams's answer is simple: Paul appealed to the emperor as a civil authority against civil charges only (namely sedition) and therefore recognized the difference between civil and religious authority. Williams next takes up the symbolism of the "sword" given by God to civil magistrates as a symbol of divine appointment and authority. He argues that the Bible distinguishes between different metaphorical swords for the spiritual and civil realms.

Truth. We must distinguish of swords.[35] We find four sorts of swords mentioned in the New Testament. First, the sword of persecution, which Herod stretched forth against James (Acts 12). Second, the sword of God's Spirit, expressly said to be the Word of God (Ephesians 6), a sword of two edges carried in the mouth of Christ (Rev. 1). . . . Third, the great sword of war and destruction, given to him that rides that terrible red horse of War,[36] so that he takes peace from the earth, and men kill one another, as is most lamentably true in the slaughter of so many hundred thousand souls within these few years in several parts of Europe, our own and others. None of these three swords [is] intended in this Scripture. Therefore, fourthly, there is a civil sword, called the sword of civil justice, which being of a material [and] civil nature—for the defense of persons, estates, families, [and the] liberties

35. The use of "swords" as a metaphor for distinctions between spiritual and civil authority is rooted in biblical allusion (Luke 22:38) and enjoys a rich history in Christian theology. For a brief review of this history, see John Witte, *Religion and the American Constitutional Experiment*, 2nd ed. (Boulder, Colo.: Westview Press, 2005), 1–17.

36. "And there went out another horse that was red: and power was given to him that sat thereon to take peace from the earth, and that they should kill one another: and there was given unto him a great sword" (Rev. 6:4).

of a city or civil state, and the suppressing of uncivil or injurious persons or actions by such civil punishment—it cannot according to its utmost reach and capacity . . . extend to spiritual and soul-causes, spiritual and soul punishment, which belongs to that spiritual sword with two edges, . . . the Word of God.

. . . That the Spirit of God never intended to direct or warrant the magistrate to use his power in spiritual affairs and religion's worship, I argue from the term or title it pleases the wisdom of God to give such civil officers: God's ministers. Now at the very first blush, no man denies a double ministry: the one appointed by Christ Jesus in his church, to gather, to govern, receive in [and] cast out, and order all the affairs of the church. . . ; [and] secondly, a civil ministry or office, merely human and civil, which men agree to continue [and] called therefore a human creation (1 Peter 2). [This civil ministry] is as true and lawful in those nations, cities, and kingdoms which never heard of the true God nor his holy Son Jesus as [it is] in any part of the world beside where the name of Jesus is most taken up. . . . All magistrates are God's ministers, essentially civil, bound to a civil work with civil weapons or instruments and paid or rewarded with civil rewards. From all which, I say . . . that this Scripture is generally mistaken and wrested from the scope of God's Spirit and the nature of the place, and cannot be truly alleged by any for the power of the civil magistrate to be exercised in spiritual and soul matters.

Peace. Against this I know many object out of the fourth verse of this chapter, that the magistrate is to avenge or punish evil.[37] From whence it is gathered that heresy . . . , being evil, ought to be punished civilly.

Truth. . . . I have proved from the scope of the place that here is not intended evil against the spiritual or Christian estate . . . , but evil against the civil state . . . , properly falling under the cognizance of the civil minister of God, the magistrate, and punishable by that civil sword of his as an incivility, disorder, or breach of that civil order, peace, and civility to which all the inhabitants of a city, town, or kingdom oblige themselves.

Peace. I have heard that the elders of the New England churches (who yet out of this Romans 13 maintain persecution) grant that the magistrate is to

---

37. "For he is the minister of God to thee for good. But if thou do that which is evil, be afraid; for he beareth not the sword in vain: for he is the minister of God, a revenger to execute wrath upon him that doeth evil" (Romans 13:4).

preserve the peace and welfare of the state, and therefore that he ought not to punish such sins as hurt not his peace. In particular, they say, the magistrate may not punish secret sins in the soul, nor such sins as are yet handled in the church in a private way, nor such sins which are private in families. And therefore they say the magistrate transgresses to prosecute complaints of children against their parents, servants against masters, wives against husbands, . . . nor such sins as are between the members and churches themselves. . . .

Truth. From thence, sweet Peace, may we well observe . . . [that] the distinction of private and public evil will not here avail, because such as urge that term evil . . . urge it strictly . . . , because heresy, blasphemy, false church, and false ministry [are] evil, as well as disorder, in a civil state. Secondly, I observe how they take away from the magistrate that which is proper to his cognizance, the complaints of servants, children, wives, against their parents, masters, and husbands. Families as families, being stones which make up the common building, are properly the object of the magistrate's care, in respect of civil government, civil order, and obedience. . . .

It is evil, says he,[38] to tolerate notorious evildoers, seducing teachers, and scandalous livers. In which speech, I observe two evils: first, that this proposition is too large and general, because the rule admits of exception, and that according to the will of God. It is true that evil cannot alter its nature but is always evil . . . , yet it must be remembered that it is one thing to command, conceal, counsel, [or] approve evil, and another thing to permit and suffer evil with protestation against it or dislike of it, at least without approbation of it. [Second], this sufferance or permission of evil is not for its own sake, but for the sake of good, which puts a respect of goodness upon such permission.

Hence it is that for God's own glory's sake (which is the highest good), he endures (that is, permits or suffers) the vessels of wrath (Rom. 9). And therefore although he be of pure eyes and can behold no iniquity, yet his pure eyes patiently and quietly behold and permit all the idolatries and profanations, all the thefts and rapines, all the whoredoms and abominations, all the murders and poisonings. And yet, I say, for his glory's sake he is patient, and long permits.

38. That is, Cotton.

Williams finishes his belabored argument over the biblical evidence against persecution by visiting (and revisiting) a few more passages. He then turns his attention from scripture to contemporary politics, arguing that religious tolera-tion was properly commended by prominent European rulers, most notably the King of Bohemia, King Steven of Poland, and King James I himself. In fact, he argues, the current practice of toleration in some regions of Europe is more con-sistent with a Christian politics than is the violent defense of religion.

Civil Promotion of Christianity Hurts the Church's Integrity More Than It Helps

Truth. . . . I affirm that that state policy and state necessity which (for the peace of the state and preventing of rivers of civil blood) permits the con-sciences of men will be found to agree most punctually with the rules of the best politician that ever the world saw, the King of kings, and Lord of lords. . . . That absolute rule of this great politician for the peace of the field (which is the world) and for the good and peace of the saints . . . I have dis-coursed of in his command of permitting the tares. . . .

Peace. I have often heard that history reports (and I have heard that Mr. Cotton himself has affirmed it) that Christianity fell asleep in Constantine's bosom and the laps and bosoms of those emperors professing the name of Christ.

Truth. The unknowing zeal of Constantine and other emperors did more hurt to Christ Jesus [and] his crown and kingdom than the raging fury of the most bloody Neros. In the persecution of the latter, Christians were sweet and fragrant, like spices pounded and beaten in mortars. But those good emperors, persecuting some erroneous persons (like Arius) and ad-vancing the professors of some truths of Christ (for there was no small number of truths lost in those times) and maintaining their religion by the material sword, I say by this means Christianity was eclipsed and the profes-sors of it fell asleep. Babel was ushered in, and by degrees the gardens of the churches of saints were turned into the wilderness of whole nations, until the whole world became Christian, or "Christendom."

Doubtless these holy men . . . intended and aimed right, to exalt Christ. But not attending to the command of Christ Jesus to permit the tares to grow in the field of the world, they made the garden of the church and field of the world to be all one, and might not only sometimes . . . persecute good wheat instead of tares, but also pluck up thousands of those precious flakes by commotions and combustions about religion, as has been since practiced in the great and wonderful changes wrought by such wars in many great and mighty states and kingdoms. . . .

When Christianity began to be choked, it was not when Christians lodged in cold prisons, but down beds of ease, and persecuted others.

Civil Rulers Not Qualified to Distinguish "True" Religion from False

Peace. He [Cotton] ends this passage with approbation of Queen Elizabeth for persecuting the Papists, and a reproof to King James for his persecuting the Puritans.

Truth. I answer, if Queen Elizabeth, according to the Answerer's tenet and conscience, did well to persecute according to her conscience, King James did not ill in persecuting to his. For Mr. Cotton must grant that either King James was not fit to be a king, had not the essential qualifications of a king in not being able rightly to judge who ought to be persecuted and who not, or else he must confess that King James and all magistrates must persecute such whom in their conscience they judge worthy to be persecuted.

I say it again (though I neither approve Queen Elizabeth or King James in such their persecutions): such as hold this tenet of persecuting for conscience must also hold that civil magistrates are not essentially fitted and qualified for their function and office except [that] they can discern clearly the difference between such as are to be punished and persecuted and such as are not. Or else if they be essentially qualified, without such a religious spirit of discerning, and yet must persecute the heretic and the schismatic, must they not persecute according to their conscience and persuasion?[39] And then doubtless (though he be excellent for civil government) may he easily . . . persecute the Son of God, instead of the son of perdition. Therefore according to Christ Jesus his command, magistrates are bound not to

---

39. Williams argues this point several times in *The Bloody Tenent,* that appointing civil magistrates as defenders of the faith logically leads to one of three conclusions: (1) all governments are properly equipped to judge spiritual matters (a point he believed Cotton would agree was clearly false); (2) the ability to discern "true" religion is a necessary condition for the legitimacy of a civil leader's authority (a politically dangerous and theologically dubious argument for a Puritan to make); or (3) each civil leader essentially defends his own personal beliefs, which leaves the fate of religion subject to the winds of political circumstance.

persecute, and to see that none of their subjects be persecuted and oppressed for their conscience and worship, being otherwise subject and
peaceable in civil obedience.

The author of An Humble Supplication *had enlisted the support of various
church fathers to the cause of religious freedom, but Cotton responded by refut-
ing such a reading of the tradition. Williams, of course, felt obliged to defend at
length the reading of the church fathers as supporting freedom of conscience.
Surprisingly for a Puritan, Williams then proceeds to ally himself with his
Catholic contemporaries on the issue of religious toleration.*

The Hypocrisy of New England's Refusal to Grant Toleration

Peace. The next passage in the Author which the Answerer descends to is
the testimony of the Papists themselves, a lively and shining testimony from
Scriptures alleged both against themselves and all that associate with them
. . . in such unchristian and bloody tenets and practices:

> As for the testimony of the Popish book (says Mr. Cotton), we weigh it not, as
> knowing whatever they speak for toleration of religion where themselves are
> under hatches, when they come to sit at stern they judge and practice quite
> contrary, as both their writings and judicial proceedings have testified to the
> world these many years.

Truth. I answer, although both writings and practices have been such, yet
the Scriptures and expressions of truth alleged and uttered by them speak
loud and fully for them when they are under the hatches: that for their conscience and religion they should not there be choked and smothered, but
suffered to breathe and walk upon the decks in the air of civil liberty and
conversation in the ship of the commonwealth, upon good assurance given
of civil obedience to the civil state.

Again, if this practice be so abominable in his eyes from the Papists—that
they are so partial as to persecute when they sit at helm and yet cry out
against persecution when they are under the hatches—I shall beseech the
Righteous Judge of the whole world to present as in a water or glass (where
face answers to face) the faces of the Papist to the Protestant. . . . When Mr.
Cotton and others have formerly been under hatches, what sad and true

complaints have they abundantly poured forth against persecution? How have they opened that heavenly Scripture (Cant. 4:8) where Christ Jesus calls his tender wife and spouse from the fellowship with persecutors in their dens of lions and mountains of leopards? But coming to the helm . . . how, both by preaching, writing, printing, and practice, do they themselves . . . unnaturally and partially express toward others the cruel nature of such lions and leopards? O, that the God of heaven might please to tell them how abominable in his eyes are a weight and a weight, a stone and a stone, in the bag of weights! One weight for themselves when they are under hatches, and another for others when they come to helm.

Nor shall their confidence of their being in the truth (which they judge the Papists and others are not in) nor the truth itself privilege them to persecute others, and to exempt themselves from persecution. For first, it is against the nature of true sheep to persecute or hunt the beasts of the forest, not even the same wolves who formerly have persecuted them. Second, if it be a duty and charge upon all magistrates in all parts of the world to judge and persecute in and for spiritual causes, then either they are no magistrates who are not able to judge in such cases, or else they must judge according to their consciences, whether pagan, Turkish, or Antichristian. Lastly, notwithstanding their confidence of the truth of their own way, yet the experience of our fathers' errors, our own mistakes and ignorance, the sense of our own weakness and blindness in the depths of the prophesies and mysteries of the kingdom of Christ, and the great professed expectation of light to come which we are not now able to comprehend, may abate the edge, yea sheath up the sword of persecution toward any, especially such as differ not from them in doctrines of repentance, or faith, or holiness of heart and life and hope of glorious and eternal union to come, but only in the way and manner of the administrations of Jesus Christ.

Who Is in a Position to Judge Whether Another Truly Fears God?

Truth. I here observe the Answerer's partiality, that none but such as truly fear God should enjoy liberty of conscience, whence the inhabitants of the world must either come into the estate of men fearing God, or else dissemble a religion in hypocrisy, or else be driven out of the world—one must follow. The first is only the gift of God, the second and third are too commonly practiced upon this ground.

Again, since there is so much controversy in the world where the name of Christ is taken up concerning [what constitutes] the true church, ministry and worship, and who are those that truly fear God, I ask: who shall judge in this case who be they that fear God? It must be granted that such as have the power of suffering or not suffering such consciences must judge. And then must it follow (as before I intimated) that the civil state must judge of the truth of the spiritual, and then magistrates—fearing or not fearing God themselves—must judge of the fear of God. Also, their judgment or sentence must be according to their conscience, of what religion so ever. . . . And lastly, since the sovereign power of all civil authority is founded in the consent of the people, [it must be] that every commonwealth has radically and fundamentally in it a power of truly discerning the true fear of God, which they transfer to their magistrates and officers, or else that there are no lawful kingdoms, cities, or towns in the world in which a man may live, and to whose civil government he may submit. And then (as I said before) there must be no world, nor is it lawful to live in it, because it has not a true discerning spirit to judge them that fear or not fear God.

Lastly, although this worthy Answerer so readily grants that liberty of conscience should be suffered to them that fear God indeed, yet we know what the ministers of the churches of New England wrote in answer to the three questions sent to them by some ministers of Old England.[40] Although they confessed [them] to be such persons whom they approved of far above themselves . . . , yet if they and other godly people with them coming over to them should differ in church constitution, they then could not approve their civil cohabitation with them, and consequently could not advise the magistrates to suffer them to enjoy a civil being within their jurisdiction. Hear, O heavens, and give ear, O earth, yea let the heavens be astonished and the earth tremble at such an answer as this from such excellent men to such whom they esteem for godliness above themselves!

Peace. Yea, but they say they doubt not if they were there but they should agree. For, say they, either you will come to us or you may show us light to come to you, for we are but weak men, and dream not of perfection in this life.

Truth. Alas, who knows not what lamentable differences have been between the same ministers of the church of England . . . ? How great the pres-

---

40. See "Mr. Cotton's Letter," note 16, in this volume.

ent differences even amongst them that fear God . . . ? Let none now think that the passage to New England by sea or by the nature of the country can do what only the Key of David can do, [that is], open and shut the consciences of men. Beside, how can this be a faithful and upright acknowledgement of their weakness and imperfection when they preach, print, and practice such violence to the souls and bodies of others, and by their rules and grounds ought to proceed even to the killing of those whom they judge so dear to them, and in respect of godliness far above themselves?

Peace. Yea, but (say they) the godly will not persist in heresy or turbulent schism when they are convinced in conscience.

Truth. . . . According to this conclusion it must follow that if the most godly persons yield not to once or twice admonition (as is maintained by the Answerer), they must necessarily be esteemed obstinate persons, for if they were godly (says he) they would yield. Must it not then be said (as it was by one, passing sentence of banishment upon some, whose godliness was acknowledged) that he that commanded the judge not to respect the poor in the cause of judgment commands him not to respect the holy or the godly person?

Hence I could name the place and time when a godly man, a most desirable person for his trade yet something different in conscience, propounded his willingness and desire to come to dwell in a certain town in New England. It was answered by the chief of the place, "This man differs from us, and we desire not to be troubled." So that in conclusion (for no other reason in the world) the poor man, though godly, useful, and peaceable, could not be admitted to a civil being and habitation on the common earth in that wilderness among them. . . .

The "Bloody Tenent" of Persecution Contradicts the Mind of Christ

Peace. Mr. Cotton concludes with a confident persuasion of having removed the grounds of that great error, viz. that persons are not to be persecuted for cause of conscience.

Truth. And I believe (dear Peace) it shall appear to them that with fear and trembling at the word of the Lord examine these passages, that the charge of error rebounds back, even such an error as may well be called the *bloody tenent,* so directly contradicting the spirit and mind and practice of the Prince of Peace, so deeply guilty of the blood of the souls under the altar persecuted in all ages for cause of conscience, and so destructive to the civil peace and welfare of all kingdoms, countries, and commonwealths.

Peace. To this conclusion (dear Truth) I heartily subscribe, and know that God, the Spirit, the Prince, the angels, and all the true awakened sons of peace will call you blessed.

Truth. How sweet and precious are these contemplations, but oh, how sweet the actions and fruitions!

Peace. Your lips drip as the honeycomb, honey and milk are under your tongue. Oh, that these drops, these streams might flow without a stop or interruption!

Truth. The glorious white troopers (Rev. 19) shall in time be mounted, and he that is the most High Prince of princes and Lord General of generals, mounted upon the Word of Truth and Meekness (Ps. 45) shall triumph gloriously and renew our meetings. But hark, what noise is this?

Peace. These are the doleful drums and shrill sounding trumpets, the roaring murdering cannons, the shouts of conquerors, the groans of wounded, dying, slaughtered, and righteous with the wicked. Dear Truth how long? How long these dreadful sounds and direful fights? How long before my glad return and restitution?

Truth. Sweet Peace, who will believe my true report? Yet true it is, if I were once believed, blessed Truth and Peace should not so soon be parted.

Peace. Dear Truth, what welcome have you found of late beyond your former times or present expectations?

Truth. Alas, my welcome changes as the times, and strongest swords and arms prevail. Were I believed in this—that Christ is not delighted with the blood of men, but shed his own for his bloodiest enemies, that by the word of Christ no man for gainsaying Christ or joining with his enemy Antichrist should be molested with the civil sword—were this foundation laid as the Magna Carta of highest liberties, and good security given to all hands for the preservation of it, how soon should every brow and house be stuck with olive branches?

Peace. This heavenly invitation makes me bold once more to crave your patient ear and holy tongue. Error's impatient and soon tired, but you are light, and like the Father of Lights unwearied in your shining. Look here what once again I present to your impartial censure.

A MODEL OF CHURCH and CIVIL POWER.
Composed by Mr. COTTON and the MINISTERS of NEW-ENGLAND,
And sent to the church at Salem, as a further Confirmation of
the bloody doctrine of PERSECUTION for cause of CONSCIENCE
Examined and Answered.[41]

Truth. What have you there?

Peace. Here is a combination of your own children against your very life and mine. Here is a model (framed by many able learned and godly hands) of such a church and commonwealth as wakens Moses from his unknown grave and denies Jesus yet to have seen the earth.[42]

Truth. Begin, sweet Peace, read and propound. My hand shall not be tired with holding the balances of the sanctuary. Put in, and I shall weigh in as is the preference of Him whose pure eyes cannot behold iniquity.

The Two Kingdoms, Church and Civil Society

Peace. Thus then speaks the preface or entrance:

Seeing God has given a distinct power to church and commonwealth, the one spiritual (called the Power of the Keys), the other civil (called the Power of the Sword) and has made the members of both societies subject to both Authorities, so that every soul in the church is subject to the higher powers in the commonwealth, and every member of the commonwealth (being a member of the church) is subject to the laws of Christ's kingdom, and in him to the censures of the church; the question is, how the civil state and the church may dispense their several governments without infringement and impeachment of the power and honor of the one or of the other, and what bounds and limits the Lord has set between both the administrations.

Truth. From that conclusion, dear Peace, that every member of the commonwealth, being a member of the church, is subject to the laws of Christ's

---

41. Williams insists that this "Model of Church and Civil Power" was prepared by Cotton and other Massachusetts divines and sent as a chastisement to the church at Salem. Cotton declared that he had no part in the document, and he denied that it was ever sent to the Salem church. But as Richard Groves points out, "Cotton was certainly aware of the piece. At the conclusion of his reply to the *Humble Supplication,* he referred to 'a treatise sent to some of the brethren late of Salem, who doubted as you do.'" Richard Groves, preface to *The Bloody Tenent of Persecution,* ed. Richard Groves (Macon, Ga.: Mercer University Press, 2001), x.

42. In other words, in Williams's estimation the "Model" reflects a failure to read the collusion of religion and civil power in Old Testament Israel as typological and therefore not applicable after Christ.

kingdom and in him to the censure of the church, I observe that they grant the church of Christ in spiritual causes to be superior and over the highest magistrates in the world, if members of the church. Hence therefore I infer [that] she may refuse to receive and may also cast forth any, yea even the highest (if obstinate in sin), out of her spiritual society. Hence in this spiritual society, that soul who has most of Christ, most of His Spirit, is most (spiritually) honorable, according to the Scriptures quoted (Acts 15:20; Isa. 49:23; Gal. 3:28). And if so, how can this stand with their common tenet that the civil magistrate must keep the First Table, set up and reform the church, and be judge and governor in all ecclesiastical, as well as civil, causes? . . .

Civil Societies Do Not Need the Church to Flourish

Peace.

Whereas diverse affecting transcending power to themselves over the church have persuaded the princes of the world that the kingdom of Christ in His church cannot rise or stand without the falls of those commonwealths wherein it is set up, we do believe and profess the contrary to this suggestion: the government of the one being of this world, the other not; the church helping forward the prosperity of the commonwealth by means only ecclesiastical and spiritual, the commonwealth helping forward her own and the church's felicity by means political or temporal; the falls of commonwealths being known to arise from their scattering and diminishing the power of the church, and the flourishing of commonwealths with the well ordering of the people (even in moral and civil virtues) being observed to arise from the vigilant administration of the holy discipline of the church. . . .

Truth. From this confession, that the church or Kingdom of Christ may be set up without prejudice of the commonwealth (according to John 18:36),[43] . . . I observe that although the Kingdom of Christ the church and the civil kingdom or government be not inconsistent (but that both may stand together), yet they are independent according to that Scripture, and therefore there may be (as formerly I have proved) flourishing common-

43. "Jesus answered, My kingdom is not of this world: if my kingdom were of this world, then would my servants fight, that I should not be delivered to the Jews: but now is my kingdom not from hence."

wealths and societies of men where no church of Christ abides. In addition, the commonwealth may be in perfect peace and quiet notwithstanding the church, the commonwealth of Christ, be in distractions and spiritual oppositions, both against their religions, and sometimes amongst themselves, as the church of Christ in Corinth was troubled with divisions and contentions.

Second, I observe it is true the church helps forward the prosperity of the commonwealth by spiritual means (Jer. 29:7). The prayers of God's people procure the peace of the city where they abide, yet that Christ's ordinances and administrations of worship are appointed and given by Christ to any civil state, town, or city as is implied by the instance of Geneva, I confidently deny. The ordinances and disciplines of Christ Jesus, though wrongfully and profanely applied to natural and unregenerate men, may cast a blush of civility and morality upon them. . . . Yet withal I affirm that the misapplication of ordinances to unregenerate and unrepentant persons hardens up their souls in dreadful sleep and dream of their own blessed estate, and sends millions of souls to hell in a secure expectation of a false salvation.

Civil Magistrates, Like Husbands, Should Respect the Conscience of Their "Spouse"

Truth. . . . Families are the foundations of government, for what is a commonwealth but a commonwealth of families agreeing to live together for common good? Now in families, suppose a believing Christian husband has an unbelieving Antichristian wife. What other charge in this respect is given to a husband (1 Cor. 7) but to dwell with her as husband, if she be pleased to dwell with him, but to be so far from forcing her from her conscience to his, that if for his conscience sake she would depart, he would not force her to tarry with him. Consequently the father or husband of the state, differing from the commonwealth in religion, ought not to force the commonwealth, nor to be forced by it. Yet is he to continue a civil husband's care, if the commonwealth will live with him and abide in civil covenant. Now as a husband, by his love to the truth and holy conversation in it and seasonable exhortations, ought to endeavor to save his wife, yet abhor to use corporal compulsion . . . , so ought the father, husband, governor of the commonwealth endeavor to win and save whom possibly he may, yet far from the appearance of civil violence. . . .

Spiritual Virtue Distinct from Civil and Moral Virtue

Peace. Dear Truth, it seems not to be unseasonable to close up this passage with a short descant upon that assertion [that], "A subject without godliness will not be *bonus vir* (a good man) nor a magistrate except he see godliness preserved will not be *bonus magistratus*."

Truth. I confess that without godliness or a true worshipping of God with an upright heart according to God's ordinances, neither subjects nor magistrates can please God in Christ Jesus and so be spiritually or Christianly good. . . . Yet this I must [remind] you of, that when the Most High God created all things [out] of nothing, he saw and acknowledged diverse sorts of goodness, which must still be acknowledged in their distinct kinds. [For example,] a good air, a good ground, a good tree, a good sheep, [or] I say the same in artificials: a good garment, a good house, a good sword, a good ship; I also add a good city, a good company or corporation, a good husband, father, master. Hence also we say, a good physician, a good lawyer, a good seaman, a good merchant, a good pilot for such or such a shore or harbor— that is, morally and civilly good in their several civil respects and employments.

Hence (Ps. 133) the church or City of God is compared to a city compact within itself, which compactness may be found in many towns and cities of the world where yet has not shined any spiritual or supernatural goodness. . . . These I observe to prove that a subject or a magistrate may be a good subject or a good magistrate in respect of civil or moral goodness (which thousands want and where it is, it is commendable and beautiful), though godliness (which is infinitely more beautiful) be wanting . . . and only proper to the Christian state, the commonwealth of Israel, the true church, the holy Nation (Eph. 2; 1 Pet. 2). Lastly, however the authors deny that there can be *bonus magistratus* (a good magistrate) except he see all godliness preserved, yet they themselves confess that civil honesty is sufficient to make a good subject. . . . Doubtless, if the law of relations holds true, that civil honesty which makes a good citizen must also (together with qualifications fit for a commander) make a good magistrate.

Civil Powers Derive from the People, but Authority over Religion Not among Them

Peace. The fourth head is the proper means of both these powers to attain their ends:

> Magistrates, as magistrates, have no power of setting up the form of church government, electing church officers, punishing with church censures, but to see that the church does her duty herein. And on the other side, the churches, as churches, have no power (though as members of the commonwealth they may have power) of erecting or altering forms of civil government, electing of civil officers, inflicting civil punishments (no not on persons excommunicate) as by deposing magistrates from their civil authority or withdrawing the hearts of the people against them to their laws, no more then to discharge wives, or children, or servants, from due obedience to their husbands, parents, or masters; or by taking up arms against their magistrates, though he persecute them for conscience. For though members of churches who are public officers also of the civil state may suppress by force the violence of usurpers . . . yet this they do not as members of the church but as officers of the civil state.

Truth. Here are diverse considerable passages, which I shall briefly examine, so far as concerns our controversy.

First, whereas they say that the civil power may erect and establish what form of civil government may seem in wisdom most meet, I acknowledge the proposition to be most true, both in itself and also considered with the end of it—that a civil government is an ordinance of God to conserve the civil peace of people so far as concerns their bodies and goods, as formerly has been said. But from this grant I infer (as before has been touched) that the sovereign, original, and foundation of civil power lies in the people. . . . And if so, a people may erect and establish what form of government seems to them most meet for their civil condition. It is evident that such governments as are by them erected and established have no more power, nor for no longer time, than the civil power or people consenting and agreeing shall entrust them with. This is clear not only in reason, but in the experience of all commonwealths, where the people are not deprived of their natural freedom by the power of tyrants.

And so if the magistrates receive their power of governing the church from the people, undeniably it follows that a people, as a people naturally considered (of what nature or nation soever in Europe, Asia, Africa, or

America), have fundamentally and originally as men a power to govern the church, to see her do her duty, to correct her, to redress, reform, and establish. And if this be not to pull God and Christ and Spirit out of heaven and subject them to natural, sinful, inconstant men—and so consequently to Satan himself, by whom all peoples naturally are guided—let heaven and earth judge.

Peace. It cannot by their own grant be denied but that the wildest Indians in America ought to (and in their kind and several degrees do) agree upon some forms of government, some more civil, . . . some less. As also that their civil and earthly governments be as lawful and true as any governments in the world, and therefore consequently their governors are keepers of the church, or both tables, if any church of Christ should arise or be amongst them. And therefore lastly, if Christ has entrusted and charged the civil power with his church, they must judge according to their Indian or American consciences, for other consciences it cannot be supposed they should have.

Truth. Again, whereas they say that outward civil peace cannot stand where religion is corrupted . . . , I answer with admiration how such excellent spirits (as these authors are furnished with, not only in heavenly but earthly affairs) should so forget, and be so fast asleep in things so palpably evident, as to say that outward civil peace cannot stand where religion is corrupt. When so many stately kingdoms and governments in the world have long and long enjoyed civil peace and quiet, notwithstanding their religion is so corrupt as that there is not the very name of Jesus Christ amongst them. And this every historian, merchant, [and] traveler in Europe, Asia, Africa, and America can testify. . . .

Laws Concerning Religion

Peace. Yea, but they say that such laws as are conversant about religion may still be accounted civil laws, as on the contrary, an oath remains religious, though conversant about civil matters.

Truth. Laws respecting religion are two-fold: First, such as concern the acts of worship and the worship itself, the ministers of it, their fitness or unfitness, to be suppressed or established. For such laws we find no footing in the New Testament of Jesus Christ. Second, laws respecting religion may be such as merely concern the civil state, bodies and goods of such and such persons, professing these and these religions. For instance, that such and such persons, notorious for mutinies, treasons, rebellions, or massacres, be disarmed. Again, that no persons—Papists, Jews, Turks, or Indians—be disturbed at their worship (a thing which the very Indians abhor to practice towards any). Also that immunity and freedom from tax and toll may be granted to the people of such or such a religion, as the magistrate pleases (Ezra 7). These and such as are of this nature, concerning only the bodies and goods of such and such religious persons, I confess are merely civil.

But now on the other hand, that laws restraining persons from such and such a worship, because the civil state judges it to be false; that laws constraining to such and such a worship, because the civil state judges this to be the only true way of worshipping God; that such and such a reformation of worship be submitted to by all subjects in such a jurisdiction; that such and such churches, ministers, or ministries be pulled down, and such and such churches, ministries, and ministrations set up; that such laws properly concerning religion, God, or the souls of men, should be civil laws and constitutions—[these kinds of laws are] as far from reason as [saying] that the commandments of Paul, which he gave the churches concerning Christ's worship (1 Cor. 11 and 1 Cor. 14), were civil and earthly constitutions, or that the canons and constitutions of either ecumenical or national synods concerning religion should be civil and state conclusions and agreements.

To that instance of an oath remaining religious though conversant about civil things, I answer and acknowledge that an oath may be spiritual, though taken about earthly business, and accordingly it will prove and only prove what before I have said, that a law may be civil though it concerns persons of this and of that religion, that is as the persons professing it are concerned in civil respects of bodies or goods. . . . Whereas if it concerns the souls and religions of men simply so considered in reference to God, it must of necessity put on the nature of a religious or spiritual ordinance or constitution. (Besides, [the example of the oath] is a most improper and fallacious instance, for an oath, being an invocation of a true or false God to judge in a case, is an action of a spiritual and religious nature whatever the subject matter be about which it is taken, whether civil or religious.) But a law or constitution may be civil or religious, as the subject about which it is conversant is either civil (merely concerning bodies or goods) or religious (concerning soul and worship).

The fifth, sixth, and seventh "heads" of the Model address the extent of the magistrate's power to make and enforce laws binding on the church. The authors of the Model try to reserve a space for conscience, especially in what they call "indifferent" matters, but they maintain that the magistrate (by virtue of his role as God's vicegerent) is obliged to enforce laws that protect the purity of Christian religion. In response, Williams repeats some of his now familiar arguments, reminding his readers of the futility of trying to force a conscience to accept matters of belief, as well as the historical evidence that coercion usually leads to more strife and violence than it does peace for the church or state. He also uses the Model's argument on "indifferent" matters against its authors, insisting that if freedom of conscience is important in indifferent and secondary matters, it is even more vital to protect it in moments of fundamental conviction and practice.

Persistency Not Necessarily a Sign of "Sinning against Conscience"

Truth. . . . [The Model's authors] propose a distinction of some sins, [that] some are against the light of conscience. . . . I have before discussed this point [regarding] a heretic sinning against the light of conscience. And I shall add that howsoever they lay this down as an infallible conclusion, that all heresy is against light of conscience, yet . . . how do all idolaters, after light [is] presented and exhortations [are] powerfully pressed, either Turks or pagans, Jews or Antichristians, strongly even to the death hold fast (or rather are held fast by) their delusions. Yea, God's people themselves, being deluded and captivated, are strongly confident even against some fundamentals (especially of worship), and yet not *against* the light but *according to* the light or eye of a deceived conscience. Now all these consciences walk on confidently and constantly even to the suffering of death and torments, and are more strongly confirmed in their belief and conscience, because such bloody and cruel courses of persecution are used toward them. . . .[44]

44. Williams is making the point here that religious error is not necessarily the product of sinning *against* conscience, but instead may be the result of staying true to an erroneous conscience. This distinction is important for Williams, because by arguing that they were punishing only those who were found guilty of sinning against conscience, the Massachusetts authorities were trying to conscript the authority of a person's own conscience as a witness against the person and in service to the establishment. By arguing against the logic of "sinning against conscience," Williams once again undercuts a major source of philosophical justification for Massachusetts's practice of religious persecution.

Magistrates Not Responsible for Squelching Religious Dissent

Peace. Their eighth question is this: What power magistrates have about the gathering of churches?

> First, the magistrate has power, and it is his duty to encourage and countenance such persons as voluntarily join themselves in holy covenant, both by his presence (if it may be) and promise of protection, they accepting the right hand of fellowship from other neighbor churches.
>
> Second, he has power to forbid all idolatrous and corrupt assemblies, who offer to put themselves under their patronage, and shall attempt to join themselves into a church-estate, and if they shall not hearken, to force them there from by the power of the sword (Ps. 101:8). For our tolerating many religions in a state in several churches, beside the provoking of God, may in time not only corrupt, leaven, divide, and so destroy the peace of the churches, but also dissolve the continuity of the state, especially ours whose walls are made of the stones of the churches; it being also contrary to the end of our planting in this part of the world, which was not only to enjoy the pure ordinances, but to enjoy them all in purity.
>
> Third, he has power to compel all men within his grant to hear the Word, for hearing the Word of God is a duty which the light of nature leads even heathens to. . . . Yet he has no power to compel all men to become members of churches, because he has not power to make them fit members for the church, which is not wrought by the power of the sword, but by the power of the Word. Nor may he force the churches to accept of any for members but those whom the churches themselves can freely approve of.

Truth. To the first branch of this head, I answer that the magistrate should encourage and countenance the church, yea, and protect the persons of the church from violence [and] disturbance. . . . 'Tis true, all magistrates in the world do this, [that is], encourage and protect that church or assembly of worshippers which they judge to be true and approve of, but not permitting other consciences than their own. It has come to pass in all ages . . . that the Lord Jesus and his Queen[45] are driven and persecuted out of the world.

To the second, that the magistrate ought to suppress all churches which he judges [to be] false, he quotes Psalm 101:8—"Betimes I will cut off the wicked of the Land, that I may cut off all evildoers from the City of Jehovah." . . . At present I answer [that] there is no holy land or city of the Lord . . . but the church of Jesus Christ . . . out of which the Lord Jesus, by his holy

45. That is, the church.

ordinances in such a government and by such governors as he has appointed, cuts off every wicked person and evildoer. . . . And the Spirit of God evidently testifies that the churches were in the cities and countries, not that the whole cities or countries were God's holy land, . . . out of which all false worshippers and wicked persons were to be cut (Rev. 2, 3). . . . If that Scripture may now literally be applied to nations and cities in a parallel to Canaan and Jerusalem since the Gospel ([that is,] this Psalm 101 be literally applied to cities, towns, and countries in Europe and America) . . . how many thousands and millions of men and women in the several kingdoms and governments of the world must be cut off from their lands and destroyed from their cities, as this Scripture speaks?

Truth and Peace go on to point out how the Model's authors contradict themselves in asserting the magistrates' responsibility to defend the purity of the church all the while New England congregations fail to separate from the national church of England. The failure to separate, says Williams, compromises the clergy's mandate to the magistrates to "cut off all evildoers" from Christ's church.

Truth. But having examined that Scripture alleged, let us now weigh their reasons. First they say [that] not cutting off by the sword but tolerating many religions in a state would provoke God. I answer . . . that no proof can be made from the institutions of the Lord Jesus that all religions but one are to be cut off by the civil sword, that national church in that typical Land of Canaan being abolished and the Christian commonwealth or church instituted. Second, I affirm that the cutting off by the sword other consciences and religions is (contrarily) most provoking to God, expressly against his will concerning the tares (Matt. 13) as I have before proved. . . . Third, let conscience and experience speak how in not cutting off their many religions, it has pleased God not only not to be provoked, but to prosper the state of the united provinces [of] our next neighbors, and that to admiration.[46]

Peace. The second reason [for suppressing heterodoxy given by the Model's authors] is that such tolerating would leaven, divide, and destroy the peace of the churches.

---

46. The reference here is to Holland.

Truth. This must also be denied upon so many former Scriptures and reasons produced, proving the power of the Lord Jesus and the sufficiency of his spiritual power in his church for the purging forth and conquering of the least evil, yea for the bringing every thought in subjection unto Christ Jesus (2 Cor. 10). I add, they have not produced one Scripture, nor can [they], to prove that the permitting of the leaven of false doctrine in the world or civil state will leaven the churches. Only we find that the permission of leaven in persons, doctrines, or practices *in* the church that indeed will corrupt and spread (1 Cor. 5; Gal. 5). But this reason should never have been alleged, were not the particular churches in New England but as so many implicit parish churches in one implicit national church. . . . We shall find lawful civil states both before and since Christ Jesus in which we find not any tidings of the true God or Christ. Lastly, their civil New England state, framed out of their churches, may yet stand, submit, and flourish, though they did (as by the word of the Lord they ought) permit either Jews or Turks or Antichristians to live among them, subject to their civil government.

Peace. One branch more . . . and it concerns the hearing of the Word, to which they say "all men are to be compelled, because hearing of the Word is a duty which even nature leads heathens to," for which [argument] they quote the practice of the Ninevites hearing Jonah, and Eglon's (King of Moab) rising up to Ehud's pretended message from God.[47]

Truth. I must deny that position: for [the] light of nature leads men to hear that only which nature conceives to be good for it, and therefore not to hear a messenger, minister, or preacher whom conscience persuades is a false messenger or deceiver . . . , as millions of men and women in their several respective religions and consciences are so persuaded, conceiving their own to be true.

Secondly, as concerning the instances, Jonah did not compel the Ninevites to hear that message which he brought to them. . . . Nor did Christ Jesus or any of his ambassadors so practice, but if persons refused to hear, the command of the Lord Jesus to his messengers was only to depart from them, shaking off the dust from their feet with a denunciation of God's wrath against them (Matt. 10, Acts 14). . . .

I desire all men, and these worthy authors of this Model, to lay their

47. Jonah 3; Judges 3:12–30.

hands upon their hearts and to consider whether this compulsion of men to hear the Word . . . carries men to be of no religion all their days, worse than the very Indians, who dare not live without religion according as they are persuaded. . . .

State Support of Clergy Violates the Conscience of Those outside the Church

Peace. . . . [The authors of the Model] affirm that the magistrate may force out the ministers' maintenance from all that are taught by them, and that after the pattern of Israel, and the argument from 1 Cor. 9 [and] Gal. 6:6.

Truth. . . . To that Scripture Gal. 6:6 ("Let him that is taught in the Word make him that teaches partaker of all his goods"), I answer: That teaching was of persons converted, believers entered into the school and family of Christ the church, which church being rightly gathered is also rightly invested with the power of the Lord Jesus to force every soul therein by spiritual weapons and penalties to do its duty. But this forcing of the magistrate is intended and practiced to all sorts of persons without as well as within the church, unconverted, natural and dead in sin. . . . Now for those sorts of persons to whom Christ Jesus sends his Word out of church estate, Jews or Gentiles,[48] . . . we never find title of any maintenance to be expected, least of all to be forced and exacted from them. By civil power they cannot be forced, for it is no civil payment or business, no matter of Caesar, but concerning God; nor can they be forced by spiritual power, which has nothing to do with those which are without (1 Cor. 5).

It is reasonable to expect and demand of such as live within the state a civil maintenance of their civil officers, and to force it where it is denied. It is reasonable for a schoolmaster to demand his recompense for his labor in his school, but it is not reasonable to expect or force it from strangers, enemies, rebels to that city, from such as come not within or else would not be received into the school. What is the church or Christ Jesus, but the city, the school, and family of Christ? The officers of this city, school, family, may reasonably expect maintenance from such [as] they minister to, but not from strangers or enemies.

Peace. It is most true that sin goes in a link, for that tenent that all the men

---

48. That is, the uncoverted or non-Christians.

of the world may be compelled to hear Christ preach (and enjoy the labors of the Teacher as well as the church itself) forces on another also as evil, that they should also be compelled to pay, as being most equal and reasonable to pay for their conversion. . . .

Truth. God gave to that national church of the Jews that excellent land of Canaan, and therein houses furnished, orchards, gardens, vineyards, olive yards, fields, and wells that they might well in this settled abundance and the promised continuation and increase of it afford a large temporal supply to their priests and Levites, even to the tenth of all they did possess. God's people are now in the Gospel brought into a spiritual land of Canaan, flowing with spiritual milk and honey, and they abound with spiritual and heavenly comforts, though in a poor and persecuted condition, therefore an enforced settled maintenance is not suitable to the Gospel, as it was to the ministry of priests and Levites in the law. . . .

Peace. Yea, but (say they) is not the laborer worthy of his hire?

Truth. Yes, from them that hire him, from the church to whom he labors or ministers, not from the civil state, no more than the minister of the civil state is worthy of his hire from the church but from the civil state (in which I grant the persons in the church ought to be assistant in their civil respects).

Peace. What maintenance (say they) shall the ministry of the Gospel have?

Truth. We find two ways of maintenance for the ministry of the Gospel, proposed for our direction in the New Testament. First, the free and willing contribution of the saints (according to 1 Cor. 16, Luke 8:3), upon which both the Lord Jesus and his ministers lived. Second, the diligent work and labor of their own hands. . . .

Israel a "Type" for the Church, Not a Pattern for Civil Enforcement of Religion

The tenth "head" of the Model asserted limited responsibility on the part of magistrates for defending and promoting sound Christian doctrine. To this Williams responds with his familiar warning (confirmed by history) that magistrates will not necessarily be faithful or learned enough to defend Christian orthodoxy. Williams then turns to the eleventh "head," which argues for magistrates' responsibility to promote right worship.

Truth. In this general head are proposed two things, first, what the magistrate *ought* to do positively concerning the worship of God, [and] second, what he *may* do in the worship of God. What he ought to do is comprised in these particulars: first, he ought to reform the worship of God when it is corrupted; second, he ought to establish a pure worship of God; third, he ought to defend it by the sword, he ought to restrain idolatry by the sword and cut off offenders, as former passages have opened. For the proof of this positive part of his duty are propounded three sorts of Scriptures: first, from the practice of the kings of Israel and Judah; second, some from the New Testament; third, from the practice of kings of other nations.

To which I answer, . . . I have often touched those Scriptures produced from the practice of the kings of Israel and Judah, yet because so great a weight of this controversy lies upon this precedent of the Old Testament, from the duties of this nature enjoined to those kings and governors and their practices . . . , I shall (with the help of Christ Jesus, the true King of Israel) declare and demonstrate how weak and brittle this supposed pillar of marble is, to bear up and sustain such a mighty burden and weight of so many high concernments as are laid upon it. In which I shall evidently prove that the state of Israel as a natural state, made up of spiritual and civil power, so far as it attended upon the spiritual was merely figurative and typing out the Christian churches consisting of both Jews and Gentiles, enjoying the true power of the Lord Jesus, establishing, reforming, correcting, defending in all cases concerning his kingdom and government. . . . I shall consider the very land and country of Canaan itself, and present some considerations proving it to be a none-such.[49] First, this land was espied out and chosen by the Lord out of all the countries of the world to be the seat of his church and people (Ezek. 20:6). But now there is no respect of earth, of places or countries, with the Lord. So testified the Lord Jesus Christ himself to the woman of Samaria (John 4), professing that neither at that mountain nor at Jerusalem should men worship the Father. While that national state of the church remained, the Tribes were bound to go up to Jerusalem to worship (Ps. 122). But now in every nation (not the whole land or country as it was with Canaan), he that fears God and works righteousness is accepted with him (Acts 10:35). This then appeared in that large commission of the Lord Jesus to his

---

49. That is, that Canaan was not meant to be a pattern for other earthly lands or kingdoms.

first ministers: Go into *all* nations, and not only into Canaan, to carry tidings of mercy. . . .

. . . [T]he partition wall is broken down, and in respect of the Lord's special propriety to one country more than another, what difference [is there] between Asia and Africa, between Europe and America, between England and Turkey, London and Constantinople? This land[50] . . . was called Emanuel's land, that is, God with us. . . . But now Jerusalem from above is not material and earthly, but spiritual (Gal. 4, Heb. 12). Material Jerusalem is no more the Lord's city than Jericho, Nineveh, or Babel (in respect of place or country), for even in literal Babel was a church of Jesus Christ (1 Pet. 5). . . .

What land, what country now is Israel's parallel and antitype but that holy mystical nation the church of God, peculiar and called out to him out of every nation and country (1 Pet. 2:9)? In which every true spiritual Naboth has his spiritual inheritance, which he dares not part with though it be to his king or sovereign, and though such his refusal cost him this present life. . . .

Peace. The English, Scotch, and Dutch are apt to make themselves the parallels, as wonderfully come forth of popery.

Truth. But first, whole nations are no churches under the Gospel. Second, bring the nations of Europe professing Protestantism to the balance of the sanctuary, and ponder well whether the body, bulk, the general or one hundredth part of such peoples be truly turned to God from popery. Who knows not how easy it is to turn, and turn, and turn again whole nations from one religion to another? Who knows not that within the compass of one poor span of twelve years of revolution, all England has become from half-Papist, half-Protestant to absolute Protestants; from absolute Protestants to absolute Papists; from absolute Papists (changing as fashions) to absolute Protestants?

. . . Only such as are Abraham's seed, circumcised in the heart, newborn,[51] Israel (or "wrestlers with God"),[52] are the antitype of the former Israel, these are only the holy Nation (1 Peter 2) wonderfully redeemed from the Egypt of this world (Titus 2:14), brought through the Red Sea of baptism (1 Cor 10)

50. Canaan.

51. That is, "born again" (John 3:3).

52. A reference to the literal meaning of "Israel," which according to Genesis is the name God gave Jacob after the patriarch's physical encounter with the Lord (Genesis 32:28).

through the wilderness of afflictions, . . . into the Kingdom of heaven begun below, even that Christian Land of Promise where flow the ever flowing streams and rivers of spiritual milk and honey. . . .

But where is now that nation or country upon the face of the earth thus clean and holy to God, and bound to so many ceremonial cleansings and purgings? Are not all the nations of the earth alike clean to God, or rather alike unclean, until it pleases the Father of mercies to call some out to the knowledge and grace of his Son, making them to see their filthiness and strangeness from the commonwealth of Israel, and to wash in the blood of the Lamb of God? This taking away the difference between nation and nation, country and country, is most fully and admirably declared in that great vision of all sorts of living creatures presented to Peter (Acts 10), whereby it pleased the Lord to inform Peter of the abolishing of the difference between Jew and Gentile in any holy or unholy, clean or unclean respect. . . .

Lastly, all this whole nation or people, as they were of one typical seed of Abraham and sealed with a shameful and painful ordinance of cutting off the foreskin (which differenced them from all the world beside), so also were they bound to such and such solemnities of figurative worships. Amongst many others I shall end this passage concerning the people with a famous observation out of Numbers 9:13, [that] that whole nation was bound to celebrate and keep the feast of the Passover in his season, or else they were to be put to death. But does God require a whole nation, country or kingdom now thus to celebrate the spiritual Passover, the supper and feast of the Lamb Christ Jesus, at such a time once a year, and that whosoever shall not so do shall be put to death? What horrible profanations, what gross hypocrisies, yea what wonderful desolations (sooner or later) must follow upon such a course?

Tis true, the people of Israel, brought into covenant with God in Abraham and so successively born in covenant with God, might (in that state of a national church) solemnly covenant and swear that whosoever would not seek Jehovah the God of Israel should be put to death (2 Chron. 15), whether small or great, whether man or woman. But may whole nations or kingdoms now . . . follow that pattern of Israel and put to death all, both men and women, great and small, that according to the rules of the Gospel are not born again, penitent, humble, heavenly, and patient? What a world of hypocrisy from hence is practiced by thousands, that for fear will stoop to give that God their bodies in form, whom yet in truth their hearts affect not? Yea also what a world of profanation of the holy name and holy ordinances of the Lord in prostituting the holy things of God . . . to profane, impenitent, and unregenerate persons? Lastly, what slaughters both of men and women must this necessarily bring into the world, by the insurrections and civil wars about religion and conscience? Yea what slaughters of the innocent and faithful witnesses of Christ Jesus, who choose to be slain all the day long for Christ's sake and to fight for their Lord and Master Christ, only with spiritual and Christian weapons?

Peace. It seems, dear Truth, a mighty gulf between that people and nation, and the nations of the world then extant and ever since.

Truth. As sure as the blessed substance to all those shadows, Christ Jesus, is come, so unmatchable and never to be paralleled by any national state was that Israel in the figure or shadow. And yet the Israel of God now, the regenerate or newborn, the circumcised in heart by repentance and mortification who willingly submit to the Lord Jesus as their only King and Head, may fitly parallel and answer that Israel in the type without such danger of hypocrisy, of such horrible profanations, and of firing the civil state in such bloody combustions, as all ages have brought forth upon this compelling a whole nation or kingdom to be the antitype of Israel.

Peace. Were this light entertained, some hope would shine forth for my return and restoration.

Truth. I have yet to add a third consideration concerning the kings and governors of that land and people. They[53] were to be (unless in their captivities) of their brethren, members of the true church of God, as appears in the history of Moses, the elders of Israel, and the judges and kings of Israel afterward. But first, who can deny but that there may be now many lawful governors, magistrates, and kings in the nations of the world, where is no true church of Jesus Christ? Second, we know the many excellent gifts wherewith it has pleased God to furnish many, enabling them for public service to their countries both in peace and war (as all ages and experience testify), on whose souls he has not yet pleased to shine in the face of Jesus Christ. Which gifts and talents must all lie buried in the earth, unless such persons may lawfully be called and chosen to and improved in public service, notwithstanding their different or contrary conscience and worship.

Third, if none but true Christians, members of Christ Jesus, might be civil

53. That is, the rulers of Israel.

magistrates, and publicly entrusted with civil affairs, then none but members of churches (i.e., Christians) should be husbands of wives, fathers of children, masters of servants. But against this doctrine the whole creation, the whole world may justly rise up in arms, as not only contrary to true piety, but common humanity itself. For if a commonwealth be lawful among men that have not heard of God nor Christ, certainly their officers, ministers, and governors must be lawful also.

Fourth, it is notoriously known to be the dangerous doctrine professed by some Papists, that princes degenerating from their religion and turning heretics are to be deposed, and their subjects actually discharged from their obedience.[54] Which doctrine all such must necessarily hold (however most loath to own it) that hold the magistrate guardian of both Tables. . . . Being thus governor and head of the church, the magistrate must necessarily be a part of it himself, which when by heresy he falls from head of the church (though it may be by truth, miscalled heresy) he falls from his calling of magistracy, and is utterly disabled from his (pretended) guardianship and government of the church.

Lastly, we may remember the practice of the Lord Jesus and his followers, commanding and practicing obedience to the higher powers, though we find not one civil magistrate a Christian in all the first churches. . . .

Peace. The liberty of the subject sounds most sweet; London and Oxford both profess to fight for it. How much infinitely more sweet is that true soul liberty according to Christ Jesus?

I know you would not take from Caesar ought,[55] although it were to give to God, and what is God's and his people's I wish that Caesar may not take. Yet for the satisfaction of some, be pleased to glance upon Josiah's famous acts in the church of God concerning the worship of God, the priests, Levites, and their services, compelling the people to keep the Passover, making

54. During the reigns of both Elizabeth and James I, Roman popes had excommunicated the English monarchs and declared that in the eyes of Catholic faith it would not be a sin to assassinate heretical (that is, Protestant) English rulers. The most notorious example of Catholics accepting the pope's invitation was the Gunpowder Plot of 1605, when English Catholic terrorists attempted to assassinate King James and most of the nation's leaders by blowing up Westminster Palace during the opening session of Parliament. The failure of the plot is the inspiration for the celebration of Guy Fawkes Night.

55. That is, "what belongs to Caesar." This is, of course, a reference to Jesus' saying, "Render therefore unto Caesar the things which are Caesar's; and unto God the things that are God's" (Matthew 22:21).

himself a covenant before the Lord, and compelling all that were found in Jerusalem and Benjamin to stand to it.[56]

Truth. To these famous practices of Josiah I shall parallel the practices of England's kings: first *de jure*, a word or two of their right, then *de facto*, discuss what has been done. First, *de jure*: Josiah was a precious branch of that royal root King David, who was immediately designed by God. And when the golden links of the royal chain broke in the usurpations of the Roman conqueror, it pleased the most wise God to send a Son of David, a Son of God, to begin again that royal line, to sit upon the throne of his father David (Luke 1:32; Acts 2:30). It is not so with the Gentile princes, rulers, and magistrates (whether monarchical, aristocratic, or democratic) who (though government in general be from God) receive their callings, power, and authority (both kings and parliaments) mediately from the people.

Second, Josiah and those kings were kings and governors over the then true and only church of God national, brought into the covenant of God in Abraham. . . . But what commission from Christ Jesus had Henry VIII, Edward VI, or any Josiah-like [leader] to force the many hundred thousands of English men and women, without such immediate signs and miracles that Israel had to enter into an holy and spiritual covenant with the invisible God, the Father of Spirits, or upon pain of death (as in Josiah's time) to stand to that which they never made, nor before evangelical repentance are possibly capable of.

Now second *de facto*, let it be well remembered concerning the kings of England professing Reformation. The foundation of all was laid in Henry VIII. The pope challenged to be the Vicar of Christ Jesus here upon earth, to have power of reforming the church and redressing abuses. Henry VIII falls out with the pope and challenged that very power to himself of which he had despoiled the pope, as appears by that act of Parliament establishing Henry VIII the supreme head and governor in all cases ecclesiastical.[57] It

56. King Josiah ruled Judah in the late seventh century B.C.E. During his reign he led a return to Deuteronomic law, endeavoring to rid Judah of the pagan cults that had infiltrated the religious life of Judah over years of corrupt leadership and occupation (see 2 Kings 22–23; 2 Chronicles 34–36). As a political authority instituting religious reform, Josiah provided another biblical template for Puritans who were inclined to believe that God still ordained magistrates as the protectors of good religion.

57. This is a reference to the Act of Supremacy of 1534, by which Henry VIII severed his nation's ties with the church in Rome and established himself as the "Supreme Head" of the church of England.

pleased the Most High God to plague the pope by Henry VIII his means, but neither pope nor king can ever prove such power from Christ derived in either of them.

Second, (as before intimated) let us view the works and acts of England's imitation of Josiah's practice. Henry VII leaves England under the slavish bondage of the pope's yoke. Henry VIII reforms all England to a new fashion, half-Papist, half-Protestant. King Edward the VI turns about the wheel of the state and works the whole land to absolute Protestantism. Queen Mary succeeding to the helm steers a direct contrary course, breaks in pieces all that Edward wrought, and brings forth an old edition of England's reformation all popish. Mary not living out half her days (as the prophet speaks of bloody persons), Elizabeth (like Josiah) advanced from the prison to the palace, and from the irons to the crown; she plucks up all her sister Mary's plants and founds a trumpet all Protestant. What sober man stands not amazed at these revolutions? And yet like mother like daughter: how zealous are we their off-spring for another impression and better edition of a national Canaan (in imitation of Judah and Josiah), which if attained, who knows how soon succeeding kings or parliaments will quite pull down and abrogate?

Thirdly, in all these formings and reformings a national church of natural, unregenerate men was . . . the subject matter of all these forms and changes, whether popish or Protestant. Concerning [a] national state [church], the time is yet to come whenever the Lord Jesus has given a word of institution and appointment. . . .

Peace. Dear Truth, you have shown me a little draught of Zion's sorrows, her children tearing out their mother's bowels: Oh, when will he that establishes, comforts, and builds up Zion look down from heaven and have mercy on her?

Truth. The vision yet does tarry (says Habakkuk) but will most surely come, and therefore the patient and believing must wait for it.[58] But to your last proposition, whether the kings of Israel and Judah were not types of civil magistrates, now I suppose by what has been already spoken these things will be evident: First, that those former types of the land, of the peo-

---

58. "And the LORD answered me, and said, Write the vision, and make it plain upon tables, that he may run that readeth it. For the vision is yet for an appointed time, but at the end it shall speak, and not lie: though it tarry, wait for it; because it will surely come, it will not tarry" (Habakkuk 2:2–3).

ple, of their worships, were types and figures of a spiritual land, spiritual people, and spiritual worship under Christ. Therefore consequently, their saviors, redeemers, deliverers, judges, and kings must also have their spiritual antitypes, and so consequently not civil but spiritual governors and rulers, lest the very essential nature of types, figures, and shadows be overthrown.

Second, although the magistrate by a civil sword might well compel that national church to the external exercise of their natural worship, yet it is not possible (according to the rule of the New Testament) to compel whole nations to true repentance and regeneration, without which (so far as may be discerned true) the worship and holy name of God is profaned and blasphemed. An arm of flesh and sword of steel cannot reach to cut the darkness of the mind, the hardness and unbelief of the heart, and kindly operate upon the soul's affections to forsake a long continued father's worship and to embrace a new, though the best and truest. This work performs alone that sword out of the mouth of Christ . . . (Rev. 1, 3).

Third, we have not one tittle in the New Testament of Christ Jesus concerning such a parallel, neither from himself nor from his ministers with whom he conversed forty days after his resurrection, instructing them in the matters of his kingdom (Acts 1). Neither find we any such commission or direction given to the civil magistrate to this purpose, nor to the saints for their submission in matters spiritual, but the contrary (Acts 4, 5; 1 Cor. 7:23; Col. 2:18).

Fourth, we have formerly viewed the very nature and essence of a civil magistrate, and find it the same in all parts of the world, wherever people live upon the face of the earth, agreeing together in towns, cities, provinces, and kingdoms. I say [it is] the same, essentially civil, both from (1.) the rise and fountain whence it springs, that is, the people's choice and free consent; and (2.) The object of it, that is, the commonwealth or safety of such a people in their bodies and goods, as the authors of this model have themselves confessed. This civil nature of the magistrate we have proved to receive no addition of power from the magistrates being a Christian, no more than it receives diminution from his not being a Christian, even as the commonwealth is a true commonwealth although it has not heard of Christianity. Christianity professed in it . . . makes it no more a commonwealth, and Christianity taken away . . . makes it nevertheless a commonwealth.

Fifth, the Spirit of God expressly relates the work of the civil magistrate under the Gospel (Rom. 13), expressly mentioning as the magistrate's object the duties of the Second Table concerning the bodies and goods of the subject. The reward or wages which people owe for such a work—tribute, toll, or custom—are wages payable by all sorts of men, natives and foreigners, who enjoy the same benefit of public peace and commerce in the nation.

Sixth, since the civil magistrate—whether kings or parliaments, states or governors—can receive no more in justice then what the people give, and are therefore but the eyes and hands and instruments of the people (simply considered, without respect to this or that religion), it must inevitably follow (as formerly I have touched) that if [we grant that magistrates have authority over the church and] magistrates have received their power from the people, then the greatest number of the people of every land have received from Christ Jesus a power to establish, correct, and reform his saints and servants, his wife and spouse, the church. And she that by the express word of the Lord (Ps. 149) binds kings in chains and nobles in links of iron must herself be subject to the changeable pleasures of the people of the world, . . . even in matters of heavenly and spiritual nature. Hence therefore in all controversies concerning the church, ministry and worship, the last appeal must come to the bar of the people or commonwealth, where all may personally meet as in some commonwealths of small number, or in greater by their representatives. Hence then no person [could be] esteemed a believer and added to the church, no officer [could be] chosen and ordained, no person [could be] cast forth and excommunicated, but as the commonwealth and people please. In conclusion, there exists no church of Christ in this land or world, and consequently no visibly Christ the Head of it, yea yet higher, consequently no God in the world worshipped according to the institutions of Christ Jesus, except the several peoples of the nations of the world shall give allowance. . . .

I may therefore here seasonably add a seventh, which is a necessary consequence of all the former arguments, and an argument itself: we find expressly a spiritual power of Christ Jesus in the hands of his saints, ministers, and churches to be the true antitype of those former figures in all the prophecies concerning Christ in his spiritual power. . . .

The Civil Magistrate's Responsibility to Religion

Truth. The civil magistrate either respects that religion and worship which his conscience is persuaded is true and upon which he ventures his soul, or else that and those which he is persuaded are false. Concerning the first, if that which the magistrate believes to be true be true, I say he owes a three-fold duty to it: First, approbation and countenance, a reverent esteem and honorable testimony (according to Isa. 49, Rev. 21), with a tender respect of truth and the professors of it. Second, personal submission of his own soul to the power of the Lord Jesus in that spiritual government and kingdom (according to Matt. 18, 1 Cor. 5). Third, protection of such true professors of Christ, whether apart or met together, as also of their estates, from violence and injury (according to Rom. 13).

Now secondly, if it be a false religion (to which the civil magistrate dare not adjoin), yet he owes first permission (for approbation he owes not to what is evil), and this according to Matthew 13:30 for public peace and quiet sake.[59] Second, he owes protection to the persons of his subjects (though of a false worship), that no injury be offered either to the persons or goods of any (Rom. 13).

Even Christian Magistrates Have No Special Jurisdiction over the Church

Peace. Dear Truth, in this eleventh head concerning the magistrate's power in worship, you have examined what is affirmed that the magistrate may do in points of worship. There remains a second [point to consider]: that which they say the magistrate may *not* do in worship. . . .

[*Truth.*] If in a ship at sea, wherein the governor or pilot of a ship undertakes to carry the ship to such a port, the civil magistrate (suppose a king or emperor) shall command the master such and such a course, to steer upon such or such a point, which the master knows is not their course, and which if they steer he shall never bring the ship to that port or harbor, what shall the master do? Surely all men will say the master of the ship (or pilot) is to present reasons and arguments from his mariners art (if the prince be capable of them), or else in humble and submissive manner to persuade the prince not to interrupt them in their course and duty properly belonging to them, that is, governing of the ship, steering of the course. If the master of

59. "Let both grow together until the harvest: and in the time of harvest I will say to the reapers, Gather ye together first the tares, and bind them in bundles to burn them: but gather the wheat into my barn" (Matthew 13:30).

the ship command the mariners thus and thus in cunning[60] the ship, managing the helm, trimming the sail, and the prince command the mariners a different or contrary course, who is to be obeyed? It is confessed that the mariners may lawfully disobey the prince and obey the governor of the ship in the actions of the ship.

What if the prince has as much skill (which is rare) as the pilot himself? I conceive it will be answered, that the master of the ship and pilot, in what concerns the ship, are chief and above (in respect of their office) the prince himself, and their commands ought to be attended by all the mariners, unless it be in manifest error, wherein it is granted any passenger may reprove the pilot. I ask if the prince and his attendants be unskillful in the ship's affairs, whether every sailor and mariner, the youngest and lowest, be not (so far as concerns the ship) to be preferred before the prince's followers, and the prince himself? And their council and advice more to be attended to, and their service more to be desired and respected, and the prince to be requested to stand by and let the businesses alone in their hands? In case a willful king and his attendants, out of opinion of their skill or willfulness of passion, would so steer the course or trim sail as that in the judgment of the master and seamen the ship and lives shall be endangered, [I ask] whether (in case humble persuasions prevail not) ought not the ship's company to refuse to act in such a course, . . . resisting and suppressing these dangerous practices of the prince and his followers, [so to] save the ship?

Last, suppose the master, out of base fear and cowardice or covetous desire of reward, shall yield to gratify the mind of the prince, contrary to the rules of art and experience, and the ship come in danger and perish, and the prince with it. If the master gets to shore, may he not be justly questioned, yea and suffer as guilty of the prince's death and those that perished with him? These cases are clear, wherein according to this similitude the prince ought not to govern and rule the actions of the ship, but such whose office and charge and skill it is.

The result of all is this: the church of Christ is the ship, wherein the prince (if a member, for otherwise the case is altered) is a passenger. In this ship the officers and governors, such as are appointed by the Lord Jesus, they are the chief, and (in those respects) above the prince himself, and are to be obeyed

---

60. According to the *Oxford English Dictionary,* "cunning" in the sense Williams uses it here meant "to direct the steering of (a ship) from some commanding position on shipboard."

and submitted to in their works and administrations, even before the prince himself. In this respect every Christian in the church, man or woman (if of more knowledge and grace of Christ) ought to be of higher esteem concerning religion and Christianity then all the princes in the world who have either none or less grace or knowledge of Christ—although in civil things all civil reverence, honor, and obedience ought to be yielded by all men. Therefore, if in matters of religion the king commands what is contrary to Christ's rule (though according to his persuasion and conscience), who sees not that (according to the similitude) he ought not to be obeyed? Yea . . . boldly with spiritual force and power he ought to be resisted. And if any officer of the church of Christ shall out of baseness yield to the command of the prince, to the danger of the church and souls committed to his charge, the souls that perish (notwithstanding the prince's command) shall be laid to his charge. . . .

Williams proceeds to respond to the twelfth and thirteenth heads of the Model, which deal respectively with the magistrate's power to censure religious deviants and call church assemblies. Williams reacts to the authors' willingness to grant limited license to civil authority on these fronts with a reprise of his previous arguments.

Truth. But to wind up all, as it is most true that magistracy in general is of God (Rom. 13) for the preservation of mankind in civil order and peace (the world otherwise would be like the sea, wherein men like fishes would hunt and devour each other, and the greater devour the less), so also it is true that magistracy in special . . . is of man (1 Pet. 2:13).[61] Now whatever kind of magistrate the people shall agree to set up, whether he receive Christianity before he be set in office or whether he receive Christianity after, he receives no more power of magistracy than a magistrate that has received no Christian-

---

61. In other words, Williams asserts that particular forms of civil government derive from popular consent, a conviction he shared with most of his Puritan colleagues. Timothy Breen has pointed out, however, that despite this general agreement on popular consent, the Puritans understood the nature of popularly conferred power in different ways. Some Puritans argued that civil leaders, once chosen by their subjects, enjoyed broad discretionary powers as the direct vicegerents of God. Others insisted that popular consent determined not only the choice of political leader but also the specific parameters of his political authority. For more on popular consent in Puritan political philosophy, see Timothy H. Breen, *The Character of the Good Ruler: A Study of Puritan Political Ideas in New England, 1630–1730* (New Haven: Yale University Press, 1970), 59–64.

ity. For neither of them can receive more than the commonwealth, the body of people and civil state, as men communicate to them and entrust with them. All lawful magistrates in the world, both before the coming of Christ Jesus and since, (excepting those unparalleled typical magistrates of the church of Israel) are but derivatives and agents immediately derived and employed as eyes and hands serving for the good of the whole. Hence they have and can have no more power than fundamentally lies in the bodies or fountains themselves, which power, might, or authority is not religious . . . but natural, human, and civil.

And hence it is true that a Christian captain, Christian merchant, physician, lawyer, pilot, father, master, and (so consequently) magistrate, is no more a captain, merchant, physician, lawyer, pilot, father, master, or magistrate than a captain, merchant, or so on of any other conscience or religion. It is true, though, Christianity teaches all these to act in their several callings to a higher ultimate end, from higher principles, in a more heavenly and spiritual manner.

Peace. O that your light and brightness, dear Truth, might shine to the dark world in this particular [point], let it not therefore be grievous if I request a little further illustration of it.

Truth. In his season God will glorify himself in all his truths, but to gratify your desire, [I answer] thus: a pagan or Antichristian pilot may be as skillful to carry the ship to its desired port as any Christian mariner or pilot in the world, and may perform that work with as much safety and speed. Yet they have not command over the souls and consciences of their passengers or mariners under them, although they may justly see to the labor of the one and the civil behavior of all in the ship. A Christian pilot performs the same work . . . from a principle of knowledge and experience, but more than this, he acts from a root of the fear of God and lives to mankind in his whole course. Second, his aim is more to glorify God than to gain his pay or make his voyage. Third, he walks heavenly with men and with God, in a constant observation of God's hand in storms and calms. . . . Lastly, the Christian pilot's power over the souls and consciences of his sailors and passengers is not greater than that of the Antichristian, otherwise than[62] he can subdue the souls of any by the two-edged sword of the Spirit, the Word of God, and by his holy demeanor in his place. . . .

62. Beyond that.

Christ Honored When the "Two Swords" Govern within Their Own Spheres

Peace. The truth is, Christ Jesus is honored when the civil magistrate, a member of the church, punishes any member or elder of the church with the civil sword, even to the death, for any crime against the civil state so deserving it; for he bears not the sword in vain. And Christ Jesus is again most highly honored when for apparent sin in the magistrate, being a member of the church (for otherwise they have not to meddle with him), the elders with the church admonish him and recover his soul, or if obstinate in sin, cast him forth of their spiritual and Christian fellowship, which doubtless they could not do were the magistrate supreme governor under Christ in ecclesiastical or church causes, and so consequently the true heir and successor of the apostles. . . .

Should Privileges and Offices of Civil Society Be Limited to Church Members?

Truth. . . . Whereas that case is put, which is nowhere found in the pattern of the first churches nor suiting with the rule of Christianity, that the commonwealth should consist [only] of church members, . . . [that is,] that none should be admitted members of the commonwealth but such as are first members of the church, . . . I say let such practices be brought to the touchstone of the true frame of a civil commonwealth and the true frame of the spiritual or Christian commonwealth, the church of Christ, and it will be seen what wood, hay, and stubble of carnal polity and human inventions in Christ's matters are put in place of the precious stones, gold and silver, of the ordinances of the most high and only wise God. . . .

Concerning the choice of magistrates, that such ought to be chosen as are church members . . . , I answer: it were to be wished that since the point is so weighty, as concerning the pilots and steersmen of kingdoms and nations on whose ability, care, and faithfulness depends most commonly the peace and safety of the commonwealths they fail in—I say it were to be wished that they had more fully explained what they intend by this affirmative, [that] magistrates ought to be chosen out of church members. For if they intend by this a necessity of convenience, that for the greater advancement of common utility and rejoicing of the people . . . it were to be desired, prayed for, and peaceably endeavored, then I readily assent to them. But if by this "ought" they intend such a necessity as those Scriptures quoted imply, that people shall sin by choosing such for magistrates as are not members of churches, . . . then I propose these necessary queries:

First whether those are not lawful civil combinations, societies, and communions of men in towns, cities, states, or kingdoms where no church of Christ is resident, yea where his name was never heard of? I add to this that men of no small note, skillful in the state of the world, acknowledge that if the world were divided into thirty parts, twenty-five of that thirty have never yet heard of the name of Christ. If their civil polities and combinations be not lawful (because they are not churches, and their magistrates church members) then disorder, confusion, and all unrighteousness is lawful and pleasing to God.

Second, whether in such states or commonwealths where a church or churches of Christ *are* resident, such persons may not lawfully succeed to the crown or government in whom the fear of God . . . cannot be discerned, nor are brothers of the church, . . . but only are fitted with civil and moral abilities to manage the civil affairs of the civil state?

Third, since not many wise and noble are called, but the poor receive the Gospel, as God has chosen the poor of the world to be rich in faith (1 Cor. 1, James 2), I ask whether it may not ordinarily come to pass that there may not be found in a true church of Christ (which sometimes consists but of few persons) persons fit to be either kings or governors, whose civil office is no less difficult than the office of a doctor or physic, a master or pilot of a ship, or a captain or commander of a band or army of men— for which services the children of God may be no ways qualified, though otherwise excellent for the fear of God and the knowledge and grace of the Lord Jesus?

Fourth, if magistrates ought (that is, ought *only*) to be chosen out of the church, I demand if they ought not also to be dethroned and deposed when they cease to be of the church, either by voluntary departure from it or by excommunication out of it, according to the bloody tenets and practice of some Papists, with whom the Protestants (according to their principles), although they seem to abhor it, do absolutely agree?

Therefore lastly, I ask if this be not to turn the world upside down, to turn the world out of the world, to pluck up the roots and foundations of all common society in the world, to turn the garden and paradise of the church and saints into the field of the civil state of the world, and to reduce the world to the first chaos or confusion? . . .

Conclusion

Peace. We have now, dear Truth, through the gracious hand of God clambered up to the top of this our tedious discourse.

Truth. O 'tis mercy inexpressible that either you or I have had so long a breathing time, and that together!

Peace. If English ground must yet be drunk with English blood, oh, where shall Peace repose her wearied head and heavy heart?

Truth. Dear Peace, if you find welcome, and the God of peace miraculously please to quench these all-devouring flames, yet where shall Truth find rest from cruel persecutions?

Peace. Oh, will not the authority of holy Scriptures, the commands and declarations of the Son of God therein produced by you, together with all the lamentable experiences of former and present slaughters, prevail with the sons of men (especially with the sons of Peace) to depart from the dens of lions and mountains of leopards,[63] and to put on the bowels (if not of Christianity, yet) of humanity each to other!

Truth. Dear Peace, Habakkuk's fishes[64] keep their constant bloody game of persecutions in the world's mighty ocean, the greater taking, plundering, swallowing up the lesser. O happy [is] he whose portion is the God of Jacob! He who had nothing to lose under the sun, but has a state, a house, an inheritance, a name, a crown, a life past all the plunderers', ravishers', murderers' reach and fury!

Peace. But lo! Who's here?

Truth. Our sister Patience, whose desired company is as needful as delightful! 'Tis like the wolf will send the scattered sheep in one; the common pirate gathers up the loose and scattered navy; the slaughter of the witnesses by that bloody Beast unites the Independents and Presbyterians. The God of Peace, the God of Truth will shortly seal this Truth, and confirm this Witness, and make it evident to the whole world—that the doctrine of Persecution for cause of Conscience is most evidently and lamentably contrary to the doctrine of Christ Jesus the Prince of Peace. Amen.

---

63. "Come with me from Lebanon, my spouse, with me from Lebanon: look from the top of Amana, from the top of Shenir and Hermon, from the lions' dens, from the mountains of the leopards" (Song of Solomon 4:8).

64. "Thou art of purer eyes than to behold evil, and canst not look on iniquity: wherefore lookest thou upon them that deal treacherously, and holdest thy tongue when the wicked devoureth the man that is more righteous than he? and makest men as the fishes of the sea, as the creeping things, that have no ruler over them?" (Habakkuk 1:13, 14).

CHAPTER FOUR

Christenings Make Not Christians

or, A Brief Discourse concerning that name *Heathen,*
commonly given to the Indians.
As also concerning that great point of their Conversion.

The brief treatise "Christenings Make Not Christians" was published in London in early 1645, as Williams was returning to Providence from his first diplomatic mission to secure a parliamentary charter for the colony. In it Williams objects to the Europeans' reference to the Native Americans as "heathens" and their extensive efforts to "civilize" them by converting them to Christianity. While he hints at the moral respect he held for the Native Americans (a respect that receives more extensive treatment in A Key into the Language of America*), the primary reason for his objections lies in his assessment of European Christianity, or "Christendom." He argues that most of Christendom—Protestant and Catholic—exhibits no more faithfulness to the true message and institutions of Christ than the Native Americans do, and thus remains every bit as "heathen" as the natives themselves. To introduce the Americans into such a perverted church institution, then, would succeed only in converting them from one damnable religion to another. Instead, he muses at the end of the treatise, perhaps their conversion should wait until the restoration of the true church at the return of Christ. Thus, in this short work we see at once the interplay of key ingredients to Williams's theological justification of religious freedom: his strict separatist ecclesiology, his millennial eschatology, his rejection of coercion as a tool for molding religion and conscience, and his positive regard for the moral capacity of human beings, even (or especially) those who exist outside the influence of "Christendom."*

The Term "Heathen" Applies Not Just to the Americans, but to All outside True Christianity

I shall first be humbly bold to inquire into the name "heathen," which the English give them and the Dutch approve and practice in their name *heydenen,* signifying "heathen" or "nations." How oft have I heard both the English and Dutch (not only the civil, but the most debauched and profane) say, "These heathen dogs, better [to] kill a thousand of them than that we Christians should be endangered or troubled with them. They have spilt our Christian blood; the best way [is] to make riddance of them, cut them all off, and so make way for Christians."

I shall therefore humbly entreat my countrymen of all sorts to consider that, although men have used . . . this word "heathen" to the Indians that go naked and have not heard of that One-God, yet this word "heathen" is most improperly, sinfully, and unchristianly so used in this sense. The word "heathen" signifies no more than "nations" or "gentiles"; so do our translations from the Hebrew . . . and the Greek . . . , in the Old and New Testament, promiscuously render these words "gentiles," "nations," [or] "heathens." Why "nations"? Because the Jews, being the only People and Nation of God, esteemed (and that rightly) all other people—not only those that went naked, but the famous Babylonians, Chaldeans, Medes, Persians, Greeks, and Romans, their stately cities and citizens—inferior themselves and not partakers of their glorious privileges, but ethnic, gentiles, heathen, or the nations of the world.

Now then, we must inquire who are the People of God, his holy nation, since the coming of the Lord Jesus and the rejection of his first typical holy nation, the Jews.[1] It is confessed by all, that the Christians, the followers of Jesus, are now the only People of God, his holy nation . . . (1 Pet. 2:9). Who are then the nations, heathen, or gentiles, in opposition to this People of God? I answer, all people, civilized as well as uncivilized, even the most famous states, cities, and kingdoms of the world. . . .

---

1. By "rejection," Williams is likely referring to the Jews' rejection of Christ as Messiah, not God's rejection of the Jews. The latter reading would be inconsistent with the Puritans' conviction that the Jews were still the chosen people of God. For a discussion of Williams's typological reading of the Hebrew Bible, see the introduction to this volume.

"Christendom" Is as Heathen as the Americans

Yea, this will by many hands be yielded, but . . . since . . . the world [is] turned Christian and the little flock of Jesus Christ has marvelously increased in such wonderful conversions, let me be bold to ask: What is Christ? What are the Christians? The Hebrew . . . and the Greek . . . will tell us that Christ was and [is] the Anointed of God, whom the prophets and kings and priests of Israel in their anointing did prefigure and type out; whence his followers are called . . . "Christians," that is, "anointed" also. So that indeed to be a Christian implies two things: first, to be a follower of that Anointed One in all his offices, [and] secondly, to partake of his anointing. . . .

To come nearer to this "Christian world"—where the world becomes Christian, holy, anointed, God's People—what says John? What says the Angel? Yea, what says Jesus Christ and his Father, from whom the Revelation came?[2] What say they to the Beast and his worshippers (Rev. 13)? If that Beast be not the Turk nor the Roman Emperor (as the grossest interpret), but either the general councils or the Catholic Church of Rome or the popes or papacy (as the most refined interpret), why then all the world . . . wonders after the Beast, worships the Beast, follows the Beast, and boasts of the Beast. There is none like him, and all people, tongues, and nations come under the power of this Beast, and no man shall buy or sell, nor live, who has not the make of the Beast in his forehead, or in his hand, or the number of his name.[3]

If this world or earth,[4] then, be not intended of the whole terrestrial globe (Europe, Asia, Africa, and America), which sense and experience denies, but of the *Roman* . . . world and the people, languages, and nations of the Roman monarchy, transferred from the Roman emperor to the Roman popes and the popish kingdoms, . . . then we know by this time what the Lord Jesus would say of the Christian world and of the Christian. Indeed

---

2. Williams is invoking the biblical Book of Revelation here, which tradition says was given to the Apostle John.

3. In other words, Williams is arguing that if Christendom is identified as that vast part of the world under the influence of Catholicism, but at the same time the Catholic Church is understood to be the Beast prophesied in Revelation (an attribution many seventeenth-century Protestants would share with Williams), then it follows that Christendom is as heathen as any non-Christian part of the world.

4. That is, Christendom.

what he says [in] Revelation 14: if any man worship the Beast or his picture, he shall drink even the dread fullest cup that the whole Book of God ever held forth to sinners.

Protestants Remain Extensions of Popish, Heathen Christendom

Grant this, say some of popish countries, that notwithstanding they make up Christendom, or [the] Christian world, yet submitting to that Beast, they are the earth or world and must drink of that most dreadful cup. But now for those nations that have withdrawn their necks from that beastly yoke, and protesting against him are not papists but Protestants, shall . . . they or any of them . . . also be called (in true Scripture sense) heathens, that is nations or gentiles in opposition to the People of God, which is the only holy nation? I answer, that all nations now called Protestants were at first part of that whole . . . Antichristian continent that wondered after [and] worshipped the Beast. This must then with holy fear and trembling (because it concerns the Kingdom of God, and salvation) be attended to, whether such a departure from the Beast and coming out from Antichristian abominations—from his marks in a false conversion and a false constitution, or framing of national churches in false ministries, and ministrations of Baptism, Supper of the Lord, admonitions, and excommunications—amounts to a true perfect hand, cut off from that earth which wondered after and worshipped the Beast, or whether, not being so cut off, they remain not *peninsula,* or necks of land, contiguous and joined still to his Christendom. If now the bodies of Protestant nations remain in an unrepentant, unregenerate, natural estate, and so consequently far from hearing the admonitions of the Lord Jesus (Matt. 18), I say they must sadly consider and know (lest their profession of the name of Jesus prove at last but an aggravation of condemnation) that Christ Jesus has said [that] they are but as heathens and publicans (v. 17). How might I therefore humbly beseech my countrymen to consider what deep cause they have to search their conversions from that Beast . . . ? And whether having no more of Christ than the name (beside the invented ways of worship, derived from or drawn after Rome's pattern), their hearts and conversations will not evince them unconverted and *unchristian Christians,* and not yet knowing what it is to come by true regeneration within, to the true spiritual Jew from without amongst the nations, that is heathens. . . .

The Error of Attempts at Mass Conversions among the Americans

Now secondly, for the hopes of conversion and turning the people of America to God: there is no respect of persons with [God], for we are all the work of his hands. From the rising of the sun to the going down thereof, his name shall be great among the nations, from the east and from the west. If we respect their sins, they are far short of European sinners; they neither abuse such corporal mercies[5] (for they have them not), nor sin they against the Gospel light (which shines not amongst them), as the men of Europe do. And yet if they were greater sinners than they are, or greater sinners then the Europeans, they are not the further from the great ocean of mercy in that respect. Lastly, they are intelligent, many very ingenious, plain-hearted, inquisitive, and (as I said before) prepared with many convictions.

Now secondly, for the Catholics' conversion [of the Americans]: although I believe I may safely hope that God has his in Rome [and] in Spain, yet if Antichrist be their false head (as most true it is), [then] the body, faith, baptism, [and] hope (opposite to the true, Ephesians 4) are all false also. Yea, consequently their preaching, conversions, [and] salvations (leaving secret things to God) must all be of the same false nature likewise. If the reports (yea some of their own historians) be true, what monstrous and most inhumane conversions have they made, baptizing thousands, yea ten thousands of the poor natives, sometimes by wiles and subtle devices, sometimes by force compelling them to submit to that which they understood not, neither before nor after their monstrous christening of them.

Thirdly, for our New England parts I can speak uprightly and confidently: I know it to have been easy for myself long [before] this to have brought many thousands of these natives, yea the whole country, to a far greater Antichristian conversion than ever was yet heard of in America. I have re-

---

5. By this phrase, Williams appears to refer to something more particular than simply bodily aid, for his parenthetical aside excuses the Americans from practicing them "for they have them not." Since implying that the Americans engaged in no mutual care would seem to contradict both historical knowledge of Native American communal practices and Williams's own testimony in the *Key to the Native Americans'* support of one another's physical needs, he must have something else in mind. The *Oxford English Dictionary* traces the phrase "corporal works of mercy" to a sixteenth-century *Manuall of Prayers* and suggests that the term referred to a specific list of mutual obligations, including "To feed the hungry. To giue drinke to the thirsty. To cloathe the naked. To visitt and ransome the Captiues. To harbour the harbourlesse. To visitt the sicke. To burie the dead." Williams's point here, then, may be that the Americans' sins "fall short of European sinners" because they lack this specific tradition of religious obligation that European Christians know but violate so routinely.

ported something in the chapter of their religion,[6] how readily I could have brought the whole country to have observed one day in seven, . . . to have received a baptism (or washing) though it were in rivers (as the first Christians and the Lord Jesus himself did), . . . to have come to a stated church meeting, maintained priests and forms of prayer, and a whole form of Antichristian worship in life and death. Let none wonder at this, for [both] plausible persuasions in the mouths of those whom natural men esteem and love [and] the power of prevailing forces and armies have done this in all the nations . . . of "Christendom."

Yet what lamentable experience have we of the turnings and turnings of the body of this land in point of religion in few years? When England was all popish under Henry VII, how easy is conversion wrought to half papist, half-Protestant under Henry VIII? From half-Protestantism, half-popery under Henry VIII to absolute Protestantism under Edward VI; from absolute Protestantism under Edward VI to absolute popery under Queen Mary; and from absolute popery under Mary to absolute Protestantism under Queen Elizabeth—just like the weathercock, with the breath of every prince.

For all this, yet some may ask, why has there been such a price in my hand not improved?[7] Why have I not brought them to such a conversion as I speak of? I answer, woe be to me if I call light darkness, or darkness light; sweet bitter, or bitter sweet. Woe be to me if I call that conversion to God which is indeed subversion of the souls of millions in Christendom, from one false worship to another, and the profanation of the holy name of God, his holy Son, and blessed ordinances. America (as Europe and all nations) lies dead in sin and trespasses. It is not a suit of crimson satin [that] will make a dead man live; take off and change his crimson into white [and] he is dead still. Off with that and shift him into cloth of gold, and from that cloth of diamonds, he is but a dead man still. For it is not a form, nor the change of one form into another—a finer, and a finer, and yet more fine— that makes a man a convert, I mean, such a conversion as is acceptable to God in Jesus Christ, according to the visible Rule of his last will and testament. I speak not of hypocrites, . . . but of a true external conversion. I say

6. A reference to Chapter 21 of *A Key into the Language of America*, Williams's anthropological and linguistic study of the customs of the Narragansett Indians.

7. The indirect reference here is to the parable of the unprofitable servant, Matthew 25:14–30.

then, woe be to me if, intending to catch men (as the Lord Jesus said to Peter),[8] I should pretend conversion and the bringing of men as mystical fish into a church-estate, that is a converted estate, and so build them up with ordinances as a converted Christian people, and yet afterward still pretend to catch them by an after conversion.[9] I question not but that it has pleased God in his infinite pity and patience to suffer this among us, yea and to convert thousands whom all men (yea, and the [converted] persons [themselves]) have esteemed good converts before. . . .

"True Conversion" to Christ Cannot Be Compelled

And lastly, it is out of [the] question to me that I may not pretend a false conversion, and a false state of worship, to the true Lord Jesus. If any noble Berean[10] shall make inquiry what is that true conversion I intend, I answer first negatively. First, it is not a conversion of a people from one false worship to another, as Nebuchadnezzar compelled all nations under his monarchy. Second, it is not to a mixture of the manner or worship of the true God, the Gold of Israel, with false gods and their worships, as the people were converted by the King of Assyria (2 Kings 17), in which worship for many generations did [the] Samaritans continue, having a form of many wholesome truths amongst them concerning God and the Messiah (John 4). Third, it is not from the true to a false, as Jeroboam turned the ten Tribes to their ruin and dispersion to this day (1 Kings 12). Fourth, it must not be a conversion to some external submission to God's ordinances upon earthly respects, as Jacob's sons converted the Shechemites (Gen. 34).[11] Fifth, it must

8. "And Jesus, walking by the sea of Galilee, saw two brethren, Simon called Peter, and Andrew his brother, casting a net into the sea: for they were fishers. And he saith unto them, Follow me, and I will make you fishers of men. And they straightway left their nets, and followed him" (Matthew 4:18–20).

9. By "after conversion" Williams is referring to repeated attempts to convert peoples from Catholicism to Protestantism or vice versa, as the political fortunes of a particular brand of Christianity changed. The religious fickleness of sixteenth- and seventeenth-century England in particular illustrated the superficiality and futility of attempts to convert the Native Americans.

10. An allusion to the Jewish nobility in Beroea, who responded to the evangelistic message of Apostles Paul and Silas with eagerness and scriptural inquiry (Acts 17:10–12).

11. Shechem was a Hivite who raped Jacob's daughter Dinah and then sought Jacob's permission to marry her. Jacob's sons deceitfully responded that such an alliance between families could only occur if Shechem and his clan were circumcised. Shechem agreed, but while he and his tribe were still recuperating from their "conversion," Dinah's brothers exacted revenge for her rape by attacking the Shechemites and killing all the males.

not be (it is not *possible* it should be, in truth) a conversion of people to the worship of the Lord Jesus by force of arms and swords of steel: So indeed did Nebuchadnezzar deal with all the world (Dan. 3), so does his antitype and successor the Beast deal with all the earth (Rev. 13).

But so did never the Lord Jesus bring any to his most pure worship, for he abhors (as all men, yea the very Indians, do) an unwilling Spouse, and to enter into a forced bed. The will in worship, if true, is like a free vote—*nec cogit, nec cogitur.*[12] Jesus Christ compels by the mighty persuasions of his messengers to come in, but otherwise with earthly weapons he never did compel nor can be compelled. The not discerning of this truth has let out the blood of thousands in civil combustions in all ages, and [has] made the whore drunk, and the earth drunk with the blood of the saints and witnesses of Jesus. And it is yet like to be the destruction and dissolution of that which is called "the Christian world," unless the God of peace and pity look down upon it, and satisfy the souls of men, that he has not so required. (I should be far yet from not securing the peace of a city, of a land, which I confess ought to be maintained by civil weapons, and which I have so much cause to be earnest with God for. Nor would I leave a gap open to any mutinous hand or tongue, nor wish a weapon left in the hand of any known to be mutinous and peace-breakers.) I know (lastly) the consciences of many are otherwise persuaded, both from Israel's state of old and other allegations. Yet I shall be humbly bold to say [that] I am able to present such considerations to the eyes of all who love the Prince of Truth and Peace that shall discover the weakness of all such allegations, and answer all objections, that have been or can be made in this point. So much negatively.

True Conversion Stems from the Preaching of Properly Commissioned Messengers of Christ

Affirmatively, I answer in general [that] a true conversion (whether of Americans or Europeans) must be such as those conversions were of the first pattern, either of the Jews or the heathens. . . . In particular, first, it must be by the free proclaiming or preaching of repentance and forgiveness of sins (Luke 24) by such messengers as can prove their lawful sending and commission from the Lord Jesus, to make disciples out of all nations and so to

---

12. Translated, "neither does he compel, nor is he compelled."

baptize or wash them . . . in the name or profession of the holy Trinity (Matt. 28:19; Rom. 10:14, 15). Second, such a conversion (so far as man's judgment can reach, which is fallible) . . . [must be] a turning of the whole man from the power of Satan to God (Acts 26). Such a change, as if an old man became a new babe (John 3), . . . amounts to God's new creation in the soul (Eph. 2:10). Third, visibly it is a turning from idols, not only of conversation but of worship (whether pagan, Turkish, Jewish, or antichristian), to the living and true God in the ways of his holy worship, appointed by his Son (1 Thes. 1:9). I know objections used to be made against this, but the Golden Rule, if well attended to, will discover all crooked swerving and aberrations.

If any now say to me, "Why then, if this be conversion, and you have such a *Key of Language*[13] and such . . . knowledge of the country and the inhabitants, why proceed you not to produce in America some patterns of such conversions as you speak of? I answer, first, it must be[14] a great deal of practice and mighty pains and hardships undergone by myself, or any that would proceed to such a further degree of the language, as to be able in propriety of speech to open matters of salvation to them. . . . Yet [in addition], I answer, if a man were as affectionate and zealous as David to build a house for God, and as wise and holy to advise and encourage as Nathan [the] attempt [of] this work, without a word, warrant, and commission . . . from God himself, they must afterwards hear a voice, though accepting good desires, yet reproving want of commission: "Did I ever speak a word, says the Lord?" (2 Sam. 7:7).

True Conversion Must Wait for the Return of Christ?

The truth is, having not been without (through the mercy of God) abundant and constant thoughts about a true commission for such an embassy and ministry, I must ingenuously confess the restless unsatisfiedness of my soul in diverse main particulars: As first whether . . . God's great business between Christ Jesus, the holy Son of God, and Antichrist, the man of sin and son of perdition, must not be first over, and Zion and Jerusalem be re-

---

13. Again, a reference to Williams's study of the language and customs of the Narragansett Indians, also published during his first return to England.
14. That is, "it would require."

built and re-established, before the Law and Word of Life be sent forth to the rest of the nations of the world who have not heard of Christ (the prophets are deep concerning this). Secondly, since there can be no preaching (according to the last will and testament of Christ Jesus) without a true sending (Rom. 14:15), where [does] the power and authority of sending and giving that Commission (Matt. 28) . . . now lie? It is here unseasonable to number up all that lay claim to this power, with their grounds for their pretenses, either those of the Romish sort or those of the Reforming or rebuilding sort, and the mighty controversies which are this day in all parts about it. . . . They may make us ashamed for all that we have done (Ezek. 43), and loath ourselves for . . . [having] broken him with our whorish hearts (Ezek. 9), to fall dead at the feet of Jesus (Rev. 1) as John did, and to weep much as he (Rev. 5), that the Lamb may please to open to us that wonderful Book, and the seven sealed mysteries thereof.

CHAPTER FIVE

The Bloody Tenent Yet More Bloody

by Mr. Cotton's endeavor to wash it white in the Blood of the LAMB,
Of whose precious Blood, spilt in the Blood of his Servants, and
Of the blood of Millions spilt in former and later Wars for conscience sake,
that Most Bloody Tenent of Persecution
for cause of conscience, upon a second Trial,
is found now more apparently and more notoriously guilty.

Between Williams's two emissary trips to London, John Cotton composed a rebuttal to The Bloody Tenent of Persecution, *published as* The Bloody Tenent, Washed, and Made White in the Blood of the Lamb *(1647). To this rejoinder Williams responded with a point-by-point refutation of Cotton's treatise, revisiting important themes from* The Bloody Tenent, *such as the distinction between spiritual righteousness and civil virtue and the inappropriateness of state power for advancing the cause of religion.* The Bloody Tenent Yet More Bloody *was published in London in 1652, and the verbal duel between these two great minds ended with Cotton's death that same year.*

To the Most Honorable, the Parliament of the Commonwealth of England

Most Noble Senators,

One of the greatest spirits and as active [a leader] as later times have yielded, Charles V, tired out with affairs of state, resigns up all, and sits down to end his days in quiet contemplation. I doubt not but many of your honorable heads have felt the thorny crown of these late years' troubles [to be] so sharp, so weighty, that your tired spirits would joyfully embrace, if not . . . a total cessation, yet like some faithful tired judge after so long and troublesome a term, at least some breathing short vacation.

Although I dare not, [for] England's peace and safety, admit desires of your total cessation or long vacation, yet common gratitude for such incomparable labors, expenses, [and] hazards, from whence the God of Heaven has vouchsafed such rare and incomparable preservations, deliverances, [and] enjoyments—I say, common gratitude cannot only wish you heartily and pray earnestly for your eternal rest and most joyful harvest in the heavens, but also all the possible breathing hours and cool retired shades of contemplation and self-enjoyment amidst the scorching travails of so many vexing and tedious actions. Ever renowned Patriots, like some grave commanders of fleets and armies who have brought their ships and followers through tempestuous storms and bloody fights to joyful rest and harbors, you cannot but look back with admiration, with praise, with resolve to cast your crowns and heads and hearts and hands (for the remaining minutes of the short candle of your life) at his feet, in whose high and most gracious hands have all your breaths and ways been.

In the review of the multitude of your actions and sufferings, your battles and victories, dangers and deliverances, you cannot (no man can) but observe and see a naked arm from heaven fighting for you, but most especially since the times and hours you gratified the Most High Eternal King of Kings (now more than ever England's king) with these two famous subsidies (if I may in humble reverence so call them): the first, of mercy and moderation to the poor oppressed consciences of the English nation, amidst the throng of which he graciously will [acknowledge], yea he has acknowledged, that some of his own dear children (the sons and daughters of the God of Heaven) have been relieved and succored by you; the second, your high and impartial drawing of the sword of justice upon the great and highest offenders. Since [these] two wonderful subsidies, the most willfully blind must be forced to see the glorious goings of the God of Heaven with your councils and armies, and the discharge of his holy promise in honoring you who have so highly (in so rare and unparalleled travails and hazards) honored him.

Concerning the first of these subsidies, I was humbly bold some few years since to present you with a conference between Peace and Truth, touching a most bloody murderous malefactor, the bloody tenent of persecution for cause of conscience—a notorious and common pirate that takes and robs, that fires and sinks the spiritual ships and vessels (that is, the consciences) of all men, of all sorts, of all religions and persuasions whatsoever. It has pleased Master Cotton (a man incomparably too worthy for such a service) to attempt the washing of this bloody tenent (as he says) in the blood of the Lamb, Christ Jesus. . . . This present discourse presents your Honors with the second part of the conference between Peace and Truth, and has examined Mr. Cotton's reply and washings.

I sum up the multitude of my thoughts touching your Honors' consideration of this point in these three most humble petitions:

First, I most humbly and earnestly beseech your Honors to mind the difference between state necessity of freedom to different consciences and the equity and piety of such a freedom. State policy and [the] necessity of affairs drew from great Constantine (with his colleague Licinius) that famous edict of freedom to all men's consciences, whom yet afterward he persecuted.[1] But a successor of his . . . , Maximilian II, comes near the life of the business when he conscientiously professed in a solemn speech to the bishop of Olmuts in Bohemia, "There is no sin ordinarily greater against God . . . than to use violence against the consciences of men."[2] Your Honors will find (if the Father of Spirits pleases to spare you time and spirits to mind this cause and controversy) that all violence to conscience turns upon these two hinges: first, of restraining from that worshipping of a god or gods which the consciences of men in their respective worships (all the world over) believe to be true; secondly, of constraining to the practicing or countenancing of that whereof their consciences are not persuaded. In the practice of both these, the histories of our own nation will tell us . . . how sharp and zealous the strongest swords of England have ever used to be. . . .

The pope, the Turk, the king of Spain, the Emperor, and the rest of persecutors, . . . while they practice violence to the souls of men and make their swords of steel co-rivals with the two-edged spiritual sword of the Son of

1. In 313 Constantine I, emperor of the western portions of the Roman Empire, and his eastern counterpart, Licinius, issued the Edict of Milan, a joint declaration of religious toleration that for the first time made it legally permissible in the empire to practice Christianity. Shortly thereafter Licinius marched against Constantine in an effort to consolidate imperial power under his own rule, and to garner the loyalty of his military he rescinded many of the protections afforded Christians under the Edict of Milan. Since no evidence exists to suggest that Constantine ever persecuted Christians after his alleged conversion, Williams's reference to persecution here refers either to Licinius's reversal or to Constantine's actions against non-Christians.

2. Maximilian II (1527–1576) was a king of Bohemia and Hungary who eventually ascended to the title of Holy Roman Emperor in 1564. Although he remained a Catholic throughout his life, Maximilian demonstrated an affection for Protestant nobility and maintained a policy of religious neutrality and freedom that provided Europe a respite from the earlier violence between Protestants and Catholics during the Reformation.

God, the basis of their highest pillars, the foundation of their glorious palaces, are but dross and rottenness. And however in our poor arithmetic their kingdoms' numbers seem great, yet in the only wise account of the Eternal, their ages are but minutes and their short periods are never accomplished. For herein the maxim is most true, in the matters of religion and conscience of men especially: the violent motion must break.

But light from the Father of Lights has shined on your eyes; mercy from the Father of Mercies has softened your breasts, to be tender [to] the tenderest part of man, his conscience. For indeed there is no true reason of policy or piety (as this discourse discovers) why that man that will subscribe (and give assurance for honest meaning) to that most prudent Act of Civil Engagement[3] (whatever his conscience be) should be deprived and robbed of the liberty of it in spiritual and religious matters.

I fear I have been long in my first petition; my second shall be brief. I most humbly and earnestly beseech your Honors in all straits and difficulties which yet you are to pass (concerning this great point of men's consciences or other high affairs): steer carefully off from one sunk rock on which so many gallant vessels have miscarried. This rock lies deeper then others, and seldom has appeared but at some dead-low water, when the Most High Judge of the whole world reckons with men or states in low conditions and debasements. I humbly beg from God the gracious continuance of his mighty angels' guard about your sitting, to preserve your Honors from the flames of wars abroad and from such flames at home, from risings, tumults, mutinies, pistols, stabs, powder-plots, [and] poison—but above all, from your own wisdom and policies in straits and difficulties. The holy history tells that on this rock[4] . . . struck the great statist Jeroboam, to the ruin of himself and his posterity. On this rock split that famous and zealous reformer Jehu. This [rock] plucked the crown from Saul's high head, when his own wisdom in straits made him presumptuous about the worship of God. This [rock] plucked off the crown, and plucked out the eyes, of Zedekiah, when in a strait he trusted not in God (as Solomon speaks) but leaned to his own understanding for his safety.

To which purpose my third petition is, that in the midst of so many great negotiations of justice, of mercy to the bodies and estates, spirits and con-

---

3. The Act of Civil Engagement to which Williams refers was a loyalty oath used during the early years of the Commonwealth period in England.

4. That is, the rock of reliance on worldly wisdom instead of on God's instruction.

sciences of so many thousands and ten thousand, you forget not to deal justly and to show mercy to yourselves. Oh, how lamentable and dreadful will it prove, if after all your high employments . . . , if in the midst of all your cares and fears and tossings about the souls and consciences and salvation of others, your own most dear and precious selves make an eternal shipwreck? Your Honors know that although men have chosen and culled you out as wise and noble, yet God has not chosen (if Paul say true) many wise and noble to eternal life and blessedness. Who can love and honor you and not cry to the God of Heaven for you, and to yourselves for yourselves? Be not so busy about the earthly estate, no nor the heavenly estate of others, as to forget to make sure your own vocation and election, and to work out your own salvation with fear and trembling.

O let not this bold cry offend, [or] though offend, yet let it thoroughly awake your noble spirits to know your dangers and hindrances (more then other men's) from a world of distractions from without [and] from pride and self-confidence within, from the flatteries of such who (hoping for rewards and morsels from you) proclaim abroad (that you may hear it)—O blessed Christian magistrates, Christian kings and queens, Christian states, Christian Parliaments, Christian armies!—so lulling your precious souls into an eternal sleep. . . .

Your Honors well remember that the main point of Luther's Reformation—and before him of the Hussites in Germany and Bohemia, and before them of the Wicklivites in England, and before them the Waldensians in France—consisted chiefly about repentance and faith in the blood of Christ. [And] the main contentions of Calvin, and since him of most Reformers, have turned upon the hinge of the *form* of the church and the administrations thereof, the lamentable though precious fuel of those fires of strife among the wisest, holiest, and most learned of the followers of Christ Jesus in these times. You know the Lord Jesus prophesied that many false churches should arise, and the Scriptures more than once give the title of Christ to the church, whence it is evident that every model, platform, and profession of a church is the profession of a various and different Christ. Your Honors also know he spoke most true . . . that said, "That which is most highly esteemed amongst men is abomination in the sight of God" (Luke 15). Hence such may the glorious profession of Christs or churches be as may ravish the eyes and hearts of men, and from which the jealous eye of the true Lord Jesus turns away with indignation, as from the false and counterfeit. . . .

On six principal pillars or foundations (says the Holy Spirit, Heb. 6:6) is built the fabric of true Christianity: on repentance, on faith, on baptism, on laying on of hands, on the resurrection, and the eternal judgment. Concerning the two middle ones of these there are and have been mighty and lamentable differences among the scholars of Jesus, who yet agree in the other four, of repentance and faith, the resurrection and eternal judgment. Whatsoever your Honors' apprehensions are of the last four, I beseech you . . . [to] make sure of the first two, and ply (with sails and oars) day and nights, and give not rest to your souls [until] you have anchored in some blessed assurance, that although you find not satisfaction in the many frames of churches pretending, yet that . . . those your very eyes which have seen so much of Christ Jesus and so many wonderful changes, and have been rotten awhile in their holes in death, shall joyfully possess and fill their holes again, and be gloriously blessed with the sight of a Redeemer, when these heavens and this earth shall pass away. For which humbly and incessantly prays your Honors' most unworthy, yet unfainedly devoted, Roger Williams.

To the Several Respective General Courts, Especially That of Massachusetts in New England

Honored and beloved Friends and Countrymen,

While you sit dry on your safe American shores (by God's most gracious providence) and have beheld the doleful tossings of so many of Europe's nations—yea of our dearest Mother, aged England—in a sea of tears and blood, I am humbly bold to present your eyes and hearts with this not unseasonable discourse of blood, of the bloody tenents of persecution, oppression, and violence, in the cause and matter of conscience and religion.

It is a second conference of Peace and Truth, an examination of the worthily honored and beloved Mr. Cotton's reply to a former conference and treatise of this subject. And although it concerns all nations which have persecuted and shed the blood of Jesus, the bloody Roman Empire (with all the savage lions, emperors, and popes thereof), the bloody monarchies of Spain and France and the rest of Europe's kingdoms and states (which under their several vizards and pretenses of service to God have in so many thousands of his servants murdered so many thousand times over his dear Son)—yea, although it concerns that bloody Turkish monarchy and all the nations of the world who practice violence to the conscience of any Christian, or Antichristians, Jews or pagans—yet it concerns yourselves (with all due respect otherwise be it spoken) in some more eminent degrees. [This is so] partly as so many of you of chief note (beside Mr. Cotton) are engaged in it, partly as New England (in respect of spiritual and civil state) professes to draw nearer to Christ Jesus than other states and churches, and partly as New England is believed to hold and practice such a bloody doctrine, notwithstanding Mr. Cotton's veils and pretenses of not persecuting men for conscience (but punishing them only for sinning against conscience!), and of . . . not persecuting, but punishing heretics, blasphemers, idolaters, [and] seducers.

It is Mr. Cotton's great mistake and forgetfulness to charge me with a public examination of his private letter to me. Whereas in truth, there never passed such letters between himself and me about this subject, as he alleges. But the prisoner's[5] arguments against persecution, with Mr. Cotton's answer (which I examined), I say these were unexpectedly and solemnly sent to me as no private thing, with earnest desire of my consideration . . . [of] them. These agitations between Mr. Cotton and others so sent to me, as also the "Model of church and Civil Power" by God's providence coming to hand, I say they seemed to me to be of too public a nature, and in which my soul not only heard the doleful cry to the Lord for vengeance of the souls under the altar, but their earnest solicitations, yea and the command of the Lord Jesus, for vindication of their blood and lives spilled and destroyed by this bloody tenent, though under never so fair and glorious shows and colors.

The Most Holy and All-Seeing knows how bitterly I resent the least difference with Mr. Cotton, yea with the least of the followers of Jesus, of what conscience or worship soever. How mournfully I remember this stroke . . . on Mr. Cotton's eye and the eyes of so many of God's precious children and servants in these and other parts, that those eyes so piercing and heavenly (in other holy and precious truths of God) should yet be so clouded over and bloodshot in this. I grieve [that] I must contest, and maintain this contestation, with (in other respects) so dearly beloved and so worthy adversaries.

And yet why mention I or respect I man that is but grass, and the children of men that must die, whose brains, eyes, and tongues (even the holiest and the highest) must shortly sink and rot in their skulls and holes. Without re-

---

5. A reference to John Murton, whom Williams believed to be the author of *An Humble Supplication*. See the introduction to this volume, especially note 13.

membering therefore who my adversary is, nor all the wormwood and gall so frequently in Mr. Cotton's reply against me, I fully and only level with an upright and single eye (the Lord Jesus graciously assisting) against that foul and monstrous bloody tenent and doctrine which has so slyly (like the old serpent, the author of it) crept under the shade and shelter of Mr. Cotton's patronage and protection.

My end is to discover and proclaim the crying and horrible guilt of the bloody doctrine, as one of the most seditious, destructive, blasphemous, and bloodiest in any or in all the nations of the world, notwithstanding the many fine veils, pretenses, and colors of not persecuting Christ Jesus but heretics, not God's truth or servants but blasphemers [and] seducers, not persecuting men for their conscience but for sinning against their conscience. My end is to persuade God's Judah (especially) to wash their hands from blood, to cleanse their hearts and ways from such unchristian practices toward all that is man, [being] capable of a religion and a conscience, but most of all toward Christ Jesus, who cries out (as he did to Saul) in the sufferings of the least of his servants: Old England, New England, King, Parliaments, General Courts, Presbyterians, Independents, why persecute you me? It is hard for you to kick against the pricks. . . .[6]

It is but humanity, it is but Christianity to exercise meekness and moderation to all men. It is human and Christian wisdom to listen to a serious alarm against a common enemy. Prove the alarm false, it may be but troublesome; prove it true, it may be destruction to have despised it. As the wounds of a lover are better then the kisses of an enemy, so says the same spirit, an open rebuke is better than secret love [Prov. 27:5].

But yet your consciences (as all men's) must be satisfied, I have therefore in all these agitations humbly presented (amongst others) two fundamental hints or considerations: first, that the people (the origin of all free power and government) are not invested with power from Christ Jesus to rule his wife (or church), to keep it pure, [or] to punish opposites by force of arms; secondly, that the pattern of the national church of Israel was a none-such,

6. According to the *Oxford English Dictionary*, to "kick against the pricks" invoked the metaphor of oxen resisting the prodding of their driver; the phrase meant "to be recalcitrant to one's own hurt." This and the previous sentence are a paraphrase of Jesus' encounter with Saul (later the Apostle Paul) on the road to Damascus, as recorded in Acts 9:5—"And he [Saul] said, Who art thou, Lord? And the Lord said, I am Jesus whom thou persecutest: it is hard for thee to kick against the pricks."

inimitable by any civil state in all or any of the nations of the world beside. (In this latter hint, I insisted more largely in my former considerations upon "[The Model of] church and Civil Power" in New England, to which Mr. Cotton replied not, and of any other replies of any to whom Mr. Cotton refers I do not yet know.)[7]

I add, it is a glorious character of every true disciple or scholar of Christ Jesus to be never too old to learn. It is the command of Christ Jesus to his scholars to try all things. And liberty of trying what a friend, yea what an (esteemed) enemy, presents has ever (in point of Christianity) proved one special means of attaining to the truth of Christ. For I dare confidently appeal to the consciences of God's most knowing servants if that observation be not true, that it has been the common way of the Father of Lights to enclose the light of his holy truths in dark and obscure (yea, and ordinarily in forbidden) books, persons, and meetings. . . .

New England voyages have taught most of our old English spirits how to put due prices upon the most common and ordinary undervalued mercies. How precious with some has been a little water? How dainty with others a piece of bread? How welcome to some the poorest housing? Yea, the very land and earth, after long and tedious passages? There is one commodity for the sake of which most of God's children in New England have run their mighty hazards, a commodity marvelously scarce in former times (though in some late years by God's most gracious and mighty hand more plentiful) in our native country: it is a liberty of searching after God's most holy mind and pleasure. . . .

Amongst the crying sins of our own or other sinful nations, [these] two are ever amongst the loudest: invented devotions to the God of Heaven, [and] secondly, violence and oppression on the sons of men, especially . . . for dissenting. Against both these, and that the impartial and dreadful hand of the most holy and jealous God . . . tear and burn not up at last the roots of these plantations, but graciously discovering the plants which are not his, he may graciously fructify and cause to flourish what his right hand will own—I say this is the humble and unfeigned desire and cry at the throne of grace of your so long despised outcast: Roger Williams.

---

7. In the *Bloody Tenent, Washed,* Cotton largely ignored the debate over "The Model," except to insist he did not participate in its writing.

To the Merciful and Compassionate Reader

While the unmerciful priests and levites turn away their cruel eyes and feet from their poor wounded neighbors, the oppressed for matters of religion and worship, it will be no ungrateful act to present your tender heart and ear, compassionate Samaritan, with the doleful cry of the souls under the altar. . . .[8] Here and there among these slaughtered heaps of saints lie (thin and rare) the slaughtered carcasses of some poor Arians or Papists or other poor deluding and deluded souls. This seeming color of impartial justice serves woefully that murderous enemy of all mankind for a stale[9] or covert under which his bloody game goes on, of persecuting (or hunting) the harmless deer, the children of the living God. For the sake of the dear saints and followers of Jesus, then, for his holy sake and truth, for the holy name and truth of the most holy Father of Lights, . . . your compassionate eye is here presented with a second conference and view of Mr. Cotton's reply, and artificial bloody washing of the bloody tenent. . . .

Touching Mr. Cotton, I present two words, first for his person, [and] secondly for his work. For his person, although I rejoice that since it pleased God to lay a command on my conscience to come in as his poor witness in this great cause (I say I rejoice it has pleased him to appoint so able and excellent and conscionable an instrument to bolt out the truth to the brain), so I can humbly say it in his holy presence, it is my constant heaviness and soul's grief to differ from any fearing God, so much more . . . from Mr. Cotton, whom I have ever desired (and still desire highly) to esteem and dearly to respect, for so great a portion of mercy and grace vouchsafed to him and so many truths of Christ Jesus maintained by him. And therefore, notwithstanding that some . . . have said that he wrote his *Washing of the Bloody Tenent* in blood against Christ Jesus and gall against me, yet if upon so slippery and narrow a passage I have slipped . . . into any . . . expression unbecoming his person or the matter . . . in hand considered, I humbly crave pardon of God and Mr. Cotton also.

Secondly, concerning his work, . . . the observant reader will soon discover that whatever Mr. Cotton's stand is, yet he most weakly provides him-

---

8. "I saw under the altar the souls of them that were slain for the word of God, and for the testimony which they held: and they cried with a loud voice, saying, How long, O Lord, holy and true, dost thou not judge and avenge our blood on them that dwell on the earth?" (Revelation 6:9, 10).

9. A deception, trap, or decoy.

self very strange reserves and retreats. To point with the finger at two or three most frequent and remarkable:

First, when he seems to be overwhelmed with the lamentable and doleful cries of the souls under the altar, crying out for vengeance on their persecutors . . . , he often retreats and professes to hold no such doctrine of persecuting the saints, nor of any for cause of conscience, nor that the magistrate should draw forth his sword in matters of religion. When it is urged that through this whole book he persecutes or hunts (by name) the idolater, the blasphemer, the heretic, and the seducer, and that to death or banishment . . . , Mr. Cotton retreats into the land of Israel, and calls up Moses and his laws against idolaters, blasphemers, [and] seducers. When he is challenged . . . for producing the pattern of a national church when he stands only for a congregational, for producing that national church of Israel . . . as a copy or sampler for the nations and peoples of the world, Mr. Cotton retreats to moral equity, that the seducer and he that kills a soul should die. When it is urged that Christ at his so long typed out coming abolished those national shadows and erected his spiritual kingdom of Israel, . . . Mr. Cotton retreats and confesses Christ's kingdom is spiritual [and] not national, but congregational, and that those Scriptures hold forth a spiritual cutting off, and he so produces them to prove the heretic so to be cut off, alleging that the question was put in general terms [and] that he knew not what persecution should be intended. . . . When all the consciences in the world cry out against him for setting up the civil power and officers and courts of civil justice to judge the convictions of men's souls and consciences, Mr. Cotton retreats to his last refuge, and says that although this be the duty of all the magistrates in the world, yet not any of them must meddle to punish in religion until they be informed ([by which he means] until he is sure they will draw their swords for his conscience and church against all others as heretical [and] blasphemous). . . .

I confess in this plea for freedom to all consciences in matters (merely) of worship, I have impartially pleaded for the freedom of the consciences of the Papists themselves, the greatest enemies and persecutors . . . of the saints and truths of Jesus. Yet I have pleaded for no more then is their due and right, and whatever else shall be the consequence, it shall stand for a monument and testimony against them, and be an aggravation of their former, present, or future cruelties against Christ Jesus the Head and all that uprightly love him, his true disciples and followers.

It is true, I have not satisfaction in the clear discovery of those holy prophesies and periods set down and prefixed by the Holy Spirit in Daniel [and] John concerning the kingdom of Christ Jesus. Yet two things I profess in the holy presence of God, angels, and men. First, my humble desires and resolution (the Lord assisting) to contend for the true and visible worship of the true and living God, according to the institution and appointment of the last will and Testament of Christ Jesus. [Secondly,] I believe and profess, that such persons, such churches are nearest to Christ Jesus on whose forehead are written these blessed characters of the true Lord Jesus Christ: first, content with a poor and low condition in worldly things; second, a holy cleansing from the filthiness of false worships and worldly conversations; third, a humble and constant endeavor to attain (in their simplicity and purity) to the ordinances and appointments of Christ Jesus; fourth, are so far from smiting, killing, and wounding the opposites of their profession and worship that they resolve themselves patiently to bear and carry the cross and gallows of their Lord and Master, and patiently to suffer with him. In the number of such his poor servants who (notwithstanding my plea against persecutors and persecution) unfeignedly desire to suffer as cheerfully with Christ Jesus, gloriously to reign with him, and desire to be, your unfeigned, though unworthiest of all the followers of Jesus, Roger Williams.

The Bloody Tenent Yet More Bloody, by Master Cotton's Attempting to Wash It with the Blood of the Lamb

Truth. Blessed be the God of truth and peace, sweet Peace, that once again we find a corner and a few hours to entertain our sweet embraces and discourses about that bloody tenent of persecution for cause of conscience.

Peace. It is indeed Jehovah's work, and it is marvelous in our eyes, that amid this world's combustions such a corner and such hours are found.

Truth. Dear friends the longer absent meet the sweeter, and have cause to spend each minute to praise him who works wonders, and this not the least [of those wonders], that we two see each other's face at all in these tempestuous days and veil of tears. How harshly were our last conferrings entertained by some? How [we] were suspected and traduced[10] for counterfeits,

---

10. To speak evil of, especially falsely or maliciously.

and our pious and peaceable meditations cruelly condemned to the devouring flames? . . .

Peace. Meanwhile 'tis yet our lamentation that so many of our darlings whom we have tendered as our eyes have both in print and pulpit cried out against us—and amongst the rest, one of your dearest eldest children, too worthy to be the defender of the bloody tenent of persecution.

Truth. Our love shall cover his shame and nakedness, and our wisdoms pity his heavy labor, Blackamore-washings, and so great expense of precious time and spirit, in laboring to wash this so deeply bloody and Blackamore[11] tenent in the blood of the Lamb of God.

Peace. [Just as] parents and true friends love and pity theirs, though sick, though froward[12] and distracted, let our bowels yearn over him who tears out ours. Who knows but once before he sleeps his last in the pit of rottenness, he may awake and give glory to the God of peace and truth, of patience and long suffering, whose thoughts, whose ways, whose love, whose pity has no bounds nor limits toward them whom he has loved before the world's foundation.

O let these blessed buds of hope and sweet desires, dear Truth, put forth in pious fruits of renewed endeavors, and let me once again prefer my suit for your impartial weighing of what replies, objections, pleadings, he has brought against us.

Truth. For the God of Peace, for the sake of the Prince of Peace, yea for his servants' sake, for Zion's sake, I will not be silent, and know at last I shall prevail to scatter and dispel the mists and fogs that for a while arise to cloud and choke us.

Peace. First, then, what cause should move this so able a defendant to leap over all our first addresses both to the High Court of Parliament and to every Reader? What may be conjectured [from the fact that he] directs a word to neither in this controversy?

Truth. I desire my rejoinder may be as full of love as truth, yet some say Master Cotton is wise and knows in what door the wind blows of late. He is

---

11. According to the *Oxford English Dictionary,* the term "Blackamore" referred literally to "a black-skinned African, an Ethiopian, a Negro; any very dark-skinned person." Additionally, however, the term could be used figuratively to refer to "blackness" or, in a more sinister vein, "a devil."

12. *OED:* "Disposed to go counter to what is demanded or what is reasonable; perverse, difficult to deal with, hard to please; refractory, ungovernable; also, in a wider sense, bad, evilly-disposed, 'naughty.' (The opposite of *toward.*)"

not ignorant [of] what sad complaints in letters, printings, [and] confer-
ences so many of God's people (and of his own conscience and judgment of
Independency) have poured forth against New England's persecuting. He
knows what bars New England's bloody tenent and practice may put to his
brothers' just desires and suits for moderation and toleration to non-con-
forming consciences. 'Tis true [that] his conscience and the credit of his
way compel his reply, but the times advise him [to respond] with as little
noise as may be, and it seems with no great willingness that that high and
searching house of England's Parliament should search and scan his meditations. . . .

The True Meaning of "Persecution of Conscience"

Peace. . . . Master Cotton first complains against the publishing of his private letter with an answer thereunto. He faults the Discusser for punishing
his conscience, against the Discusser's own tenent of liberty of conscience
. . . in first publishing to the world before private admonition and telling the
church. . . .[13]

Truth. To my knowledge there was no such letter or intercourse passed
between Master Cotton and the Discusser, but what I have heard is this: one
Master Hall of Roxbury[14] presented the prisoner's arguments against persecution to Master Cotton, who gave this present controverted answer. With
which Master Hall, not being satisfied, sent to the Discusser, who never saw
the said Hall nor those arguments in writing, though he well remembered
that he saw them in print some years since. Apprehending no other but that
Master Cotton's answer was as public as Master Cotton's profession and
practice of the same tenent was and is, what breach of rule can Master Cotton say it was to answer that in the streets which Master Cotton proclaims
on the housetop? . . . Does [Master Cotton] indeed plead for liberty of conscience? Let the following discourse and this present passage manifest how
tender he is of his own conscience and of the liberty of it, but how censori-

13. "Moreover if thy brother shall trespass against thee, go and tell him his fault between thee and
him alone: if he shall hear thee, thou hast gained thy brother. But if he will not hear thee, then take
with thee one or two more, that in the mouth of two or three witnesses every word may be established. And if he shall neglect to hear them, tell it unto the church: but if he neglect to hear the
church, let him be unto thee as an heathen man and a publican" (Matthew 18:15–17).
14. John Hall of Roxbury emigrated to Boston two years after Williams, living in Massachusetts
and Connecticut from 1633 until his death in 1673.

ous and senseless of the pangs and agonies of other men's conscience and spirits and sorrows [is he] . . . !

Peace. Complains Master Cotton of persecution for such dealings against him? I never heard that disputing, discoursing and examining men's tenents or doctrines by the Word of God was, in proper English acceptance of the word, persecution for conscience. Well had it been for New England [if] no servant of God nor witness of Christ Jesus could justly take up [any] other complaint against New England for other kinds of persecution! Surely the voice of Christ Jesus to Paul—"Saul, Saul, why persecutest thou me?"—was for another kind of persecution.

Truth. Dear Peace, if the bishops of old England or New had never stirred up the civil magistrate to any other suppressing of men's consciences, nor no other persecuting, than discussing [and] disputing, they should never have needed to have been charged so publicly in the face of the world with the bloody tenent of persecution for cause of conscience. . . . Persecution for conscience is, in plain English, hunting for conscience. Master Cotton . . . much desires to have the word "persecution" changed for the word "punishing," a term more proper to true justice. But is this not the guise and profession of all that ever persecuted or hunted men for their religion and conscience? Are not all histories and experiences full of the pathetic speeches of persecutors to this purpose? You will say you are persecuted for your conscience, you plead conscience, [but] you are a heretic; the devil has deceived you, [and] your conscience is deluded. . . .

Persecution for cause of conscience is not only when a man is punished for professing such doctrines and worships as he believes to be of God, but also when he is punished for renouncing such doctrine and not practicing such worships which he believes are not of God. . . .

Peace. 'Tis woefully true, that the peace of the saints and the peace of the world have been lamentably broken and distracted in punishing or persecuting men, but especially the saints, upon both these grounds. But yet the records of time and experience will tell us that since the Apostasy from the truth of Jesus, the rising of Antichrist, and the setting up of many state religions, the sorest and most frequent punishing or hunting of the children of God has been . . . for not bowing down to the state images, for not coming to church, for not obeying the laws, for withstanding the king's, queen's, or Parliament's proceedings. . . .

Truth. I here first observe (as also in other places) Master Cotton's acknowledgement and profession of what a man may be punished for: a fundamental error, persisting in it and seducing others—all [of] which are spiritual matters of religion and worship, for which he decrees from the magistrate death or banishment. And yet elsewhere in many other passages, he professes against all persecution for conscience. If Master Cotton should so fall and be so dealt with by the civil state, would not Master Cotton conscientiously be persuaded of the truth of what he held, though accounted by others fundamental error, obstinacy, [and] heresy? Will Master Cotton think that death or banishment would be wholesome and Christian means and remedies to change and heal his conscience? Granting the civil magistrate must punish him with death or banishment (to prevent the infection of others), does he not make the magistrate, yea the civil state (whatever state he lives in), the judge of his conscience and errors? Confessing now that to worship God with a common prayer was his sin, and yet it was his conscience that he might so do, if the magistrate had judged it to be a fundamental error, he grants he might then have put him to death or banishment. . . . Yet he has a proviso and a retreat against this assault, professing that if the magistrate be not rightly informed, he must stay his proceedings. . . .

Peace. What is this but in plain English to profess that all the magistrates and civil powers throughout the whole world, although they have command and power from Christ Jesus to judge in matters of conscience, religion, and worship . . . , that they do not cut off the heretic, blasphemer, [or] seducer, except they be of Master Cotton's mind and conscience . . . ? [In other words,] they must suspend their duty and office in this case until they be better informed, that is, until they be of his mind. . . .

Persecution of Conscience Threatens Both Civil and Spiritual Peace, Justice, and Order

Truth. We are wont, when we speak of keeping or breaking the peace, to speak of words or actions of violence, sedition, [or] uproar. For actions of the cases, pleas, and traverses may be and yet no peace broken, when men submit to the rule of state for the composing of such differences. Therefore it is that I affirm that if any of Christ's church have difference with any other man in civil and human things, he ought to be judged by the law: But if the church has spiritual controversies among themselves or with any other, . . .

all this may be and yet no civil peace broken. Yea, among those that profess the same God and Christ as the Papists and Protestants, or the same Muhammad as the Turks and Persians, there would no civil peace be broken (notwithstanding their differences in religion) were it not for the bloody doctrine of persecution, which alone breaks the bonds of civil peace, and makes spiritual causes the causes of their bloody dissentions. . . . Hence then, I affirm that there is no doctrine, no tenent so directly tending to break the cities' peace as this doctrine of persecuting or punishing each other for cause of conscience or religion.

Again, . . . although it is most true that sooner or later the God of heaven punishes the nations of the world for their idolatries [and] superstitions, yet Master Cotton himself acknowledges . . . that there are many glorious flourishing cities all the world over wherein no church of Christ is extant. Yea, the commonwealth of Rome flourished five hundred years together before ever the name of Christ was heard in it, which so great a glory of so great a continuance mightily evinces the distinction of the civil peace of a state from that which is Christian religion. It is true (as Master Cotton tells us) that the Turks have plagued the Antichristian world for their idolatries. Yet history tells us that one of their emperors . . . first broke up and desolated two most glorious and ancient cities, Constantinople (which had flourished 1120 years since its first building by Constantine) and Athens (which from Solon's giving of it laws had flourished two thousands years, notwithstanding their idolatries).

It is apparent, then, that the Christian religion gloriously flourished (contrary to Master Cotton's observation) when the Roman Emperors took not power to themselves to reform the abuses in the Christian church, but persecuted it; and then the church was ruined and overwhelmed with apostasy and Antichristianism when the emperors took that power to themselves. And then it was (as Master Cotton elsewhere confesses) that Christianity lost more, even in Constantine's time, than under bloody Nero [or] Domitian.

Peace. It cannot be denied, dear Truth, but that the peace of a civil state . . . was and is merely and essentially civil. But Master Cotton says further [that] although the inward peace of a church is spiritual, yet the outward peace of it magistrates must keep in a way of godliness and honesty (1 Tim. 2:1).

Truth. The peace of a church of Christ (the only true Christian state, nation, kingdom, or city) is spiritual, whether internal in the soul or external in the administration of it, [just] as the peace of a civil state is civil, internally in the minds of men and externally in the administration and conversation of it. . . .

Peace. Lastly, says he, the church is a society, as well as the societies of merchants [and] drapers, and it is just to preserve the society of the church as well as any other society.

Truth. When we speak of the balances of justice, we must distinguish between the balances of the sanctuary and the balances of the world or civil states. It is *spiritual* justice to preserve spiritual right, and for that end the spiritual king thereof has taken care. It is *civil* justice to preserve the civil rights, and the rights of a civil society ought justly to be preserved by a civil state, and yet if a company of men combine themselves into a civil society by voluntary agreement, and voluntarily dissolve it, it is not justice to force them to continue together. . . .

But lastly, if it be justice to preserve the society of the church, is it not partiality in a mere civil state to preserve only one society, and not the persons of other religious societies and consciences also? But the truth is, this mingling of the church and the world together, and their orders and societies together, does plainly [disclose][15] that such churches were never called out from the world, and that this is only a secret policy of flesh and blood, to get protection from the world and so to keep (with some little stilling of conscience) from the cross or gallows of Jesus Christ. . . .

The true and living God is the God of order—spiritual, civil, and natural. Natural is the same ever and perpetual, [while] civil alters according to the constitutions of peoples and nations. Spiritual he has changed from the national in one figurative land of Canaan to particular and congregational churches all over the world. To confound and abrogate spiritual, natural, or civil order is to exalt man's folly against the most holy and incomprehensible wisdom of God. . . .

"Blind Conscience" Justifiably Punished Only When Its Error Leads to Crimes against Others

Truth. [Cotton's] first words (*We approve no persecution for conscience*) fight against his whole endeavor in this book, which is to set up the civil

---

15. Originally "discover."

throne and judgment-seat over the consciences and souls of men, under the pretense of preserving the church of Christ pure, and punishing the evil of heresy [and] blasphemy. [It is as if Cotton were saying], "We hold no man is to be persecuted for his conscience, unless it be for a conscience which we judge dangerous to our religion. No man is to be persecuted for his conscience, unless we judge that we have convinced or conquered his conscience. . . ."

There is a self-conviction which some consciences smite and wound themselves with. But to submit these consciences to the tribunal of the civil magistrate, and powers of the world, how can Master Cotton do this and yet say no man is to be persecuted for his conscience?

Peace. Alas, how many thousands and millions of consciences have been persecuted in all ages and times in a judicial way, and how have their judges pretended victory and triumph, crying out, "We have convinced (or conquered) them, and yet are they obstinate."

Truth. Hence came that hellish proverb, that nothing was more obstinate then a Christian, under which cloud of reproach has been overwhelmed the most faithful, zealous, and constant witnesses of Jesus Christ.

Peace. But, says Master Cotton, some blinded consciences are judicially punished by God, as his in Ireland that burned his child in imitation of Abraham.

Truth. In such cases it may be truly said [that] the magistrate bears not the sword in vain for either the punishing or the preventing of such sins, whether uncleanness, theft, cruelty, or persecution. And therefore such consciences as are so hardened by God's judgment as to smite their fellow servants, under the pretense of zeal and conscience, . . . they ought to be suppressed and punished, to be restrained and prevented. And hence is seasonable the saying of King James, that he desired to be secured of the Papists concerning civil obedience,[16] which security by wholesome laws and other ways (according to the wisdom of each state) each state is to provide for itself even against the delusions of hardened consciences, in any attempt which merely concerns the civil state and commonwealth. . . .

---

16. Williams's reference to King James's toleration of Catholics is based on this quotation from *An Humble Supplication:* "I gave good proofe that I intended no persecution against them for conscience cause, but only denied to be secured for civil obedience, which for conscience cause they are bound to performe." Samuel Caldwell, editor of the Narragansett edition of this treatise, identifies the original source for this quote as the *Workes of the Most High and Mightie Prince James* (London, 1616), 248.

The Parable of the Wheat and Tares Revisited

Peace. In this chapter,[17] four answers were given by the Discusser to that great objection of the mischief that the tares will do in the field of the world, if let alone and not plucked up.[18] The first was that if the tares offend against civility or [the] civil state, God has armed the civil state with a civil sword. Master Cotton replies, what if their conscience incites them to civil offenses?

Truth. I answer, the conscience of the civil magistrate must incite him to civil punishment. . . . If the conscience of the worshippers of the Beast incite them to prejudice prince or state, although these consciences be . . . persuaded of the lawfulness of their actions, yet so far as the civil state is damaged or endangered, I say the sword of God in the hand of civil authority is strong enough to defend itself, either by imprisoning or disarming or other wholesome means—while yet their consciences ought to be permitted in what is merely a point of worship, as prayer and other services and administrations.

Hence the wisdom of God in Romans 13 (reckoned by Master Cotton the Magna Carta for civil magistrates dealing in matters of religion), I say, there it pleases God expressly to reckon up the particulars of the second table, chalking out (as it were) by his own finger the civil sphere or circle in which the civil magistrate ought to act and execute his civil power and authority.

Peace. The second answer of the Discusser was that the church or spiritual city has laws and armories to defend itself. Master Cotton [objects],[19] saying that if their members be leavened with Antichristian idolatry and superstition, and yet must be tolerated in their idolatry and superstitious worship, will not a little leaven leaven the whole lump? And how then is the church guarded?

Truth. The question is whether idolatrous and Antichristian worshippers may be tolerated in [the] *civil state.* . . . Master Cotton answers no, [for] they will do mischief. The [Discusser's] reply is [that] against any civil mischief (though wrought conscientiously) the civil state is strongly guarded. Secondly, against spiritual mischief, the church or city of Christ is guarded with

---

17. Most of Williams's discussion of the parable in this text follows closely the argument in *The Bloody Tenent* and so is not reprinted here.

18. The objection is, of course, Cotton's.

19. Originally "excepteth."

heavenly armories. . . . In the church of Christ, such worshippers ought not to be tolerated, but cast out.

That is true, says Master Cotton, but yet their leaven will spread. I answer, what is this but to make the most powerful appointments of Christ Jesus, those mighty weapons of God, terrible censures and soul-punishments in his kingdom, but as so many wooden daggers and leaden swords, children's bull-beggars,[20] and scarecrows, and upon the point so base and beggarly that without the help of the cutler's shop or smith's forge, the church or kingdom of Christ cannot be purged from the leaven of idolatry and superstition? . . .

Truth. . . . If a man calls Master Cotton murderer [or] witch with respect to civil matters, I say the civil state must judge and punish the offender, else the civil state cannot stand, but must return to barbarism. But if a man calls Master Cotton murderer [or] witch in spiritual matters, as deceiving and bewitching the people's souls, if he can prove his charge, Master Cotton ought to give God the glory and repent of such wickedness. If he cannot prove his charge, but slanders Master Cotton, the slander is of no civil nature and so not proper to any civil court, but is to be cast out (as we commonly see suits of law rejected when [they are] brought into courts which take no proper cognizance of such cases).

Peace. What relief then has Master Cotton, or any so charged in this case?

Truth. The court of heaven, the church of Christ, calls such a slanderer to repentance (whether he be within the church or without, though orderly proceeding lies only against him that is within). If he be obstinate, how dreadful is the sentence against such a slanderer, both on earth and in heaven? How dreadful the delivering up to hardness of heart (a greater plague on Pharaoh than all the devouring plagues of Egypt), how dreadful the delivering up to Satan . . . ! There is no reason in the world, therefore, for thieves and murderers to be tolerated until the last day without sentence and punishment, because transgressors against [a] spiritual state may be tolerated to live in the world yet punished for spiritual transgression with a greater censure and sorer punishment than if all their bones and flesh were racked and torn in pieces with burning pincers.

Peace. Master Cotton and others will say that the idolaters and seducers were censured spiritually under Moses, and yet were they also put to death.

Truth. I desire Master Cotton to show me under Moses such spiritual cen-

---

20. A ghost or terror.

sures and punishments, besides the cutting off by the civil sword. Which if he cannot do—and that since the Christian church antitypes the Israelite and the Christian laws and punishments the laws and punishments of Israel concerning religion—I may truly affirm that civil state which may not justly tolerate civil offenders yet may most justly tolerate spiritual offenders, of whose delinquency it has no proper cognizance. . . .

Christ Did Not Use Civil Weapons against the "Blasphemy" of the Pharisees

Peace. . . . Master Cotton elsewhere will not only have sheep fed, but the wolves driven from the fold [and] their brains beaten out. And not only by the pastors (or spiritual shepherds) but also by the civil magistrate, and to that end, he [the magistrate] is to be stirred up by the shepherds, the ministers of Christ.

Truth. Such exciting and stirring up of the civil magistrate, if it were Christ's will, how can the apostles be excused, or the Lord Jesus himself, for not stirring up the civil magistrates to his duty against these scribes and Pharisees (the wolves and foxes, as Master Cotton here calls them)?

Peace. Neither the doctrine nor their offense at it, says Master Cotton, was fundamental, nor had the civil magistrate established a law about doctrine or offenses of this nature. Besides, Christ gave his disciples a charge to be wise as serpents, and he himself would not meddle with the Pharisees until the last year of his ministry, lest their exasperation might have been some hindrance to his ministry before his hour was come. . . .

Master Cotton, who argues so much against the permitting of blasphemers to live in the world, may here call to mind that if ever blasphemy were uttered against the Son of God, it was uttered by the Pharisees in Matthew 12, when they imputed the casting out of the devils to the power of the devil in Christ Jesus. And yet we find not that Christ Jesus stirred up the civil magistrates to any such duty of his to put the blasphemers to death, nor the heretics the Sadducees, who denied that fundamental [doctrine of] the resurrection.

Truth. It is most true, that the cause needs no such weapons, nor spared he the Pharisees for fear of their exasperations, but poured forth on their faces and bosoms the sorest vials of the heaviest doom and censure that can be suffered by the children of men, that is, [the] impossibility of repentance and forgiveness of sins either in this or the world to come. And for the present, at every turn he concludes them hypocrites [and] blind guides, [who] could not escape the judgment of hell. . . .

If it were the duty of the ministers of Christ to stir up the civil magistrate against such hypocritical and blasphemous Pharisees, could Christ Jesus himself or his servants the Apostles be excused for not complaining to the Roman state against them, so leaving the blame upon the conscience of the governors, if the land were not purged of such blasphemers and fundamental opposers of the Son of God?

Let me end, sweet Peace, with the bottom of all such persecutions: Satan rages against God and his Christ; that devil that casts the saints into prison . . . would cast Christ himself into prison again, and to the gallows again, if he came again in person into any ([even] the most refined) persecuting state in the world. . . .

False Religion Deserves Spiritual, Not Civil, Punishment

Peace. This chapter contains a twofold denial: first, says Master Cotton, we hold it not lawful for a Christian magistrate to compel by the civil sword either Pharisee, pagan, or Jew to profess his religion.

Truth. He who has deceived himself with a bad commodity puts it off as good to others: Master Cotton believes, and would make others believe, that it is no compulsion to make laws (with penalties) for all to come to church and to public worship. . . . In our fathers' days, [civil compulsion presented] a sufficient trial of their religion, [requiring of them] consenting to or dissenting from the religion of the times. . . .

Peace. Master Cotton [also] denies that a blind Pharisee may be a good subject, and as peaceable and profitable to the civil state as any, since they destroyed the civil state by destroying Christ.

Truth. When we speak of civil states and their administrations, it is most improper and fallacious to wind or weave in the consideration of their true or false religions. It is true, idolatry brings judgment in God's time . . . ; notwithstanding, there is a present civil state of men combined to live together there in a commonwealth, which God's people are commanded to pray for (Jer. 29:7), whatever be the religion there publicly professed. Besides, the Pharisees destroying Christ were guilty of blood and persecution, which is more than idolatry, and cries to heaven for vengeance.

Peace. It cannot therefore with any show of charity be denied but that diverse priests of Babel might be civil and peaceable, notwithstanding their religion and conscience.

Truth. Yea, it is known by experience that many thousands of Mahumetan, popish, and pagan priests are in their persons . . . as civil and courteous and peaceable . . . as any of the subjects in the state they live in. . . .

Peace. . . . Master Cotton says: he that corrupts a soul with a corrupt religion lays a spreading leaven which corrupts a state . . . , and therefore it is *lex talionis* that calls for not only soul for soul, but life for life.[21]

Truth. Your tender brain and heart cannot let fly an arrow sharp enough to pierce the bowels of such a bloody tenent!

Peace. The flaming jealousy of that most holy and righteous Judge, who is a consuming fire, will not ever hear such tenents and behold such practices in silence!

Truth. Sweet Peace, long and long may the almond tree flourish on Master Cotton's head in the arms of true Christianity and true Christian honor,[22] and let New England's colonies flourish also (if Christ so please) until he comes again the second time. But that he who is love itself would please to tell Master Cotton and the colonies (and the world!) the untrueness, uncharitableness, unmercifulness, and unpeaceableness of such conclusions! For is not this the plain English and the bottom [of Master Cotton's point, that] if the spirit of Christ Jesus in any of his servants . . . shall persuade one soul . . . to come out of Babel, to refuse to bow down to and to come out from communing with a state's golden image, to not touch what is persuaded is an unclean thing—that that man or woman who was the Lamb's and the Spirit's instrument thus to enlighten and persuade one soul, he has (says this tenent) laid a leaven which corrupts the state . . . ? [And] that leaven shall bring the captivity, ruin, and destruction of the state, and therefore *lex talionis,* not only soul for soul in the next, but also life for life in this present world.

Peace. All your witnesses in all ages, dear Truth, have born the brand and

---

21. The term *lex talionis* refers to the biblical law of retribution, "an eye for an eye, a tooth for a tooth."

22. Ecclesiastes 12:5.

black mark of seducers, and still shall, even Christ Jesus himself, to the last of his holy army and followers against his enemies. . . .

Truth. . . . No pious and sober man can hold all men devoid of conscience to God except himself. In all religions, sects, and consciences, the sons of men are more or less zealous and precise, though it be in falsehood. . . . Let it be granted that a soul is corrupted with a false religion, and that that false religion, like leaven, in time has corrupted the state. Yet first, that state or land is none else but a part of the world, and if so . . . it is but natural, and so lies (as the whole world does) in wickedness. And so, as a state or part of the world, [it] cannot but alter from one false way or path to another (upon this supposition as before, that no whole state, kingdom, city, or town is Christian in the New Testament). Secondly, grant this state to be so corrupted or altered from one corrupt religion to another, yet that state may [for] many ages enjoy civil peace and worldly prosperity, as all history and experience testifies. Thirdly, that idolatry may be rooted out, and another idolatrous religion of the conqueror (as in the Roman and other conquests) brought in, or the religion may be changed something to the better by the coming of new princes to the crown, as we see in Henry VIII, King Edward, and Queen Elizabeth in our own nation and of late times. Lastly, a soul or souls thus leavened may be reduced by repentance, as often it pleases God so to work. . . .

Peace. How grievous is this language of Master Cotton, as if he had been nourished in the chapels and cloisters of persecuting prelates and priests, the Scribes and Pharisees? As if he never had heard of Jesus Christ in truth and meekness. For surely (as the Discusser observed) Christ Jesus never appointed the civil sword an antidote or remedy in such a case, notwithstanding Master Cotton replies that the civil sword was appointed a remedy in this case by Moses, not Christ (Deut. 13).

Truth. Moses in the Old Testament was Christ's servant, yet Moses being but a servant dispensed his power by carnal rites and ceremonies, laws, rewards, and punishments in that holy nation and that one land of Canaan. But when the Lord Jesus the Son and Lord himself was come, to bring the truth, life, and substance of all those shadows, to break down the partition-wall between Jew and Gentile, and to establish the Christian worship and kingdom in all nations of the world, Master Cotton will never prove from any of the books and institutions of the New Testament that to those spiritual remedies appointed by Christ Jesus against spiritual maladies, he added the help of the carnal sword. . . .

Civil Magistrates Rightly Defend Freedom of Religion, but Not Religion Itself

Truth. I grant [that] the civil magistrate is bound to countenance the true ministers of Christ Jesus, to encourage, protect, and defend them from injuries. But to send them armed (as the pope's legates and priests) with a sword of steel, and to compel people to hear and obey them, this savors more of the spirit of the pope, his courses and practices, yea of Muhammad his musclemen [and] dirges, than the Lamb of God and his followers. . . .

Peace. Next, Master Cotton demands what reason can be given why the magistrate ought to break the teeth of lions ([that is,] ought to suppress such as offer civil violence) and not of the wolves that make havoc of their souls, who are more mischievous than the lion, as the pope of Rome [is more dangerous] than the pagan emperors? He wonders [why] the Discusser should favor the pope more than the emperor, except it be that he [identifies]²³ with the Antichrist rather than with Caesar.

Truth. . . . The civil state and magistrate are merely and essentially civil, and therefore cannot reach (without transgressing the bounds of civility) to judge in matters spiritual, which are of another sphere and nature then civility is. Now it is most just and proper that if any member of a *civil* body be oppressed, the body should relieve it, as also it is just and proper that the *spiritual* state or body should relieve the soul of any in that spiritual combination oppressed. . . .

Peace. It is (indeed) one thing to prohibit the pope, the prelates, the Presbyterians, the Independents, or any [others] from forcing any in the matters of their respective consciences, and accordingly to take the sword from such men's hands or (as their executioners) to refuse to use it for them. It is another thing to leave them freely to their own consciences to defend themselves as well as they can by the two-edged sword of the Spirit, which is the Word of God. . . .

Truth. The renowned Parliament of England has justly deserved a crown of honor to all people for breaking the teeth of the oppressing bishops and

23. Originally "symbolizes."

their courts. But to wring the sword out of the hands of a few prelates and to willingly suffer it to be wrung by their own hands by many thousand Presbyterians or Independents, what is [that] but to change one wolf or lion for another, or instead of one, to let loose the dens of thousands?

Peace. But why should Matter Cotton insinuate the Discusser to glance a more obsequious eye upon the pope than upon the emperor?

Truth. I fear Master Cotton would create some evil opinion in the heart of the civil magistrate, that the Discusser is (as the bloody Jews told Pilate) no friend to Caesar. Whereas upon a due search it will be found clear as the light that it is impossible that any that subscribe *ex animo* to the bloody tenent of persecution can *(ex animo)* be a friend to magistracy. The reason is [that] all persecutors, whether priests or people, care only for such magistrates as suit . . . the great bloody end of persecution, [from] whom they either hope to borrow the sword or whom they hope to make their executioners. Their very principles also lead them necessarily to depose and kill their heretical, apostate, blaspheming magistrates.

Peace. But why should Master Cotton insinuate any affection in the Discusser to that tyrant of all earthly tyrants, the pope?

Truth. To my knowledge, Master Cotton and others have thought the Discusser too zealous *against* the bloody Beast. Yea, and who knows not this to be the ground of so much sorrowful difference between Master Cotton and the Discusser, that the Discusser grounds his separation from their churches upon their not separating from that man of sin? For Old England, having compelled all to church, compelled the Papists and the pope himself in them. The daughter New England, separating from her mother in old England, yet maintains and practices communion with the parishes of the old. Who sees not then but by the links of this mystical chain, New England churches are still fastened to the pope himself?

Spiritual Faithfulness and Civil Loyalty

Peace. Master Cotton's third reply is this, that it is not like such Christians who grow false and disloyal to their God will be faithful to their prince, and therefore consequently the civil magistrate must see that the church degenerate and apostate not, at least so far as to provoke Christ to depart from them.

Truth. This is indeed the downright most bloody and popish tenent of persecuting the degenerate, heretical, and apostate people, of deposing—yea, and killing—apostate and heretical princes and rulers! The truth is [that] the great gods of this world are god-belly, god-peace, god-wealth, god-honor, and god-pleasure. These gods must not be blasphemed, that is, [no] evil spoken of [them], no, not provoked. The servants of the living God, being true to their Lord and Master, have opposed his glory, greatness, and honor to these gods and to such religions, worships, and services as commonly are made but as a mask or veil . . . of these gods.

Peace. If this be the touchstone of all obedience, will it not be the cut-throat of all civil relations, unions, and covenants between princes and peoples, and between the people and people? For may not Master Cotton also say [that a certain person] will not be a faithful servant, nor she a faithful wife, nor he a faithful husband, who grows false and disloyal to their God? And indeed, what . . . has this truly ranting doctrine . . . wrought but confusion and combustion all the world over?

Truth. Concerning faithfulness, it is most true that godliness is profitable for all things, all estates, all relations. Yet there is a civil faithfulness, obedience, honesty, [and] chastity even amongst such as own not God nor Christ, else Abraham and Isaac dealt foolishly to make leagues with ungodly princes. Besides, the whole Scripture commands a continuance in all relations of government, marriage, [and] service, notwithstanding that the grace of Christ had appeared to some and the rest (it may be a husband, a wife, a magistrate, a master, [or] a servant) were false and disloyal in their several kinds and ways [before] God, or wholly ignorant of him. . . .

Can the sword of steel or arm of flesh make men faithful or loyal to God? [Does God care] for the outward loyalty or faithfulness, when the inward man is false and treacherous? Or is there not more danger (in all matters of trust in this world) from a hypocrite, a dissembler, a turncoat to his religion (from the fear or favor of men) than from a resolved Jew, Turk, or Papist who holds firm to his principles? Or lastly, if one magistrate, king, or Parliament calls this or that heresy [or] apostasy, and makes men say so, will not a stronger magistrate, king, Parliament, [or] army . . . call that heresy and apostasy Truth and Christianity, and make men call it so? And do not all experiences (and our own most lamentable in the changes of our English religions) confirm this?

As carnal policy ever falls into the pit, it digs and trips up its own heels. So I shall end this passage with two paradoxes, and yet (dear Peace) you and I have found them most lamentably true in all ages. . . . First, then, the straining of men's consciences by civil power is so far from making men faithful to God or man that it is the ready way to render a man false to both! My ground is this, [that] civil and corporal punishment do usually cause men to play the hypocrite, and dissemble in their religion, to turn and return with the tide, as all experience in the nations of the world does testify now. The binding and rebinding of conscience, contrary [to] or without its own persuasion, so weakens and defiles it that it (as all other faculties) loses its strength, and the very nature of a common honest conscience. Hence it is that even our own histories testify that where the civil sword and carnal power have made a change upon the consciences of men, those consciences have been given up, not only to spiritual but even to corporal filthiness, and bloody and mad oppressing each other (as in the Marian bloody times).

Peace. Indeed, no people [are] so enforced as the Papists and the Mahumetans, and no people more filthy in soul and body, and no people in the world more bloody and persecuting. But I listen for your second paradox.

Truth. Secondly, this tenent of the magistrates, keeping the church from apostatizing by practicing civil force upon the consciences of men, is so far from preserving pure religion that it is a mighty bulwark or barricade to keep out all true religion (yea, and all godly magistrates) from ever coming into the world.

Peace. Doubtless this will seem a hard riddle, yet I presume not too hard for the fingers of time and truth to untie, and render easy.

Truth. Thus I untie it: if the civil magistrate must keep the church pure, then all the people of the cities, nations, and kingdoms of the world must do the same and much more, for primarily and fundamentally *they* are the civil magistrate: Now the world . . . lies . . . in wickedness, and consequently according to its disposition endures not the light of Christ nor his golden candlestick the true church, nor easily chooses a true Christian to be her officer or magistrate, for she . . . suspects their faithfulness.

Peace. Hence indeed is it (as I now conceive) that so rarely this world admits or not long continues a true servant of God in any place of trust and credit, except [by] some extraordinary [overpowering] hand of God, or [except] his servants by some base stairs of flattery or worldly compliance ascend the chair of civil power. . . .

The Spiritual "Sword," Not the Civil Sword, the Proper Tool for Conversion

Truth. It is not the magistrates' work and office in the civil state to convert the heart in true repentance to God and Christ. The civil state respects conformity and obedience to civil laws, though indeed the works and office of the ministers of Christ Jesus are commonly laid upon the magistrates' shoulders and they, pretending themselves the ministers of Christ Jesus armed with the two-edged sword of the Spirit of God (the Word of God), do commonly fly to and put more confidence in the sword of steel in the hand of their civil ministers, the magistrates.

Peace. The sword of steel has done wonderful things throughout the whole world in matters of religion![24] Woeful and wonderful . . . have been the religious changes [in] the English nation, and that by the power of the civil sword, backward and forward, and that in the space of a few years, in the reign of four or five princes! But this (says Master Cotton) is no more than befell the church of Judah in the days of Ahaz, Hezekiah, Manasseh, and Josiah.

Truth. England's changes will be found upon examination incomparably greater . . . than the changes of the church of Judah were. And yet this instance will not infringe [on the point], that the civil sword of the magistrate . . . is ordinarily able to turn about a nation . . . to and from a truth of God, in national hypocrisy. And therefore most wisely has the Most Holy and Only Wise . . . abolished his own national and state church, whether explicit or implicit, that the two-edged sword of the Word of the Lord in the mouths of his true messengers might alone be brandished and magnified. . . .

The Lord Jesus, commanding [us] to give God the things that be God's, and to Caesar the things that be Caesar's, gives all his followers a clear and glorious torch of light to distinguish between offenders against God in a spiritual way and offenders against Caesar, his laws, state, and government in a civil way.

It is true, flatterers and time-servers used to make religion and justice the two pillars of a state, and so indeed do all such states in the world as maintain a state religion, invented and maintained in civil policy to maintain a civil state. But all men that have tasted of history or travel are sufficient wit-

---

24. Here Williams means "wonderful" as a negative, as in an awesomely bad occurrence.

nesses to these two particulars: first concerning justice, that if the sword and balances of justice . . . be not drawn and held forth against scandalous offenders against [the] civil state, that civil state must dissolve little by little from civility to barbarism, a wilderness of life and manners.

Peace. Yea, the very barbarians and pagans of the world themselves are forced, for their holding and hanging together in barbarous companies, to use the ties and knots and bands of a kind of civil justice against scandalous offenders against their commonwealth and profit.

Truth. But too many thousands of cities and states in the world have and do flourish, for many generations and ages of men, wherein (whatever Caesar gets) God cannot get one penny of his due in any bare permission or toleration of his religion and worship.

Peace. Dear Truth, these two points being so constantly proved, I can but wonder that Master Cotton, or any servant of Christ Jesus, should cry out to the Caesars of this world to help the eternal God to get his due, because Christ Jesus grants them a civil sword in civil cases to preserve their civil states from barbarism and confusion.

Truth. That worthy emperor, Antoninus Pius, in his letters for the Christians, plainly tells the governors of his provinces that the gods were able to punish those that sinned against their worship—evidently declaring, by that light of conscience and knowledge which God had lighted up in his soul, the vast difference between offenders in the civil state and offenders against the true and only religion and worship, about which the whole world disagrees. . . .

Peace. Ah, dear Truth, is there is no balm in Gilead, no balances, no sword of spiritual justice in the city and kingdom of Christ Jesus, but that the officers thereof must run to borrow Caesar's? Are the armories of the true King Solomon, Christ Jesus, disarmed? Are there no spiritual swords girded upon the thighs of those valiant ones that should guard his heavenly bed, except the sword of steel be run for from the cutler's shop? Is the religion of Christ Jesus so poor and so weak and feeble grown, so cowardly and base . . . that neither soldiers nor commanders in Christ's army have any courage or skill to sufficiently withstand in all points a false teacher, a false prophet, a spiritual cheater or deceiver?

Truth. This must all that follow Jesus bitterly lament, that not a spiritual sword or spear is to be found in the spiritual Israel of God. . . .

Peace. Now whereas it was added that a civil sword hardens the followers

of false teachers in the suffering of their leaders, and begets an impression of
the falsehood of that religion which cannot uphold itself all the world over
but with such instruments of violence, Master Cotton replies that the magistrate ought not to draw out his sword against seducers until he has used all
good means for conviction. [But] he then says he should be cruel to Christ's
lambs in sparing the foxes.

Truth. Who knows not this to be the plea and practice of all popish persecutors in all ages, to compass sea and land to reduce the heretic to the union
and bosom of the church, not only with promises [and] threats but oftimes
with solemn disputations, . . . before they come to the definitive sentence
and deliver him to the secular power, and so to the use of those desperate
remedies of hanging [and] burning? How do the bloody popes and the
bloody Bonners,[25] in their hypocritical letters and bloody sentences, profess
their lamentable grief at errors and heresies, their clemency and mercy and
great pains taken to reduce that wandering, to return the lost child, to heal
the scabbed sheep? Yea, and when they are forced—as they say, for the saving of the flock from infection—to deliver such sheep to the secular power
as their butchers and executioners, yet beseech they that power in the bowels
of Christ Jesus to minister justice with moderation (and that most hypocritically without shame), that if it be possible, the heretic's soul may be
saved. . . .

Peace. Master Cotton will here blame the alleged of this: for the popish religion is false, but theirs [is] true.

Truth. It is true the Papists' religion is false, yet Master Cotton cannot pass
without suspicion to be too near of kin to the bloody Papist, to whom they
are so near in practice! The Lord Jesus gave an everlasting rule to his poor
servants, to discern all false prophets by their fruits and bloody practices.
But . . . the Holy Spirit of God, in 2 Timothy now insisted on,[26] not only
commands Timothy to exhort the opposite, but patiently to wait and attend
God's will, if peradventure God will give repentance, that they may recover
themselves.

Peace. Master Cotton will not deny, together with meek exhortation, patient waiting.

---

25. Cardinal Edmund Bonner (1500–1569) was a Catholic bishop and an enemy to the Puritans
under Queen Mary.
26. 2 Timothy 2:24–26.

Truth. Why then does he limit the Holy One of Israel to days or months? Three months was by the law (in Massachusetts in New England) the time of patience to the excommunicate, before the secular power was to deal with him! But we find no time limited, nor no direction given to Timothy or his successors to prosecute the opposite before Caesar's bar, in case God vouchsafed not repentance upon their means and waiting. Christ Jesus has not been without bowels of compassion in all his gracious care and provision he has made for his sheep and lambs, against the spiritual wolves and foxes, although we read not a word of the arm of flesh and sword of steel appointed by himself for their defense in his most blessed last will and Testament.

Lastly, to that instance of the Donatists and Papists suppressed by the civil sword, no question but [that] a civil sword is able . . . to make a whole nation . . . of hypocrites. And yet experience also testifies (however Master Cotton makes it but accidental) that it is the common and ordinary effect of the civil sword drawn forth (as they say) against heretics [and] seducers to harden the seducers and seduced by their sufferings, and to beget no other opinion in their hearts than of the cruelty and weakness of the heart and cause of their persecutors. . . .

"True" Religion Cannot Justify Persecution, for Everyone Thinks Their Religion True

Peace. Touching the edict of Antonius Pius concerning persecution of Christians, and the opinion it begat in their hearts of the cruelty of their persecutors, Master Cotton answers first [that] the pagan religion is not of God, but the religion of Christians came down from heaven in the Gospel truth.

Truth. This is most true to him that believes that there is but one God, one Lord, one Spirit, one baptism, [and] one body according to Christ Jesus his institution; and that . . . all other gods, lords, spirits, faiths, baptisms, or churches are false. But what is this to many millions of men and women in so many kingdoms, nations, cities, and parts of the world who believe [just] as confidently their lies of many gods and christs, all [of] which they believe (as the Ephesians of their Diana, and . . . as Master Cotton of the way of his religion) come down from heaven?

Peace. Doubtless according to their belief all the peoples of those nations, kingdoms, and countries wherein the name of Christ is sounded, whether of the Greek church or the Latin, whether of popish or Protestant profession, will say as Master Cotton, "my religion came down from heaven in the Gospel of Truth."

Truth. Now then, either the sword of steel must decide this controversy (according to the bloody tenent of persecution) in the suppressing of heretics, blasphemers, idolaters, and seducers by the strength of an arm of flesh, or else the two-edged sword of the Spirit of God, the Word of God coming out of the mouth of Christ Jesus in the mouths of his servants, which will either humble and subdue the rebels, or cut most deep and kill with an eternal vengeance. . . .

Truth. What true reason of justice, peace, or common safety of the whole can be rendered to the world [to explain] why Master Cotton's conscience and ministry must be maintained by the sword more than the consciences and ministries of his other fellow-subjects? Why should he be accounted . . . at the bar of civil justice a soul-savior, and all other ministers of other religions and consciences soul-murderers, and so be executed as murderers or forced to temper or turn from their religion, which is but hypocrisy in religion against their conscience, which is ten thousand times worse, and renders men, when they sin against their conscience, not only hypocrites but atheists, and so fit for the practice of any evil murders, adulteries, [and] treasons? . . .

Agreement in Religion Not Necessary to Make Good Citizens

Peace. . . . [Master Cotton] confesses . . . that those wolves of which Paul warns the elders at Ephesus were mystical and spiritual wolves, yet he adds that such cannot be good subjects, loving neighbors, [and] fair dealers because they spiritually are not such. . . .[27]

Truth. I desire that this reply be well pondered, for it will be found dangerously destructive to the very roots of all civil relations, converse, and dealings—yea, and any civil being of the world itself! For if none be peaceable subjects, loving neighbors, [or] fair dealers but such [as are] of Master Cotton's conscience and religion (which he conceives to be the only true religion), what will become of all other states, governments, cities, towns, peoples, families, [and] neighbors upon the face of the earth? I say, what will be-

27. The reference is to Acts 20.

come of them (especially if power were in Master Cotton's hand to deal with them as wolves)?

Peace. Alas, too frequent experience tells us, in all parts of the world, that many thousands are far more peaceable subjects, more loving and helpful neighbors, and more true and fair dealers in civil conversation than many who account themselves to be the only religious people in the world. . . .

Truth. Hence was it . . . from such misapplied Scriptures in their churches (for commonly where state religions are set up, the magistrate is but the ministers' cane, through whom the clergy speaks) that in their solemn civil General Court, at the banishment of one poor man among them hunted out [as] a wolf (or heretic), the governor who then was, standing up, alleged for a ground of their duty to drive away such by banishment that famous charge of Christ Jesus to his ministers and church at Rome (Rom. 16:17): mark them that cause divisions contrary to the doctrine which you have received, and avoid (that is, by banishment).[28] By all [of] which and more it may be found how Satan has abused their godly minds and apprehensions in causing them so to abuse the holy writings of truth and Testament of Christ Jesus, and that however they deny it in express terms, yet by most impregnable consequence and implication they make up a kind of national church, and (as the phrase is) a Christian state and government of church and commonwealth, that is, of Christ and the world together. . . .

Truth. Why, was not the state of England, [and] the kings and queens and parliaments thereof, lawful as kings and states, though overwhelmed . . . with the Romish abominations? If such wolves, whores, and witches could yield no civil obedience, could they then exercise (by the same argument) any civil authority? And shall we then conclude all the former popish kings and parliaments (and consequently, laws) unlawful, because in spiritual things they were as wolves, tearing and burning the poor sheep of Christ? Will it not then be unlawful for any man that is persuaded [that] the whole nation where he lives is idolatrous [and] spiritually whorish, I say [will it not be] unlawful for him to live in such a state, although he might with freedom to his own conscience? [Where] will such kind of arguing drive at last, but to pluck up the roots of all states and peoples in the world as not capable of

28. Williams is, of course, referring to his own trial and banishment, during which John Haynes was governor.

yielding civil obedience or exercising civil authority, except such people . . .
are of Master Cotton's church and religion.

Peace. Methinks experience (were there no Scripture nor reason) might
tell us how peaceable and just neighbors and dealers many thousands and
millions of Jews, Turks, Antichristians, and pagans are to be found, notwithstanding their spiritual whoredoms [and] witchcrafts. . . .

Cotton's Defense of Religious Persecution Resembles the Spanish Inquisition

Truth. I have here in this discourse shown with what honorable and tender respect every civil magistrate is bound to honor and tender Christ Jesus
in his Christian sheep and shepherds, but that it is against Christianity for
the civil magistrate or civil state to imagine that all a whole nation was or
ever will be called to the union of God's Spirit in communion with God in
Christ. Also, it is against civil justice for the civil state or officers thereof to
deal so partially in matters of God as to permit to some the freedom of their
consciences and worships but to curb and suppress the consciences and
souls of all others of their free-born people. . . .

Peace. . . . Master Cotton [argues that] it is no Spanish Inquisition to preserve the sheep of Christ from the ravening of the wolves, but rather the
practice of the Discusser promotes the principal end of the Spanish Inquisition, to advance the Romish tyranny, idolatry, and apostasy by proclaiming
impunity to their whorish and wolfish emissaries.

Truth. If the nations of the world must judge (as they must, by Master
Cotton's doctrine) who are Christ's sheep and who are wolves, which is a
whore (spiritually) and which the true spouse of Christ, and accordingly
persecute the whores and wolves, this then they must do according to their
conscience, or else (as Master Cotton [says] elsewhere) they must suspend
What is this but either to set up a Spanish Inquisition in all territories, or
else to hand up all matters of religion (by this suspension he speaks of) until
the civil states of the world become Christian and godly and able to judge
And what is this in effect but to practice the very thing which he charges on
the Discusser, that is, a proclaiming an impunity all the world over, except
only in some very few and rare places where some few godly magistrate
may be found rightly informed, that is, according to [Master Cotton's] conscience and religion?

Peace. Yea, further (which I cannot without great horror observe) what is this but to give a woeful occasion at least to all magistrates in the world (who will not suspend their bloody hands from persecuting until Master Cotton shall absolve them from their suspension, and declare them godly and informed and fit to draw their swords in matters of religion) . . . to persecute (as most commonly they have ever done and do) Christ himself, the Son of God in his poor saints and servants.

Truth. Yea, if Master Cotton and [the] friends of his conscience should be cast by God's providence . . . under the reach of opposite swords, will they not produce Master Cotton's own bloody tenent and doctrine to warrant them (according to their consciences) to deal with him as a wolf, an idolater, a heretic, and as dangerous an emissary and seducer as any whom Master Cotton so accounts?

But lastly, Master Cotton has no reason to charge the Discusser with an indulgence or partiality toward Romish and wolfish emissaries, his judgment and practice is known [to be] so far different, that for departing too far from them (as is pretended) he suffers the brands and bears the marks of one of Christ's poor persecuted heretics to this day. All that he pleaded for is an impartial liberty to their consciences in worshipping God, as well as to the consciences and worships of their other fellow subjects. . . .

Catholics Can Distinguish between Religious Deference to the Pope and Civil Obligation

Truth. . . . King James, concerning the Oath of Allegiance (which he tendered to the Papists, and which so many Papists took), professed that he desired only to be secured for civil obedience, [and] to my understanding did as much as say that he believed that a Papist might yield civil obedience, as they did in taking this oath as quiet and peaceable subjects, some of them being employed in places of trust, both in his and in Queen Elizabeth's days. [For] though it be a popish tenent that the pope may so do,[29] and though Bellarmine[30] and others have maintained such bloody tenents, yet it is no general tenent of all Papists, and it is well known that a famous popish king-

---

29. That is, order Catholics to disobey Protestant civil leaders.

30. Robert Bellarmine (1542–1621) was a Jesuit theologian (later canonized) who engaged in a battle of letters with King James I in 1608 over the question of Catholic loyalty to both pope and secular monarch.

dom, the whole kingdom of France assembled in Parliament in the year
1610, condemned to the fire the book of Johannes Marianus for maintaining
that very tenent. And two months after, Bellarmine's book itself was condemned to the fire also by the same Parliament for the same detestable doctrine (as the Parliament called it), as tending to destroy the higher powers
which God has ordained, stirring up the subjects against their princes, absolving them from their obedience, stirring them up to attempt against their
persons and to disturb the common peace and quiet. . . .

Peace. This passage being so late and so famous in so near a popish country, I wonder how Mr. Cotton could chain up all Papists in an impossibility
of yielding civil obedience, when a whole popish kingdom breaks and abhors the chains of such bloody and unpeaceable doctrines and practices.

Truth. Experience has proved [it] possible for men to hold other main
and fundamental doctrines of that religion and yet renounce the authority
of the pope, as all of England did under King Henry VIII. . . . But grant the
English Catholics maintain the supreme authority of the pope, even in England, it must be considered and declared how far. If so far as to own his
power of absolving [citizens] from obedience, . . . the wisdom of the state
knows how to secure itself against such persons. But if only as head of the
church in spiritual matters, and they give assurance for civil obedience, why
should their consciences more then others be oppressed? . . . What is [it]
that has rendered the Papists so enraged and desperate in England [and] Ireland, what is it that has so embittered and exasperated their minds, but the
laws against their consciences and worships?

. . . Against the fear of evil practices the wisdom of the state may securely
provide, by just cautions and provisos [such as] subscribing the civil engagement, yielding up their arms . . . , being noted (as the Jews are in some parts)
by some distinction of or on their garments, or otherwise according to the
wisdom of the state. And without such . . . sufficient cautions given, it is not
civil justice to permit justly suspected persons, dangerous to the civil peace
to abide out of places of security and safe restraint.

Peace. If such a course were steered with consciences of that religion, yet
there are some weighty objections concerning the body of the people. First
there will always be danger of tumults and uproars between the Papists and
the Protestants.

Truth. Sweet Peace, . . . it is too fully and lamentably true that the congregations or churches of the several sorts . . . as (in whole or in part) separate

from the parish worship and worshippers are far more odious to, and do more exasperate a thousand times, the parish assemblies than the Papists or Catholics themselves are or do. So that if the people were let loose to take their choice of exercising violence and fury either upon a Popish or a Separatist Protestant assembly, it is clear from the greater corrivalry and competition made by the Protestants that separate . . . [that] the rage of the people would mount up incomparably fiercer against the one than the other. Hence it was [that] the Papists found ever more favor with the last two kings and their bishops than the so-called Puritans did. . . .

Enforced Religious Conformity Is "Soul Rape"

Truth. . . . The forcing of a woman, that is, the violent action of uncleanness upon her body against her will, we count a rape. By proportion, that is a spiritual or soul rape which [forces] . . . the conscience of any person to acts of worship. . . . This forcing of conscience was in a high measure the branded sin of that great typical Machiavellian, Jeroboam, who made Israel to worship before the golden calves. . . . Indeed, what is this before the flaming eyes of Christ, but as . . . some lustful ravisher deals with a beautiful woman, first using all subtle arguments and gentle persuasions to allure to their spiritual lust and filthiness, and where the conscience freely cannot yield to such lust and folly . . . then a forcing it by penalties, penal laws, and statutes? . . . What is it to force a Papist to church but a rape, a soul rape? He comes to church, that is, comes to that worship which his conscience tells him is false, and this to save his estate [and] credit. What is this in a Papist, but a yielding unwillingly to be forced and ravished? Take an instance of holy Cranmer[31] and many other faithful witnesses of the truth of Jesus, who being forced or ravished by terror of death, subscribed, abjured, [and] went to Mass, but yet against their wills and consciences. In both these instances of Papist and Protestant, Mr. Cotton must confess a soul ravishment, for the conscience of a Papist is not convinced that it is his duty to worship God by the English common prayer-book or directory. And the consciences of many are not convinced but that it is their sin to come to either the Papists' or

---

31. Archbishop Thomas Cranmer (1489–1556) was the chief architect of the English Reformation under Henry VIII and Edward VI; he was martyred in the return to Catholicism during Queen Mary's reign.

common Protestants' worship. So both Papist and Protestant are forced and ravished by force of arms (as a woman by a lustful ravisher) against their souls and consciences. . . .

In holy Scripture are many expressions of holiness, gravity, love, [and] meekness [that] are yet wrested by us poor men to unholy and unchristian ends and purposes. How many woefully pervert grave and heavenly passages and expressions of holy Scripture to base and filthy feasting? How many take from some sharp expressions of Christ Jesus and Paul license to rail and call men all to naught, in wrath, revenge, and passion? And how many, trampling upon the heads and consciences of all men out of pride and false zeal, are ready (not in a holy meek and Christian way but in a Pharisaical, bishop-like, and pope-like way) to roar and thunder out against God's meekest servants the odious terms "heretics," "schismatics," "blasphemers," [and] "seducers"—terms which, though used in holy Scripture, yet never [used] in such a way as commonly and constantly the bloody and persecuting express themselves in. . . .

Denial of Public Benefits or Office as Much Persecution as Imprisonment

Truth. Mr. Cotton indeed agrees . . . in general . . . that the Gospel is not to be propagated by sword, but in particulars he affirms [that] the blasphemer, the idolater, the heretic, [and] the seducer [are] to be persecuted. In general he says the magistrate may not constrain any to believe and profess the truth, yet in particulars thus far he says a man may be constrained by the magistrates' withdrawing countenance and favor, encouragement and employment from him—which [by] affirming, what else does he affirm but that he may be constrained, deposed, punished, that is, persecuted?

Peace. Indeed such kind of punishment as to displace men, to keep them out from all offices or places of trust and credit because of difference of conscience, may prove in the particular a greater affliction and punishment [than] a censure, a fine, imprisonment, yea sometimes more bitter to some spirits then death itself. . . .

Truth. Yes, and there is a moral virtue, a moral fidelity, ability, and honesty which other men (beside church members) are, by good nature and education, by good laws and good examples, nourished and trained up in—[so] that civil places of trust and credit need not be monopolized into the hands of church members (who sometimes are not fitted for them), and all others deprived and despoiled of their natural and civil rights and liberties.

Peace. But what say you (dear Truth) to Mr. Cotton's apology for New England . . . ? He says he does not know of any constraint upon any to come to church [or] to pay church duties, and says it is not so in his town.

Truth. If Mr. Cotton be forgetful, surely he can hardly be ignorant of the laws and penalties extant in New England that are (or, if repealed, have been) against [those who] absent themselves from morning and evening church, and for non-payment of church duties, although [they be not] members. For freedom of not paying in his town, it is to their commendation and God's praise, who has showed him and others more of his holy truth. Yet who can be ignorant of the assessments upon all in other towns, of the many suits and sentences in courts for non-payment of church duties, even against such as are not church members, of the motions and pleadings of some (not the meanest) of their ministers for tithes? And however for my part I believe Mr. Cotton ingeniously willing that none be forced expressly to pay to his maintenance, yet I question whether he would work if he were not well paid. And I could relate also what is commonly reported abroad, that the rich merchants and people of Boston would never give so freely if they were forced, yet now they are forced to give for shame (I take it) in the public congregation. . . .

The State of Religious Freedom in New England

Peace. Concerning Tertullian's speech, and especially that branch that ["by the law of natural equity, men are not to be compelled to any religion, but permitted to believe or not believe at all"], Mr. Cotton answers that they do permit the Indians [to practice their religion privately] but it will not therefore be safe to tolerate the public worship of devils or idols. The Discusser replied that they do permit the Indians in their paganish worship, and therefore were partial to their countrymen [in their application of religious intolerance]. Mr. Cotton answers that is not true, [for] they do so permit the Indians [only] whatever they may do privately. . . . And [as] for their countrymen, for the most part they worship God with them, [while] they [who] are distant have liberty of public prayer and preaching by such as [they] themselves choose without disturbance. . . .

Truth. I answer, it is one thing to connive at a strange Papist in private devotions on shore or in their vessels at anchor. [It is] another thing to permit Papists, Jews, and Turks the free and constant exercise of their religion and worship, in their respective orders and assemblies, were such inhabitants amongst them.

Peace. Doubtless the bloody tenent cannot permit this liberty, to neither the Papists, the Jews, the Turks, [nor] the Indians, nor does their practice toward their countrymen hold forth a show of such a freedom or permission.

Truth. I wonder why Mr. Cotton writes that the most part of the English [people] worship God with them, and the absent rest have liberty to choose their preachers! Since Mr. Cotton knows the petitions that have been presented for liberty of conscience in New England, and he cannot but also know the imprisoning and fining of some of the petitioners.

Peace. It may be [that] Mr. Cotton will use the common objection that some part of their petition tended to disturbance in civil things.

Truth. Some of their petitions were purely for liberty of conscience, which some in office (both in church and state) favored (as is reported), if not promoted. If others of some part of them might be judged offensive against laws made, yet why then has not the liberty of their conscience (in points of worship) been granted to them? [Why were they denied liberty] when they complained . . . that they have been forced to stay the baptizing of other men's children while their own might not be admitted, and therefore earnestly sued for ministers and congregations after their own free choice and consciences, which have ever been denied to them?

Peace. It is said that their ministers, being consulted with, utterly denied to yield to any such liberty.

Truth. They might justly fear that if such a window were opened . . . , the New England congregations and churches would be as thin as the Presbyterians complained theirs to have been, when the people once began to taste the freedom and liberty of their consciences from the slave's whip. . . .

The Apostate Church and God's Faithful "Witnesses"

Peace. What sound and modest reason can be . . . pretended why the holy ordinances, appointments, and provisions of the Lord Jesus . . . should be so weak in suppressing the enemies of his kingdom, that all the counsel, order, and power he has left in his absence are not able to resist the infection of false doctrine without the help of the powers of the world (his professed enemy) . . . ? Oh, what should be the mystery, that the two-edged sword of God's mighty Spirit is sufficient for conviction, for conversion, mortification, expiation, [and] salvation, but yet not powerful enough against infection?

Truth. The clergy . . . in all ages since the Apostasy have (like some proud and dainty servants) disdained to serve a poor [and] despised Christ, a carpenter, one that came at last to the gallows. And therefore have they ever framed to themselves rich and lordly, pompous and princely, temporal and worldly christs, instead of the true Lord Jesus Christ, the spiritual King of his saints and people. And however it suits well the common end to retain the name of Christ . . . , yet most sure it will be found that a temporal crown and dignity, sword and authority, wealth and prosperity is the white that most of those called scholars, ministers, [or] bishops aim and level at. . . .

Peace. It is objected [that] the temporal church of the Jews was assisted and protected with a temporal sword.

Truth. The Spirit of God tells us (Heb. 8 and 10) of a worldly sanctuary of a weak and old vanishing covenant, that is, a national covenant and ordinances of a Jewish church.

Peace. It is again said, "how can the Discusser extol the sword of the Spirit only, [but] acknowledge no churches?"[32]

Truth. Although the Discusser cannot to his soul's satisfaction conclude any of the various and several sorts of churches extant to be those pure golden candlesticks framed after the first pattern (Rev. 12:20), yet does he acknowledge [that there are] golden candlesticks of Christ Jesus extant—those golden olive trees and candlesticks, his martyrs or witnesses standing before the Lord and testifying his holy truth during all the reign of the Beast (Rev. 11:4). Hence, although we have not satisfaction that Luther or Calvin, or other precious witnesses of Christ Jesus, erected churches or ministries after the first pattern . . . , yet does he affirm them to have been prophets and witnesses against the Beast, furnished sufficiently with spiritual fire in their mouths, mightily able to consume or humble their enemies, as Elijah did with the captains sent out against him (2 Kings 1:10). . . .

Truth. Search his will and Testament and we find no other but spiritual

---

32. A reference to Williams's infamous dissatisfaction with the purity, and therefore the legitimacy, of any organized church.

means prescribed and bequeathed by the Lord Jesus to Paul, to Peter, or to any of the holy apostles or messengers.

Peace. I must acknowledge that the poor servants of Christ, for some hundreds of years after the departure of the Lord, enjoyed no other power, no other sword or shield, but spiritual, until it pleased the Lord to try his children with liberty and ease under Constantine (a sorer trial than befell them in three hundred years of persecution). Under [that] temporal protection, munificence, and bounty of Constantine, together with his temporal sword drawn out against her spiritual enemies, the church of Christ soon surfeited[33] on the too much honey of worldly ease, authority, profit, and pleasure. . . .

The Church in New England a "State Church"

Peace. But what think you of his confidence . . . that the Discusser will never be able to make [the argument] that the church in New England is implicitly a national and state church?

Truth. His own words seem to prove it, for if it be *a* church and not *churches* of New England . . . , it can be no other but a national [church], as the English, Scotch, and French churches [are]. . . . The several plantations or colonies of one religion or way of worship make up one colony or province of Englishmen in this part or tract of America. I cannot therefore properly call the church of New England a national church, but a provincial church [or] a state church cast in the mold of a national church, [divided][34] into so many parishes not expressly and explicitly, but implicitly and secretly. . . . The nature of a particular church of Christ is to be one, two, or three (more or less) in towns or cities . . . , but the nature of the state church is when the whole state is turned into a state church in so many parishes or divisions of worshippers, and it is made odious and intolerable for any part of this city [or] state not to attend the common worship of the city, sanctify the holy times, and contribute to the holy officers, but instead to walk in another way. [This] is the general state and practice of New England.

That is a national and state church where the civil power is continued the head thereof, to see to the conforming or reforming of the church, the truth

33. Meaning "overindulged."
34. Originally "distinct."

or falsehood of the churches, ministries . . . , ordinances, [and] doctrine. In the particular churches of Christ Jesus, we find not a tittle of the power of the civil magistrate or civil sword in spiritual cases. But it is impossible but that . . . a civil or temporal church [be] subject to the changes of a changeable court or country, and the interpretations and expoundings of Scripture to what the court or country is subject to approve or disapprove of. It is a national or state church where the . . . pretended heretic, blasphemer, or seducer is some way or another punished [by] or put forth from the state or country itself, by death or banishment. Whereas particular churches put forth no further than from their particular societies, and the heretics [and the like] may still live in the country . . . unmolested by them.

That church cannot be otherwise than a national or state church where the maintenance of the worship, priests, and officers is a state maintenance, provided by the care and power of the state, who . . . pays their ministers or servants their wages. Whereas the maintenance of the worship and officers of a particular church we find (by Christ's testament) to be cared for sufficiently by Christ's power, and means [within] the church. . . .

If Mr. Cotton can disprove the truth and substance of these and other particulars alleged . . . , the Discusser must acknowledge his error. But if Mr. Cotton cannot, as I believe he cannot (whatever flourish a wit may pretend), [may] the God of mercy pardon what Mr. Cotton has done in ignorance, and awaken him and others who cause his people to go astray. . . .

Peace. O, that all God's sheep in New England and such as judge themselves their shepherds may truly judge themselves at the tribunal of their own consciences in the presence of the Lord, in the upright examination of these particulars! . . .

Cotton Deceives Himself in Claiming That New England Does Not Persecute Conscience

Peace. It is untrue, says Mr. Cotton, that we restrain men from worship according to conscience, or constrain them to worship against conscience, or that such is my tenent or practice.

Truth. Notwithstanding Mr. Cotton's cloak, that is, that they will not meddle with the heretic before he has sinned against his own conscience, and so persecute him only for sinning against his own conscience, yet I earnestly beseech every reader to ponder seriously the whole stream and series of Mr. Cotton's discourse, propositions, [and] affirmations through the whole book, and he shall then be able to judge whether it be untrue that this doctrine tends to [neither] constrain nor restrain conscience. For the matter of fact, how can he, with any humility before the flaming eyes of the Most High, cry out [that they engage in] no such practice when, first, their laws cry out a command under penalty for all to come to church ([even if they be not] members) . . . , and a cruel law is yet extant against Christ Jesus, muffled up under the hood or veil of a law against Anabaptism?[35] Secondly, their practice—their imprisonments, finings, whippings, banishments—cry in the ears of the Lord of Hosts, and the louder because of such unchristian fig leaves [and] cloaks.[36]

Peace. Let it be granted, says Mr. Cotton, that we did both, yet this did not make laws to bind conscience, but [to bind] the outward man only! Nor would we think it fit (says he) to bind the outward man against conscience.

Truth. I cannot discern the coherence of these three affirmations: 1. We restrain no man from worship according to conscience; 2. We make laws but to bind the outward man only; and yet again 3. we think [it] not meet to bind the outward man against conscience. Mr. Cotton lived once under popish law, [required] to wear a fool's coat or surplice on his back and to make conjuring crosses with his fingers; why should he say that [those] laws went beyond his back and his fingers? Oh, let not Mr. Cotton put so far off the bowels of compassion toward Christ Jesus and his followers, yea toward all men, as to bind their backs, their necks, their knees, and their hands . . . to or from worship, and yet say he [only] binds the outward man!

Yea, and let not such uprightness, candor, and integrity as Mr. Cotton has been noted for be blemished with such an evasion as this, that when it comes to himself, his own conscience or his friends, . . . then he shall fly to his third evasion, saying, "We think it not meet to bind the outward man against conscience"—[by which he means] "against our consciences, whatever becomes (sink or swim) of other men's. . . ."

35. Contrary to Cotton's denials, it was a matter of record in the Massachusetts Bay Colony that failure to attend church could result in a fine and the persistent public objection to infant baptism (one of the fundamental tenets of the Anabaptist communities) could result in banishment from the colony.

36. That is, louder because of their attempts to cover up their sins with theological justification.

Laws That "Bind" Conscience

Peace. In the next passage Mr. Cotton (though with another heart, yet) in the language and tongue of the Pharisees seems to take part with the prophets against the persecuting fathers, and among many things he prohibits magistrates this one, that they must not make laws to bind conscience.

Truth. What is a law, but a binding word, a commandment? What is a law to bind conscience, but a commandment that calls for obedience? And must we raise up such tumults, such tragedies, and fill the face of the world with streams of blood about the Christian magistrates reforming religion, establishing religion, killing the heretic, blasphemer, idolater, seducer, and yet all this without a law, that may in the name of Christ exact obedience?

Peace. I wonder what we shall think of those laws and statutes of Parliament in old or New England that have bound the people's consciences, at least so far as to come to the parish church, improving (as Mr. Cotton says) the power and authority over their bodies for their souls' good? What shall we call all those laws, commandments, statutes, injunctions, directions, and orders that concern religion and conscience?

Truth. The plain truth is [that] Mr. Cotton's former reforming zeal cannot be so utterly extinguished as to forget the name and notion of Christian liberty, although in this bloody discourse he has well nigh (if not wholly) sold away the thing! The conscience (says he) must not be bound to a ceremony (to a pretended indifferent ceremony), and yet throughout this discourse he pleads for the binding of it from these and these doctrines, from these and these worships, and binding to this or that worship—I mean, to come to the public town or country worship! Just for all the world, as if a woman should not be bound to make a curtsy or salutation to such a man, but yet she should be bound . . . to come to his bed at his pleasure. Worship is a true or false bed (Cant. 1:16). . . . Confounding the nature of civil and moral goodness with religious is as far from goodness as darkness is from light. . . .

Peace. In the next place Master Cotton denies to compel to the truth by penalties, but only by withdrawing such favors as are comely and safe for such persons.

Truth. I have formerly answered . . . that a great load may be made up by parcels and particulars as well as by one mass or bulk. The backs of some men, especially merchants, may be broken [just as well] by withdrawing from them some civil privileges and rights which are their due as by afflicting them in their purses or flesh upon their backs. Christ Jesus was of another opinion . . . , that it is not lawful to deprive Caesar the civil magistrate, nor any that belong to him, of their civil and earthly rights. I say in this respect that even though a man is not godly, a sincere Christian or church member, yet to deprive him of any civil right or privilege due to him as a man, a subject, a citizen, is to take from Caesar that which is Caesar's, which God endures not, though it be given to himself.[37]

Peace. Experience oftentimes tells us that however the stream of just privileges and rights has (out of carnal policy) been stopped by God's people, when they have got the staff into their hands (in diverse lands and countries) yet has that stream ever returned, to the greater calamity and trial of God's people.

Truth. But (thirdly) it has been noted that even in New England penalties by law have been set to force all to come to church, which will appear upon a due search to be nothing else but an outward profession of force and violence for that doctrine which they suppose is the truth.

Peace. Concerning coming to church, we tolerate (says Master Cotton) Indians, Presbyterians, Antinomians, and Anabaptists, and compel none to come to church against their conscience, and none are restrained from hearing even in England.

Truth. Compelling to come to church is apparent whether with or against their conscience—let every man look to it! The toleration of Indians is against professed principles, and against the stream of all [Cotton's] present dispute. . . . It is true [that] this toleration is a duty from God, but [it is] a sin in them because they profess it their duty to suppress idolatry [and] blasphemy. . . .

Peace. But is there any such and professed toleration of Presbyterians Antinomians, [and] Anabaptists as is here insinuated?

Truth. I know of no toleration of Presbyterians, Antinomians, [and] Anabaptists worshipping God in any meetings separate from the common assemblies. . . . Communion is twofold: first, open and professed among church members, secondly, secret and implicit in all such as give their presence to such worship without witnessing against them. For otherwise how can a Papist satisfy the law compelling him to come to church, or a Protestant satisfy a popish law in popish countries but by this cloak or covering

37. Mark 12:17.

hiding and saving themselves by bodily presence at worship, though their heart be far from it.

Peace. Whereas it was said that conscionable Papists and all Protestants have suffered upon this ground, especially of refusing to come to each others' church or meeting, Mr. Cotton replies that they have suffered upon other points. . . .

Truth. It is true, many have suffered upon other points, but upon due examination it will appear that the great and most universal trial has been, amongst both Papists and Protestants, about coming to church, and . . . of countenancing what they believe false by their presence and appearance.

Believing Your Religion to Be Right Does Not Justify Forcing It on Others

Peace. Mr. Cotton in the next passage, being charged with partial dealing and a double weight and measure (one for himself and another for others), in effect answers that it is a true and just complaint against persecution and persecutors, but not against them, for they are righteous and not apostates, seducers, heretics, idolaters, [and] blasphemers.

Truth.[38] What does Master Cotton answer but what all religions, sects, and several sorts of worshippers in the world . . . plead: we are righteous!

Peace. Yea, the very Turks and Mahumetans challenge to themselves true faith in God, yea, whether Jews, Antichristians or Christians, they all call themselves . . . right believers.

Truth. It is not so great wonder, then, if the popish and Protestant sects and ministers of worship cry out (as men used to do in suits of law and pretenses to the crown), "We are righteous, my title is good, and the best! We are holy, we are orthodox and godly! You must spare us, believe us, honor us, feed us, protect and defend us in peace and quietness! Others are heretics, apostates, seducers, idolaters, blasphemers! Starve them! Imprison them! Banish them! Yea, hang them, burn them with fire and sword, pursue them!" . . .

---

38. The Caldwell manuscript identifies the speaker here as Peace, but the sequence of the conversation, not to mention the substance of the comment, suggests that this is a misprint.

The Civil Sword Is Never Used Properly for Christ When Used to Persecute Conscience

Truth. Yea, it is most woefully found evident that the best religion . . . , yea, the most holy and pure and only true religion and worship appointed by God himself, is a torment to that soul and conscience that is forced, against its own free love and choice, to embrace and observe it. And therefore whether the religion be good or naught (as Mr. Cotton here distinguishes) there ought to be no forcing, but the soul and mind and conscience of man—that is, indeed, *the man*—ought to be left free. . . .

Peace. But what say you to his unmerciful conclusion, [in the face of] the bloodshed and destruction of so many thousands and millions formerly and lately slain . . . by this bloody tenent of persecution—yea, the late and lamentable streams of English blood, the blood of our neighbors, friends, brothers, [and] parents poured forth by these late . . . bishops' wars? Mr. Cotton's conclusion is that the revealed will of God . . . is fulfilled in their just execution, whether they belong to God or not!

Truth. I wish Mr. Cotton more mercy from God and a more merciful mind towards the afflicted, and I say as the Lord Jesus said in the case of offense: Great offenses, national offenses will come for religion's sake, for national religion's sake, but woe to those that bear the guilt of so many thousand slaughters, murders, ravishings, [and] plunderings! The pope, the bishops, the Presbyterians, [and] the Independents, so far as they have been authors or actors in these horrible calamities out of the persuasion of the bloody tenent of persecution for religion and conscience—the voice of so many rivers of blood cry to heaven for vengeance against them!

Peace. But may not (blessed Truth) the sword of civil power which is from God (Rom. 13:4) be drawn and drunk with blood for Christ's sake? What say you to (among the many examples of religious wars) the most famous battles of Constantine against the bloody persecutor Maxentius? Was not Constantine Christ's champion, as once that valiant Scanderbeg called himself against the bloody Turks?[39]

---

39. Scanderbeg (ca. 1404–1468) was an Albanian national hero who, though raised in the Muslim faith as a captive of the Ottoman Empire, renounced Islam and returned to defend his homeland when the Ottomans attempted to invade Albania in 1443. In his struggle against the Ottomans, Scanderbeg allied himself with the Roman papacy, going so far as to enlist in the brief and ill-fated crusade called by Pope Pius II in 1463.

Truth. Sweet Peace, the sword of civil power was God's sword, committed by God's most wise providence into the hands of that famous Constantine; doubtless his war was righteous and pious insofar as he broke the jaws of the oppressing, persecuting lions that devoured Christ's tender lambs and sheep. And famous was his Christian edict . . . when he put forth that imperial Christian decree, that no man's conscience should be forced, and for his religion (whether to the Roman gods or the Christian) no man should be persecuted or hunted. When Constantine broke the bounds of this his own and God's edict and drew the sword of civil power in the suppressing of other consciences for the establishing of the Christian, then began the great mystery of the church's sleep, the gardens of Christ's churches turned into the wilderness of national religion, and the world (under Constantine's dominion) to the most unchristian Christendom. . . .

Why should Mr. Cotton couple murderers and adulterers with apostates and seducers? Does not even the natural conscience and reason of all men put a difference? Do not even the bloodiest popes and cardinals, Gardiners and Bonners, put a difference between the crimes of murder, treason, [and] adultery (for which, although the offender repent, yet he suffers punishment) and the crimes of heresy [and] blasphemy (which, upon recantation and confession, are frequently remitted)? . . .

A Proper Typological Reading of the Old Testament
Offers No Moral Support for Persecution

Peace. It is true, says Mr. Cotton, what the Discusser says, that Christ Jesus gave no ordinance, precept, or precedent in the Gospel for killing men for religion, and no more (says he) for the breach of civil justice. Civil magistrates therefore must either walk without rule or fetch their rules of righteousness from Moses and the prophets, who have expounded him in the Old Testament.

Truth. If Mr. Cotton pleases more awfully to observe and weigh the mind of Christ Jesus [in] his New Testament in this point, he will not only hear him subscribing to Caesar's right in civil matters, but also his servant Peter establishing all other forms of civil government which the peoples or nations of the world shall invent or create for the civil being, commonwealth, or welfare. Yea, he may remember that Christ Jesus by his servant Paul commanded the magistrate to punish murder, theft, and adultery, for he expressly named these civil transgressions together with the civil sword, the avenger of them (Rom. 13). . . .

Peace. I cannot well conceive what Mr. Cotton means by saying that Moses and the prophets expounded Christ Jesus in the Old Testament.

Truth. Nor I. They did speak or prophesy of Christ, they did type or figure him to come with his sufferings and glory, but (as John says) grace and truth came by Jesus Christ, that is, the fulfilling, opening, and expounding came by Jesus Christ. . . .

Peace. But . . . (says Mr. Cotton) here was no type nor figure for actions of *moral justice;* though sometimes extraordinary yet they are never figurative, [except] with such as turn all the Scriptures into an allegory.

Truth. To make the shadows of the Old Testament and the substance or body of the New all one is to confound and mingle heaven and earth together, for the state of the law was ceremonial and figurative. . . . And I believe that it might not only be said that Abraham's lying with his handmaid Hagar was an allegory, but that the whole church of Israel, root and branch, from first to last included figurative and allegorical kernels, were the husks and shells disclosed with more humbly and spiritual teeth and fingers.

Peace. I cannot but assent to you, that to render the Old Testament allegorical in a humble sobriety, your instance with many more gives sufficient warrant.

Truth. Yet I add (in answer to Mr. Cotton's charge of turning all Scripture into an allegory) that to deny the history of either Old or New Testament, or to render the New Testament (which expounds and fulfills the ancient figures) allegorical, are both absurd and impious.

Peace. But how (says Mr. Cotton) can an act of moral righteousness be figurative?

Truth. There is a fallacy in this term ["moral righteousness"], for Mr. Cotton himself has acknowledged a two-fold righteousness: a spiritual righteousness of the church, and a civil [righteousness] of the commonwealth. Mr. Cotton also acknowledges Israel to be a typical people, their land a typical land, their ministry and worship typical! How can Mr. Cotton then deny but that the weapons of this people, their punishments and rewards, . . . were figurative and ceremonial also? And so not parts of moral civil righteousness, or common to all other nations and peoples in the world. . . .

The Danger of Punishing Persons for "Sinning against Conscience"

Truth. . . . Let Mr. Cotton's conclusions in the beginning of this book be remembered, wherein he maintains that a man of erroneous and blind conscience in fundamental and weighty points, and persisting in the error of his way, is not persecuted for cause of conscience but for sinning against his conscience. Whence it follows that the civil courts of the world must judge whether the matter be fundamental and weighty, whether the party has been rightly once and twice admonished, and whether he persists in the error of his way (that is, whether he be obstinate after such admonition) and must then be persecuted—though . . . not for cause of conscience, but for sinning against his conscience. . . .

Let Mr. Cotton then please to understand . . . that his bloody tenent is a bitter root of many bitter branches, not only bitter to spiritual tastes, but even to the taste of civility and humanity itself. . . .

The Father of Lights has of late been graciously pleased to open the eyes of not a few of his servants to see that Mr. Cotton's distinction [of not persecuting a man for his conscience, but for sinning against his conscience] is but a fig leaf to hide the nakedness of that bloody tenent, for the civil court must then judge when a man sins against his conscience, or else [the magistrate] must take it from the clergy upon trust that the poor reputed heretic does so sin.

Peace. Mr. Cotton adds that it is aggravation of sin to hold or practice evil out of conscience.

Truth. True, but I also ask, does not that persecutor who hunts or persecutes a Turk, a Jew, a pagan, an Antichristian (under pretense that this pagan, this Turk, this Jew, [or] this Antichristian sins against his own conscience), does not this persecutor, I say, hold a greater error than any of the four, because he hardens such consciences in their errors by his persecution, and that also to the overthrowing of the civil and human society of the nations of the world in point of civil peace?

Peace. Well, dear Truth, you may enjoy your own holy and peaceable thoughts, but Mr. Cotton ends this chapter with hope that the reputed bloody tenent appears whited in the blood of the Lamb, and tends to save Christ's sheep from devouring, to defend Christ's truth and to maintain and preserve peace in church and commonwealth.

Truth. Sweet Peace, that which has in all ages poured out the precious blood of the Son of God, in the blood of his poor sheep, shall never be found whited (as Mr. Cotton insinuates) in the blood of this most heavenly Shepherd! That which has maintained the works of darkness [for] sixteen hundred years under the bloody Roman emperors and more bloody Roman popes has never tended to destroy, but build and fortify such hellish works. That which all experience since Christ's time has shown to be the great fire-brand or incendiary of the nations has poured out so many rivers of blood about religion, and that among the so-called Christian nations. That tenent, I say, will never be found [to be] a preserver but a bloody destroyer, both of spiritual and civil peace. . . .

Granting Catholics Religious Liberty to Be Preferred over Intolerance

Truth. There is a spiritual peace in the matters of Christ's kingdom and worship, and in the particular consciences and souls of his servants. There is a civil peace in the quiet enjoyment of each man's property, in the combination of towns, cities, [and] kingdoms. But neither of these will Mr. Cotton prove the Discusser proclaims to such Antichristians or enemies of Christ Jesus who persecute and oppress Jew or Gentile upon any civil or spiritual pretense. 'Tis true, the consciences and worships of all men [that are] peaceable in their way he affirms ought not to be molested, and though not approved yet permitted, and (although no spiritual, yet) a civil peace proclaimed to their outward man while peaceable in civil commerce. To persecutors he not only proclaims God's spiritual and eternal judgments, but temporal [judgments] also, and affirms that all persecutors of all sorts (and especially the bloody Whore of Rome, who has so long been drunk with the blood of the saints) ought by the civil sword to be restrained and punished as the destroyers of mankind and all civil and peaceable being in the world according to the height of their cruel and murderous oppressions.

Peace. But toleration of her, says Mr. Cotton, brings her in the back door and so we may come to drink deeply of the cup of the Lord's wrath and be filled with the cup of her plagues.

Truth. There are two opinions which have bewitched the nations professing the name of Christ: first, that a national church or state is of Christ's appointing, [and] second, that such a national church or state must be maintained pure by the power of the sword. While Mr. Cotton prays against the bewitching of the Whore's cup, O that the Father of Lights might graciously please to show him the depth of her witchcrafts and his own most woeful delusions in both these! In vain does Mr. Cotton fear partaking of her sins and plagues by a mere toleration of her worship in a civil state, while he forgets the three great causes of her downfall and desolation and partakes of any of them (Rev. 18)—that is, her worldly pomp and pleasure, her spiritual whoredoms and invented worships, and her cruelty and bloodshed, especially against the consciences of the saints or holy ones of Jesus. . . .

God's Moral Law Manifests Itself Differently in the Laws and Customs of Particular Societies

Truth. . . . Grant [that] Christ came not to destroy the moral law of the Ten Commandments . . . nor secondly the judicials of moral equity (that is, such as indeed concern life and manners, according to the nature and constitution of the several nations and peoples of the world).

Peace. Pardon me, dear Truth, but a word of explication before you proceed; your addition—according to the nature and constitution of the peoples and nations of the world—will not be allowed.

Truth. Without this I cannot allow of Moses his judicials to bind all nations of the world. . . . My reason is this: that people of Israel to which those judicial laws and punishments were prescribed was . . . a miraculous people or nation. . . . And therefore being a people of such miraculous considerations, means, and obligations, the breach of even moral laws concerning life and manners and civil estate might be more transcendently heinous and odious in them than in the other several nations and peoples of the world, many thousands and millions whereof never so much as heard of the name of the God of Israel.

Peace. If men see cause to ordain a court of chancery and erect a mercy seat to moderate the rigor of laws that cannot be justly executed without the moderate and equal consideration of persons and other circumstances, methinks that the Father of mercies (though he be Justice itself) cannot be justly imagined to carry all judicial or civil laws or sentences by one universal strictness through all the nations of the earth. . . . Dear Truth, the Scriptures are full and many arguments might be drawn out this way, but please you to pitch upon an instance whereby we may the sooner finish this digression.

Truth. Take that great case of the punishment of adultery. I confidently affirm that the conscience of the magistrate may out of faith execute other punishments besides stoning to death, which was the punishment of that sin in Israel. For although . . . that was the law of judgment in the Old Testament (and there is no other particularly expressed in the New), yet the conscience of the magistrate may know, first, that the carriage of the Lord Jesus about this case, when the question was precisely put to him, was extraordinary and strange. For . . . he condemns the sin, yet he neither confirms nor annuls this punishment, but leaves the question . . . and leaves the several nations of the world to their own several laws and agreements . . . , according to their several natures, dispositions, and constitutions, and their common peace and welfare. Second, the Lord Jesus approves of the several human ordinances . . . which the several peoples and nations of the world shall agree upon their common peace and subsistence. Hence are the several sorts of governments in the nations of the world which are not framed after Israel's pattern. And hence consequently the laws, rewards, and punishments of several nations vastly differ from those of Israel, which doubtless were unlawful for God's people to submit to, except Christ Jesus had (at least in general) approved such human ordinances . . . of men for their common peace and welfare.

Peace. Methinks Mr. Cotton and such as literally stick to the punishment of adultery, witchcraft, and [other crimes] by death must either deny the several governments of the world to be lawful (according to that of Peter) and that the nature and constitutions of peoples and nations are not to be respected, but all promiscuously forced to one common law, or else he must see cause to moderate this their tenent, which [otherwise] proves as bloody a tenent in civil affairs as persecution in religious affairs.

Truth. Yea, of what woeful consequence must this prove to the state of Holland and the Low-Countries, to the state of Venice, to the cantons of Switzerland, to our own dear state of England and others who have no king as Israel's last established government had. . . .

Peace. To end this passage upon the former grounds, methinks the conscience of a New England magistrate . . . may in faith execute any other punishment (according to established law) besides death upon adulterers. And the New England colonies may be exhorted to rectify their ways and to moderate such laws which cannot possibly put on the face of moral equity from Moses.

Truth. Your satisfaction, dear Peace, now presupposed, I proceed and grant . . . that Christ Jesus neither abrogated Moses' morals nor [his] judicials, yet who will deny that Moses established (besides the two former) a third, that is, laws merely figurative, typical, and ceremonial, proper and peculiar to that land and people of Israel? Those laws necessarily wrapped up that nation and people in a mixed constitution of spiritual and temporal, religious and civil, so that their governors of civil state were governors of the church, and the very land and people were by such governors to be compelled to observe a ceremonial purity and holiness. But Christ Jesus erected another commonwealth, the . . . Christian commonwealth or church, that is, not whole nations, but in every nation where he pleases his Christian congregation [to be]. . . .

Conclusion: The Bloody Tenent of Persecution

Truth. Dear Peace, our golden sand is out, we now must part with a holy kiss of heavenly peace and love. Mr. Cotton speaks and writes his conscience, yet the Father of Lights may please to show him that what he highly esteems as a tenent washed white in the Lamb's blood is yet more black and abominable in the most pure and jealous eye of God. . . . For myself, I must proclaim before the most holy God, angels, and men that whatever other white and heavenly tenents Mr. Cotton holds, yet this [one] is a soiled, black, and bloody tenent.

A tenent of high blasphemy against the God of peace, the God of order, who has of one blood made all mankind to dwell upon the face of the earth, now all confounded and destroyed in their civil beings and subsistence by mutual flames of war from their several respective religions and consciences.

A tenent warring against the Prince of Peace, Christ Jesus, denying his appearance and coming in the flesh to put an end to . . . the shadows of that ceremonial and typical Land of Canaan.

A tenent fighting against the sweet end of his coming, which was not to destroy men's lives for their religions, but to save them, by the meek and peaceable invitations and persuasions of his peaceable wisdom's maidens.

A tenent foully charging his wisdom, faithfulness, and love [with] so poorly providing such magistrates and civil powers all the world over as might effect so great a charge pretended to be committed to them.

A tenent lamentably guilty of his most precious blood, shed in the blood of so many hundred thousand of his poor servants by the civil powers of the world, pretending to suppress blasphemies, heresies, idolatries, and superstition.

A tenent fighting with the spirit of love, holiness, and meekness, by kindling fiery spirits of false zeal and fury, when yet such spirits know not of what spirit they are. . . .

A tenent against which the blessed souls under the altar cry loud for vengeance, this tenent having cut their throats, torn out their hearts, and poured forth their blood in all ages, as the only heretics and blasphemers in the world.

A tenent which no uncleanness, no adultery, incest, sodomy, or bestiality can equal, this ravishing and forcing (explicitly or implicitly) the very souls and consciences of all the nations and inhabitants of the world. A tenent that puts out the very eye of all true faith, which cannot but be as free and voluntary as any virgin in the world in refusing or embracing any spiritual offer or object.

A tenent loathsome and ugly in the eyes of the God of heaven, and serious sons of men—I say, loathsome with the palpable filth of gross dissimulation and hypocrisy. Thousands of peoples and whole nations compelled by this tenent to put on the foul vizard of religious hypocrisy for fear of laws, losses, and punishments, and for the keeping and hoping for of favor, liberty, [and] worldly commodity.

A tenent woefully guilty of hardening all false and deluded consciences (of whatsoever sect, faction, heresy, or idolatry . . .) by cruelties and violence practiced against them, all false teachers and their followers (ordinarily) contracting a . . . steely hardness from suffering for their consciences.

A tenent that shuts and bars out the gracious prophecies and promises and discoveries of the most glorious Son of Righteousness, Christ Jesus, that burns up the holy Scriptures and forbids them . . . to be read in English, or that any trial or search or (truly) free disquisition be made by them, when the most able, diligent, and conscionable readers must pluck forth their own eyes and be forced to read by the . . . clergy's spectacles.

A tenent that seals up the spiritual graves of all men, Jews and Gentiles, and consequently stands guilty of the damnation of all men, since no preachers nor trumpets of Christ himself may call them out but such as the several and respective nations of the world themselves allow of.

A tenent that fights against the common principles of all civility and the very civil being and combinations of men in nations [and] cities, by commixing (explicitly or implicitly) a spiritual and civil state together and so confounding and overthrowing the purity and strength of both.

A tenent that kindles the devouring flames of combustions and wars in most nations of the world, and (if God were not infinitely gracious) had almost ruined the English, French, Scotch, Irish, and many other nations. . . .

A tenent that bows down the backs and necks of all civil states and magistrates, kings and emperors, under the proud seat of that man and monster of sin and pride, the pope, and all popish and proud clergymen, rendering such laics and seculars (as they call them) but slavish executioners . . . of their most imperious synodical decrees and sentences.

A tenent that renders the highest civil magistrates and ministers of justice (the fathers and gods of their countries) either odious or lamentably grievous to the very best subjects, by either clapping or keeping on the iron yokes of cruelest oppression. No yoke or bondage [is] comparably so grievous as that upon the neck of men's religion and consciences.

A tenent, all sprinkled with the bloody murders, stabbings, poisonings, pistolings, [and] powder-plots against many famous kings, princes, and states, either actually performed or attempted, in France, England, Scotland, the Low-Countries, and other nations.

A tenent all red and bloody with those most barbarous and tiger-like massacres of so many thousand and ten thousands formerly in France, and other parts, and so lately and so horribly in Ireland—of which, whatever [other] causes be assigned, this chiefly will be found the true [cause], and while this continues (that is, violence against conscience) this bloody issue sooner or later must break forth again . . . in Ireland and other places, too.

A tenent that stunts the growth and flourishing of the most likely and most hopeful commonwealths and countries, while the best consciences and the best deserving subjects are forced to fly (by enforced or voluntary banishment) from their native countries, the lamentable proof whereof England has felt in the flight of so many worthy English into the Low Countries and New England, and from New England into Old again and other foreign parts.

A tenent whose gross partiality denies the principles of common justice, while men weigh out to the consciences of all others that which they judge not fit nor right to be weighed out to their own—since the persecutor's rule is to take and persecute all consciences, only he himself must not be touched.

A tenent that is but Machiavellian, and makes religion but a cloak or stalking horse to [the] policy and private ends of Jeroboam's crown and the priests' benefit.

A tenent that corrupts and spoils the very civil honesty and natural conscience of a nation, since conscience to God violated proves . . . ever after jaded . . . , loose and unconscionable in all converse with men.

Lastly, a tenent in England most unseasonable, as pouring oil upon those flames which the high wisdom of the Parliament, by easing the yokes on men's consciences, had begun to quench. . . .

Peace. . . . It gives me wonder that so many and so excellent eyes of God's servants should not espy so foul a monster, especially considering the universal opposition this tenent makes against God's glory and the good of all mankind.

Truth. There have been many foul opinions with which the old serpent has infected and bewitched the sons of men. . . . But this tenent is so universally opposite to God and man, so pernicious and destructive to both . . . that like the Powder-plot, it threatens to blow up all religion, all civility, all humanity—yea, the very being of the world and the nations thereof—at once. . . .[40]

Peace. He that is the father of lies and a murderer from the beginning knows this well, and this ugly Blackamore needs a mask or vizard. . . .[41] The dreadful righteous hand of God, the eternal and avenging God, is pulling off these masks and vizards, that thousands and the world may see this bloody tenent's beauty.

Truth. But see (my heavenly sister and true stranger in this sea-like restless, raging world) see here what fires and swords [have] come to part us! Well, our meetings in the heavens shall not thus be interrupted, our kisses thus distracted, and our eyes and cheeks thus wet, unwiped. For me, though censured, threatened, persecuted, I must profess while heaven and earth lasts that no one tenent that either London, England, or the world does harbor is so heretical, blasphemous, seditious, and dangerous to the corporal, to the spiritual, to the present, to the eternal good of all men, as the bloody tenent (however washed and whited), I say, as is the bloody tenent of persecution for cause of conscience.

40. A reference to the Gunpowder Plot of 1605, when English Catholic terrorists attempted to assassinate King James and members of Parliament by blowing up Westminster Palace during Parliament's opening session.

41. See note 11.

The Fourth Paper Presented by Major Butler

to the Honorable Committee of Parliament for the Propagating
[of] the Gospel of Christ Jesus

Early in 1652, during Williams's second return to London, the publication of a Socinian catechism in London disrupted the general spirit of religious tolera- tion that had followed the Independents to power. In reaction to the appearance of this heretical tract, the prominent Independent minister John Owen pro- tested to Parliament, which soon after appointed a small committee—known as the Committee for Propagating the Gospel—to consider proposals for strength- ening the cause of Christian religion in England. Owen and some allies from among the Independent ministry offered no fewer than fifteen such proposals, advising the committee to recommend a state-supported church that would ban non-Christian groups and extend toleration to dissenting Christian sects only under certain limits. Responding to the restrictions on religious liberty explicit in this petition, William Butler, a major in Cromwell's army, presented to the committee four counterproposals that rejected the idea of an established church and advocated wide toleration in matters of religion. Roger Williams found Butler's proposals to his liking, so much so that in March 1652 he republished them with commentary, along with a supporting letter from Christopher Goad and a copy of the original fifteen proposals from the Independent ministers. Williams's contribution to this debate, here preceded by his account of the pro- posals and counterproposals to which he was responding, provides a concise summary of his views on religious liberty.

The Humble Proposals of the Ministers who presented the petition to the Parliament [on] February 11 . . . for the furtherance and propagation of the Gospel in this nation, wherein they, having had equal respect for all persons fearing God, though of differing judgments, do hope also that they will tend to union and peace:

1. That persons of godliness and gifts in the universities and elsewhere, though not ordained, may be admitted to preach the Gospel, being approved when they are called thereunto.

2. That no person shall be admitted to trial and approbation[1] unless he bring a testimonial of his piety and soundness in the faith, under the hands of six godly ministers and Christians gathered together for that end and purpose, to whom he is personally known—of which number two at the least [are] to be ministers.

3. That a certain number of persons, ministers and others of eminence and known ability and godliness, be appointed to sit in every county to examine, judge, and approve all such persons as being to preach the Gospel, [having] received testimony as above. And in case there shall not be found a competent number of such persons in the same county, that others of one or more neighbor counties be adjoined to them.

4. That care be taken for the removing . . . of the ministers who are ignorant, scandalous, nonresident, or disturbers of the public peace, and of all schoolmasters who shall be found popish, scandalous, or disaffected to the government of the Commonwealth.

5. That to this end, a number of persons, ministers and others of eminent piety, zeal, faithfulness, ability, and prudence, be appointed by authority of Parliament to go through the nation, to inquire after, examine, judge of, and eject all such persons as shall be found unfit for the ministry or teaching of schools, being such as above described.

6. That for the expediting of this work, these persons may be assigned in several companies or committees, to the six circuits of the nation, to reside in each of the counties for such a convenient space of time as shall be requisite, until the work is done. And calling to their assistance in their respective circuits such godly and able ministers and others in each of the counties where they shall reside, to assist them in this work as they shall think fit.

---

1. That is, examination for the ministry.

7. That these persons so sent and commissioned may be empowered before they depart out of each county to return and to represent to Parliament the names of fit and sufficient persons, ministers and others to be appointed and approved of, such as shall be called to preach the Gospel in such counties. And in the meantime, the persons so commissioned as aforesaid shall have power while they reside in each county to examine, judge, and approve of such persons as having a call to preach the Gospel in such counties. . . .

8. That it be proposed that the Parliament be pleased to take some speedy and effectual course, either by empowering the persons in the several counties to be appointed for trial and approbation of such persons as shall be called to preach the Gospel there, or in such other way as they shall think fit, for the uniting and dividing of parishes in the several counties and cities within this Commonwealth, in reference to the preaching of the Gospel there, saving the civil rights and privileges of each parish.

9. That all ministers so sent forth and established be enjoined and required to attend the solemn worship of God in prayer, reading and preaching the Word, catechizing and expounding the Scriptures as occasions shall require, visiting the sick, and instructing from house to house, residing among the people to whom they are sent, and using all care and diligence by all ways and means to win souls to Christ.

10. That it is desired, that no persons be required to receive the Sacrament further then their light shall lead them to. Nor [should any] person sent forth to preach and already placed, or which shall be placed in any parish within this nation, be compelled to administer the Sacrament to any but such as he shall approve of as fit for the same.

11. That a law may be provided that all persons whatsoever within this nation be required to attend to the public preaching of the Gospel every Lord's Day, in places commonly allowed and usually called churches, except such persons as through scruple of conscience do abstain from those assemblies.

12. That whereas diverse persons are unsatisfied to come to the public places of hearing the Word, upon his account that those places were dedicated and consecrated, that the Parliament will be pleased to declare that such places are made use of and continued only for the better convenience of persons meeting for public worship of God and upon no other consideration.

13. That all persons dissenting from the doctrine and way of worship

owned by the state (or consenting to [it] and yet not having advantage or opportunity of some of the public meeting places commonly called churches) be required to meet (if they have any constant meetings) in places publicly known, and to give notice to some magistrate of their place of ordinary meetings.

14. That this Honorable Committee be desired to propose to the Parliament that such who do not receive but oppose those principles of Christian Religion without acknowledgement whereof the Scriptures do clearly and plainly affirm that salvation is not to be obtained (as those formerly complained of by the ministers), may not be suffered to preach or promulgate anything in opposition to such principles.[2]

15. And further, that the Parliament be humbly desired to take some speedy and effectual course for the utter suppressing of that abominable cheat of judicial astrology, whereby the minds of multitudes are corrupted and turned aside from depending upon the Providence of God, to put their trust in the lies of men and delusions of Satan.

Certain Proposals from the Scriptures, Humbly Presented to the Honorable Committee for the Propagating of the Gospel

Proposal 1: It is humbly proposed whether Jesus Christ, the Lord of the Harvest, does not send forth laborers into his vineyard, furnishing them by his Spirit and bearing witness to their labors, without the testimony and reward of men? (Matt. 9:38; Matt. 10:5–16; Acts 4:19–20; Eph. 4:11; 1 Cor. 12:3; Gal. 1:12; John 10:11; James 2:1)[3]

Proposal 2: It is humbly proposed whether it be not the will or counsel of God that there must be heresies, yea damnable heresies, that such who are approved may be made manifest? And whether it be not the pleasure of God that the judgment and condemnation of such false teachers and heretics be left to himself? (Matt. 13:24; Acts 5:34–40; 1 Cor. 11:19; 2 Peter 2:1; Jude 3, 4, 15; 2 Tim. 2:24–26; Luke 9:49–50)

---

2. Williams appended a note to this proposal: "Upon occasion of which motion, the ministers were desired to instance [that is, to give particular examples of the principles of religion to which they referred], who therefore presented fifteen Fundamentals, the copy whereof is not yet come to my hand."

3. The scripture references appended to each of the proposals were written out in Williams's original rendition.

Proposal 3: It is humbly proposed whether for the civil powers to assume a judgment in spirituals[4] be not against the liberties given by Christ Jesus to his people? (Rom. 14:4; 1 Cor. 7:23; Gal. 1:16; Heb. 11:6; 1 John 4:1; Rom. 14:23)

Proposal 4: Whether it be not the duty of the magistrate to permit the Jews, whose conversion we look for, to live freely and peaceably amongst us? (Rom. 2)

A Testimony to the Fourth Paper Presented by Major Butler to the Honorable Committee for Propagating the Gospel

It is my humble petition to the God of Heaven, to vouchsafe [on] that Honorable Committee [the] time and hearts to examine the Scriptures alleged in that Paper, and at present that they may please to weigh . . . this humble explication of the Four Proposals.

First, as to the first Head, viz. of Christ Jesus sending forth his own Messengers: I humbly pray it may be remembered that there is a twofold Ministry of Christ Jesus, 1. the one of Pastors and Teachers, feeding the flocks already Christian and converted; 2. the other of Messengers or Apostles, sent forth to convert and beget to Christ. Of this [latter] sort I humbly conceive is the sending now in debate before you, and of this sort is that sending and questioning so large and punctual (Rom. 10). How can they preach, except they be "apostlized," or sent? Upon which distinction I humbly offer three things to be necessarily supposed: first, apostolic gifts and abilities in the men sent; secondly, a greater spiritual power in the senders according to the rule, "Greater is the sender than the sent;" thirdly, it supposes an unconverted estate in the people to whom such Messengers are sent to preach and baptize. Which are three such knots that none that I know of professing Christ Jesus these many hundred years has been able to untie, and to prove such a ministry extant, otherwise than by some (seemingly) prudential inventions, or the power of the sword. Yet,

Secondly, Christ Jesus did immediately send forth his Messengers . . . first to the Jews (Matt. 10), afterwards to all nations (Matt. 16). Christ Jesus did immediately send forth by his Spirit, and mediately by the church at Antioch (Acts 13). He immediately stirred up Paul and Apollos, not only

---

4. That is, spiritual matters.

without civil but also without spiritual and church power. Yea, since the Apostasy and [the] rising of Antichrist, He has in all ages stirred up his Prophets to witness in poor and mournful sackcloth (Rev. 10, 11, and 14)— the Waldenses, the Wicklevists, the Hussites, the Lutherans, and the Calvinists, [for example].

These Protestant witnesses could never clear up their functions or ministries (as bishops or presbyters), yet doubtless has Christ Jesus endowed them with prophetical gifts of translating and expounding the Scriptures. I say, they were as prophets immediately stirred up by Christ Jesus, who doubtless now has stirred up more than ever were in this nation men of prophetical gifts and spirits—gentlemen, lawyers, physicians, soldiers, tradesmen—some adorned with human learning, others only with the Scriptures. And doubtless such is the faithfulness and love to his chosen, that he will yet stir up his witnesses and prophets, yea and in the time Apostles and Messengers, to the nations of the world, whose gifts, calling, work, and wages shall all be from Himself.

Lastly, as to those terms of testimony, or reward of men: I am far from obstructing any countenance or encouragement to any whom Christ Jesus stirs up. This only I say: 1. it seems to be an ungospel or unchristian task put upon the civil state, to grant licenses (as [do] the bishops) for preaching. 2. It is not hard to guess, that were it not for the magistrates' pay and sword, very few would be found to solicit his text or testimony. But doubtless such preachers who (either above or under board) make a bargain for so [and] so much, without which they will not be sent, I humbly conceive they can never be said to be sent by Christ Jesus, although all the civil powers in the world should subscribe to their commissions and sending.

To the second Head, of permitting false teacher and heretics: I am humbly confident that (from the Scriptures alleged) it will appear to be the will of God that Christians and Antichristians, the wheat and the tares, should be permitted to dwell, to trade, to live and die in the common field of the world together.[5] [Furthermore,] upon a due survey it will be found, that the Lord Jesus Christ himself (and his servants) have most commonly been accounted, and have suffered as, the greatest deceivers, seducers, heretics, and blasphemers in the world. . . .

---

5. The reference here is to Jesus' parable of the wheat and tares (Matthew 13), a favorite biblical appeal for Williams and others in the toleration debate. For more on Williams's interpretation of this parable, see the introduction to this volume.

To the third Head, concerning [the] civil magistrates' commission in spirituals, I humbly conceive:

1. That in these late years God has made it evident that all civil magistracy in the world is merely and essentially civil, and that the civil magistrate can truly take cognizance of nothing, as a civil magistrate, but what is proper and within his civil sphere. The magistrate, if a saint, has a spiritual power, [as] so have all saints; and he that partakes more of Christ's Spirit has more of Christ's power, whatever his outward condition be.[6]

2. By the last Will and Testament of Christ Jesus, we find not the least title of commission to the civil magistrate (as civil) to judge and act in the matters of his spiritual Kingdom.

3. That great pretence from the Land of Canaan, and the Kings of Israel and Judah, has been in these late years proved but weak and sandy, and the Lord Jesus Christ himself to be the Antitype of all those figures, the King and Head of all the Israel of God. . . .[7]

Hence, although it be the duty of kings, queens, [and] magistrates to be nursing fathers and mothers to the saints, although it be the saints' duty to pray for the magistrates, that they live peaceably under them in all godliness and honesty (Jer. 29 and 1 Tim. 2), yet suppose the magistrates be ever so ungodly, idolatrous, blasphemous, [and] bloody (as they were in the first three hundred years after Christ). Yet Christ Jesus failed not, nor will, to preserve his saints in the power and spirit of true Christianity and godliness. And contrarily, the saints never discovered so bright an image of Christ Jesus since, in those times wherein Constantine and so many after him have used and drawn their civil swords in spiritual causes.

Our Fathers before us in England, though famous for civil laws and wars and victories, yet have they but trod the round and walked in a circle—plant and pluck up, plant and pluck up—as we their children do, and all for want of commissions from Christ Jesus, and his instructions and promises in such a work. The Parliament established King Henry VIII as Head of the Church; this Supremacy has continued in four Protestant princes

---

6. Williams's point here is that a Christian magistrate's political authority and his religious status have nothing to do with each other. The Christian ruler may have as little or as much "spiritual power" in church affairs as any other Christian (dependent upon his personal piety), but that religious standing cannot increase or detract from his authority in civil matters.

7. A reference to the controversy—well played in *The Bloody Tenent* and its sequel—over whether or not to interpret typologically the biblical precedent of civil leaders with religious authority in ancient Israel. For more on this debate, see the introduction to this volume.

since.[8] Yet first, what disagreements about the title? For while the clergy have preached the *Jus Divinum*[9] of the princes [and] authority in spirituals after the pattern of the kings of Israel and Judah, the truth is that Parliaments and people since have pleased that princes could not receive but what the Parliaments gave them, and the Parliaments could not give them but what the people gave the Parliament, their representatives, which could not possibly be a spiritual and soul-power.

Secondly, the work has never prospered, but succeeding times, more enlightened by Christ Jesus, have still been breaking down and pulling up. For instance, the Protestant bishops with their English Common Prayer supplanted the popish bishops and their Latin Mass. The Presbyterians and Scotch directories, after some disputes, at last rout the Protestant bishops and their Common Prayers. Now the Parliament, being graciously pleased to remind[10] the Providence of the Most High in using instruments of various consciences in their late service, cannot but expect to be solicited by some of these consciences, and to be zealously told that Christian kings and magistrates succeed the kings of Israel and Judah in the power of establishing religion and reforming it, of defining doctrines (especially fundamentals), of punishing the contrary as heretics, of granting licenses and authority to preachers, of seeing their wages paid them—and therefore that they are bound, as they will answer to God, to Christ, to their own souls and the souls of others, to settle Religion [and] to establish something.

But, my humble prayer shall be to Him that is only wise, so to guide this renowned Parliament, that they may see and shun the rocks on which our fathers (as touching a state religion) both Papist and Protestant have made most woeful shipwreck. . . .

Hence, O that it would please the Father of Spirits to affect the heart of the Parliament with such a merciful sense of the soul-bars and yokes which our fathers have laid upon the neck of this nation, and at last to proclaim a true and absolute soul-freedom to all the people of the land impartially, so that no person be forced to pray nor pay otherwise then as his soul believes

---

8. That Williams slightly revises history to locate the power behind the Act of Supremacy principally with Parliament and not with Henry testifies to his political acumen. In other words, Williams knew how to appeal to the collective ego of his audience.

9. "Divine right," a reference to the political theory that argued that kings derive their authority from God as his vicegerents on earth, independent of popular consent.

10. That is, remember.

and consents. This act, as I believe it to be the absolute will of God as to this and all the oppressed nations of the world, so will this most prudent state find it to be a principal expedient [to] two great ends: first, the easing and sweetening [of] the minds of the people of this nation, who have so long cried out of burden; secondly, the preventing [of] all the clerical designs of one sort or another, when the whole people of the nation shall be engaged as one man to maintain that power that has from Heaven set them free from so great and so long continued slavery. Such a service for God and the nation cannot but be attended with many objections—as also [with] some merciful and humane consideration (at least for a season) [for] such of the clergy whom any town or people of the nation shall not freely close with in worship and maintenance—to all which the wisdom of the Most High is infinitely able to direct the Commonwealth's High Senate of Parliament, and doubtless will, if they humbly see their want and beg supply from him.

Upon the Scriptures, and the fourth Head, as touching the Jews: I humbly conceive it to be the duty of the civil magistrate to break down that superstitious wall of separation (as to civil things) between us Gentiles and the Jews, and freely (without their asking) to make way for their free and peaceable habitation amongst us. And the rather, because that People, however for a season under a most terrible eclipse, yet

1. The Holy Scripture says that they are a beloved people, and beloved (as we sometimes love unworthy children) for their Father's sake.

2. They are a people above all the peoples and nations in the world, under most gracious and express promises.

3. We Gentiles by their fall have had the occasion of our rising to the blessed and joyful knowledge of a Savior.

4. Their rising again to own and embrace Christ Jesus is promised to be as life from the dead, not only to themselves, but as to the propagating of Christ Jesus to other peoples.

5. Out of some kind of sense of these things, we pretend to look and long and pray for their return and calling.

6. As other nations, so this especially and the kings thereof have had just cause to fear, that the unchristian oppressions, incivilities, and inhumanities of this nation against the Jews have cried to Heaven against this nation and the kings and princes of it. What horrible oppressions and horrible slaughters have the Jews suffered from the kings and peoples of this nation, in the reigns of Henry II, John, Richard I, and Edward I, concerning which not

only we but also the Jews themselves keep chronicles? For the removing of which guilt and the pacifying of the wrath of the Most High against this nation, and for the furthering of that great end of propagating the Gospel of Christ Jesus, it is humbly conceived to be a great and weighty duty which lies upon this state, to provide (on the Jews' account) some gracious expedients for such holy and truly Christian ends.

Lastly, I humbly crave leave to say that I am not without thoughts of many objections, and cannot without horror think of the Jews' killing of the Lord Jesus, of their cursing themselves and their posterity; of the wrath of God upon them; of their denying the fundamentals of all our Christian worship; of some crimes alleged for which they have been so afflicted by this nation; of their known industry of enriching themselves in all places where they come. But I dare not prejudice the high wisdom and experience of the state, abundantly rich and able to provide answerable expedients, if once it please the Most High to affect their honorable breasts with the piety and equity, the duty and necessity of so great a work.

CHAPTER SEVEN

The Examiner Defended in a Fair and Sober Answer

to the Two and Twenty Questions
which lately examined the Author of *Zeal Examined*

In the onslaught of pamphleteering in England during the spring of 1652 appeared a defense of religious freedom entitled Zeal Examined. *The tract, published anonymously but likely written by Sir Henry Vane, was an attempt to counter the public perception of advocates of religious freedom as reckless "enthusiasts." Following quickly on the heels of its appearance was* The Examiner Examined, *an anonymous critique of* Zeal Examined *from one loyal to the idea of religious establishment.* The Examiner Examined *offered twenty-two objections to the points made in* Zeal Examined, *calling into question the logical and theological foundation for a principle of religious liberty. Because Vane was preoccupied with "Publike affairs," Williams took it upon himself to respond to each of these challenges in his own anonymously issued tract, published later that same year and entitled* The Examiner Defended. *In this treatise, Williams succinctly summarizes some of his most important biblical, logical, and empirical arguments against persecution and uniformity.*

. . . This ship of the commonwealth (like that gallant ship now going forth and so called) must share her weals and woes in common.[1] As the one, so the other has its dangers of rocks and sands, storms and tempests, want of

---

1. The preface to this treatise, in which Williams explains the circumstances for its writing and offers a dissertation on truth, is here omitted.

provisions, sickness and diseases, treacherous and professed enemies, fires, leaks, and mutinies. I humbly beg of God and wish to both their fair winds and weathers, plentiful provisions, unanimity and peace, preservations, victories, bon-voyages, and joyful anchoring in their desired ports and harbors. Such woes and weals are common to all that fail in either.

Now in a ship there is a whole and there is each private cabin. A private good engages our desires for the public and raises cares and fears for the due prevention of common evil. Hence it is that in a ship all agree (in their commanding orders and obeying stations) to give and take the word, to stand to the helm and compass, to the sails and tackling, to the guns and artillery. This is, this *must* be done in [each] artificial and in each civil ship and commonwealth. Hence, not to study, not to endeavor the common good, and to exempt ourselves from the sense of common evil is a treacherous baseness, a selfish monopoly, a kind of tyranny, and tends to the destruction both of cabin and ship, that is, of private and public safety.

I hope it will not therefore be offensive that into the great and common treasury I cast my mite and say [that] Christ's interest is the commonwealth's. Christ's interest in that sheet anchor[2] [with] which this ship has ridden and can only ride in safety. All power in heaven and earth is his. If England makes peace with him and allies with him, though every dust of the field were an army and every drop of the ocean sprung up a navy against us, yet our tranquility should not be shortened, our commonwealth, our Parliament, [and] our peace should flourish.

But where is that man whose case is not right? Where is the conscientious Papist or Prelatist or Presbyterian or Independent that assumes not thus? And (in some sense) I verily believe they all say true. . . . I know each sect is apt to plead, "My interest being Christ's, the purse and the sword of the state is not only mine, but it is Christ's due." But I also maintain that it is not true civility [and] not true Christianity that draws the sword for one or [the] other. Christ's interest in this commonwealth (or any) is the freedom of the souls of the people. I confess that all nations, all peoples, kings, princes, and judges ought to kiss the Son, to be nursing fathers and mothers to Christ Jesus and his followers. But what a dreadful mistake is this, that no people must live but Christians! That the many millions of millions in our own and other nations of the world must either at the shaking of a sword fall down

2. A sheet anchor was a large supplemental anchor that was intended for use in an emergency.

before Christ, or with the edge of it be cut off for idolaters, heretics, blasphemers (or evil speakers) against Christ and his religion! . . .

Who sees not this to be the design and the decree of heaven, to bring into the light and to breaks to pieces the . . . iron yokes and chains upon the souls and consciences of men? Who sees not with holy fear and wonder that this his decree has begun to break the arms and necks of all persecutors, both popish and Protestant? What eye so weak but may observe how little and how seldom it pleased the God of heaven to go out with our armies, until this interest of the Son of God (soul-freedom) began to be seen and served by our armies, and that they fought not for one sect or conscience, but . . . against tyranny and persecution of any conscience? Till then the balance turned not, and our armies could hardly be said to prosper, and I verily believe still shall, and the commonwealth of England and the Parliament thereof still flourish, till that fateful hour when they shall cease to break the yokes (the soul-yokes especially) and to the let the oppressed go free. . . .

Who but soul oppressors can be unwilling that men's consciences be free to see with their own eyes, and themselves to be judges of the path they choose, in which they hope to find eternal life and blessedness? Who but tyrants and oppressors can be grieved that the souls of men should choose whom to hear, what and with whom to pray, whom and how to pay and maintain according to the abilities and consciences? . . . Against many objections, I briefly oppose my answer to these two and twenty questions. . . .[3]

The sum of the first question: whether the civil magistrate who knows the doctrine of salvation be not bound as a nursing father to provide saving food for the people, and to provide that poison be kept from them?

I answer and ask, first, whether this prophesy of kings and queens being nursing fathers and nursing mothers to the saints be not (as many wise and godly take it) a peculiar prophesy and promise to that peculiar and distinct nation and people of God, the Jews, and whether these words—*I will lift up mine hand to the Gentiles* (Isaiah 49:22)—be not a character fixing this prophesy to that yet beloved people? And so consequently . . . all those bloody persecutors (Papists and Protestants) who have . . . [drawn] this shaft out of this quiver of Scripture, whereby to pierce the tender heart of Christ Jesus, yea, and all [who] give power to the civil magistrate in spiritu-

---

3. That is, the questions posed by the author of *The Examiner Examined* against the defense of religious liberty in *Zeal Examined*.

als from this Scripture, have . . . most ignorantly profaned this prophesy, and that to usurpation over the temple of God (the consciences of God's own people) and to bloody violence against their bodies, although under a cloak of providing wholesome food for their children and prohibiting poison. . . .

I ask whether the office of kings and queens be not (in the ship of all commonwealths in the world) merely and essentially civil, just as [is] the office of a captain or master of a ship at sea, who ought of all his passengers to be honored and respected, paid and rewarded for his service. But as to the consciences of the passengers—whether Jews, Turks, Persians, Pagans, Papists, [or] Protestants—whom he transports from port to port upon a civil account of payment and recompense, I ask whether he goes not beyond the sphere of his activity if he acts by any authority restraining them from their own worship, or constraining them to his? . . .

[I ask] whether kings and queens and other princes receive not all their power and authority from the several and respective peoples . . . ? Accordingly, . . . has [it] not been declared by the Parliament that the fountain and original of all authority and rule is the people, consenting and agreeing in their several combinations, by themselves or their deputies, for their better subsistence in peace? And consequently . . . have the nations and people of the world in their mere natural and national capacities any one jot of spiritual and divine power with which to entrust their magistrates and officers? And if, upon due weighing in the balance of the sanctuary, it be found that they have not, is not this challenging of spiritual power to judge and determine what is soul food and soul poison—I mean in a coercive way, binding all souls and the very souls of them that sent them, and who neither did nor could commit such power to them—is not this, I say, a soul rape and tyranny, and a mere policy of Satan, deceiving (too often) honest and zealous minds. . . ?

As to the matter of fact, do not all histories and all experience demonstrate that most of . . . those kings, queens, princes, and magistrates (popish and Protestant) that have pretended to this power of judging [between] saving food and poison have grossly mistaken the poison of Satan's inventions, superstitions, and will-worship for that wholesome and heavenly food pretended? And with bloody hands have [they] forced this poison down the throats of thousands and millions, or else forced and fired them out of the world with barbarous persecutions, if any have been enlightened by Christ Jesus to discern this poison and to refuse it. . . .

The sum of the fourth question: Whether the magistrate be not bound to love God and to advance his glory, true worship, and service, and the good of his people, with all his might?

I ask (as before) whether the magistrate, being the civil officer of the people, has any might, authority, or power but what the people commit to him? And whether any people will or can entrust such a power to the civil magistrate to compel their souls or consciences to his? Secondly, whether the Spirit of God speaks not expressly that the weapons of Christians are not sword and might, but the spirit, and whether his spiritual weapons (2 Cor. 10) be not sufficiently and abundantly able and mighty to bring down every stronghold and every high thing and every imagination and thought to the obedience of Jesus Christ? And whether any carnal might ever did or can effect [anything][4] in Christianity but the storming of the nations into an Antichristian hypocrisy and compliance?

Thirdly, [I ask] whether this principle of the magistrate putting forth his carnal might in spirituals has not constantly occasioned the magistrate (according to the mistakes of his own conscience) to promote superstition and idolatry, and also has rendered the strongest sword to be the measure and standard of all religion in the world . . . ?

Fourthly, I ask where Christ Jesus (the only lawgiver to Christians) has appointed, in his holy Testament, the civil sword [as] the judge and defender of his religion and worship? And why has he not furnished his civil magistrates of justice in the world with such hearts and spirits, but contrarily has called few of them to the profession of his name? And [I ask] whether he has not ever furnished . . . his spiritual ministers and messengers with spiritual might and power sufficiently and abundantly efficacious for the propagating of his holy name and truth, and for the confounding of Antichrist and Antichristians by the breath of his mouth, that two-edged sword of his Spirit?

Fifthly, [I ask] whether Christianity did ever so flourish as when the people of God, in the first three hundred years of Christ, had no might but that of Christ's spiritual weapons? And when it pleased God to raise up Constantine to give some rest to his people from persecution, whether Christianity did most flourish in the first time of Constantine when he, with his colleague Licinius, published the edict of freedom of religion to his

---

4. Originally "ought," by which Williams clearly meant "aught."

subjects, or in his aftertimes, when he compelled all the world to Christianity . . . ?

Lastly, I ask whether this principle of the magistrate employing the carnal sword or might in spirituals has not in all histories and experience been the firebrand that his kindled such devouring flames of war about religion, in . . . both popish and Protestant countries? And whether it did not kindle our late wars and occasion all the dreadful calamities between the bishops and the presbyters, which proved fatal to them both? And whether all these experiences are not the voice of God out of the whirlwind, to waken all the magistrates of the world to keep within the civil sphere of civil jurisdiction and dominion?

The sum of the fifth question: whether the people be not bound to pray for magistrates, that under them we may live a peaceable and quiet life in all godliness and honesty? And whether the magistrate is not bound to that for which the people pray? . . .

I ask whether in the present state and juncture of affairs in England, wherein . . . every sect, every order, and [every] conscience pleads the integrity and purity of their way, and the people of God themselves are so divided and differently persuaded as of late, . . . to blood and dreadful slaughters—I ask whether we may pray (without profaning of the holy name of God and the guilt of the breach of the civil peace of the nation) that God would send such magistrates who should authoritatively judge, whose conscience, whose worship, [and] whose godliness is true, and [who would] accordingly maintain that godliness, defend that faith, advance that worship and service of God . . . [and] prohibit by his carnal sword all other consciences, worships, and godliness as schismatic, heretical, seditious, and blasphemous? How much rather ought we to pray that it may please the most holy and only wise God to vouchsafe such a spirit of godliness and wisdom to the rulers of this commonwealth, that the civil rights may be preserved and civilities may flourish in righteousness and mercy, even in the midst of so much spiritual division and opposition, which are and must be greater and greater, in all nations of the world, when once the chains and yokes of implicit faith . . . are torn off . . . the souls and necks of the people. . . .

The sum of the thirteenth question: whether since idolatry was punished by the light of nature (as Job acknowledged, Job 31:28), the magistrate ought not much more to punish it in the Gospel's light? . . .

It is true, as Solomon said, [that] the spirit of a man is the candle of the Lord, searching all the inward parts of the belly. It is an excuser and an accuser, a secretary, a sergeant, an adversary, a judge, and [an] executioner within the bosom of mankind. But yet I ask how far this spirit of man, this candle of Jehovah, has searched and . . . possibly may search into all the inward parts of the belly or heart of man as touching this great mystery of true or false deities and their respective worships? . . . I ask if natural wisdom (that candle or light remaining in man) be not twofold: first, that which is common to all mankind in general, to the . . . lowest, the vulgar; secondly, that which is more noble and high, in degrees refined and elevated by finer animal spirits, by education, by study, by observation, [or] by experience. And I ask whether these lights and greatest candles can attain, by their utmost activity, to a true and saving Gospel knowledge, even of God himself? And therefore, whether the place of Romans 1—*They knew God*—can amount to [anything] more (even in the princes of natural knowledge, Plato, Seneca, and Aristotle) [than] a confession of a deity, a godhead above us, in us, about us; an invisible might power, creating, ruling, ordering all things; as also a conviction of blessedness in the favor of this deity and of cursedness in disunion from it?

But now let's descend to *cultus institutus* and *cultus naturalis,* an instituted and a natural worship. Come to the light of nature worshipping this deity. Come to the seven precepts of Noah, which . . . both Jews and other ancients talk of. And then I ask if it be not a downright doctrine of free will in depraved nature, if it be not to run point blank against all the histories of the nations and all present experience of mankind in all known parts of the world, to attribute so much light to any of the . . . sons of nature as to attain a spiritual and saving knowledge of God, to attain . . . the mystery of the Father and of the Son, God manifested in flesh, by whom creation and redemption are wrought, to the matter of true worship, or to anything but *Splendidum Peccatum* without the revelation of the Word and Spirit of God out of his absolutely free and peculiar grace and mercy in Christ Jesus?[5]

Hence I ask if from this corruption of nature it has not sprung that the

5. Williams here disputes the assumption of the questioner, that idolatry is condemned both by faith and by "natural conscience." True to his Calvinist roots, Williams draws a distinction between natural knowledge and saving knowledge. Natural knowledge refers to the capacity with which all human beings are created to exercise reason, to live morally (with the help of natural conscience), and to order society together. By contrast, true knowledge of God is only available to those blessed with faith in Jesus Christ (in other words, the elect). For more on the distinction between natural knowledge and knowledge for salvation, see John Calvin, *Institutes of the Christian Religion,* 2 vols., trans. Ford Lewis Battles, ed. John T. McNeill (Philadelphia: Westminster Press, 1960), Book II, chapter 2.

wisest nations, councils, and parliaments have run into such monstrous opinions about the gods and the number of them, and so many monstrous and horrible and . . . ridiculous kinds . . . of worship? Thus did the Chaldeans, the Egyptians, the Persians, the Greeks, the Romans, and all the generations and nations of men to this day. . . .

I readily acknowledge that . . . in all . . . cases wherein civility is wronged, in the bodies and goods of any, the civil sword is God's sword . . . for the suppressing of such practices and appearances, yea and the very principles of them, and for the encouragement and applause of the contrary. . . . But yet I ask whether Paul spoke [anything][6] in the first [chapter] of Romans of any human . . . judgment upon the nations of the world for their mere idolatries (thus most dreadfully plagued already by the most righteous Judge of the whole world) . . . ?[7] I ask further whether . . . seeming incivilities which the light of nature more fairly may condemn and hale before the civil tribunal, yet may not be such? [They may be] so circumstantiated with impressions from heaven that they ought not so suddenly and easily to be condemned and punished, but with a more tender and observant eye be distinguished. For . . . what shall be said to that very common and constant practice of circumcision, commanded by God himself to the Jews and now entertained by one of the greatest empires of the world, the Turks? May it not be . . . argued to be against the light of nature, although the Jews might plead [that] the institution of this ordinance was from heaven and the Lord of nature, [and] that it was done in so solemn and religious a way? . . . Or if the Mother of the Lord Jesus had brought forth her Son amongst us, and . . . without the company of her husband, yet who can be so impious against God and so unchristian and blasphemous against Christ Jesus as to question but that the most civil and the severest judge, upon due examination of the whole matter might rationally and judicially have pronounced to have found no violence of civility, no wrong to the bodies or goods of any (the proper object and cause of all civil officers), but contrarily a most holy and glorious appearance of the living God and gloriously free from such impurities with which even the religion of the whole nations are defiled? . . .

The sum of the fourteenth question: whether, since idolatry plagues upon

6. Originally "ought," by which Williams clearly meant "aught."
7. In other words, Williams distinguishes between the deviant practices Paul isolates in Romans 1 and the religious beliefs in which they were rooted. Williams implies that the practices themselves could be subject to civil punishment, but not the beliefs that inform them.

the people, the magistrate ought not to deliver the people from those plagues by removing idolatry?

I ask, . . . did not God wink at the nations (Acts 17), and is he not still pleased to wink at those numberless nations of the world to whom the sound of a savior reaches not? How wonderful are the dominions of the . . . many millions of millions of the sons and daughters of men who in all ages and nations pass on in outward peace, prosperity, and glory, amongst *some* of whom God may call some to fear him and love the Lord Jesus. But for any of these *nations* to become Christians . . . I ask whether such a thing [is to] be found in Christ's Testament, or be in experience true of the body of this or any other nation?

. . . Whatever be the pretense and mist which Satan casts, I ask . . . whether all violence in religion be not for some sinister cause and interest? . . . What a wonderful noise and sound have those three Greek names—idolatry, heresy, and blasphemy—made in the world, to the scaring and fright of poor people in both popish and Protestant countries. But let the zeal of the most zealous outcries be examined in plain English, and let the zealous . . . impartially examine, and it shall be found that the bottom and root of the matter is a plain merchandizing with the word of God . . . , a very sale of law and gospel, Moses and Christ, heaven and hell, God himself and the souls of men. I truly honor the many excellent persons and the excellent abilities . . . of many that have professed and do the nation's ministry and service. I confess there is a due of temporals[8] to such a minister of spirituals, but withal I ask, what is it but a trade and living, but a merchandizing for gain, when men profess they cannot, without so much or so much, preach Christ Jesus?[9] Surely the Apostasy has been most wonderful and dreadful. . . .

Lastly, I ask whether . . . we may not discern false doctrines, tenents, and opinions by the horrible fruits which this bitter root has brought forth, to the slaughter of so many thousands . . . , religiously and zealously . . . hunting one another as wild beasts, monsters, idolaters, heretics, [and] blasphemers—yea and which may cause a soul truly in love with Christ Jesus to tremble? This, above all others, has been that bloody knife that has so many thousand and ten thousand times stabbed the Lord Jesus to the heart, in the

8. That is, the means for temporal sustenance.

9. See *The Hireling Ministry* (the next selection in this volume) for Williams's elaboration on this subject.

bloody hunting of so many his servants and followers, as the greatest heretics [and] blasphemers in both this and other nations. . . .

The sum of the . . . seventeenth question: whether idolaters may not be convicted by acts as well as a murderer, and thereby the heart of the idolater is discovered? For the murderer is discovered guilty because of malice in his heart. . . .

As to the instance of murder, I ask if there be not three apparent differences between civil crimes against the state and those of spiritual nature against God [and] his worship? First, there are no generations of men (nor ever were in this world) but [those who] by the dark light of nature have condemned these four sins as inconsistent [with] the converse of man with man: murder, adultery, theft, and lying. But all the generations and nations of men have most constantly differed . . . about the true God and his ways of worship. Second, those four sorts of sinners—murderers, adulterers, thieves, and liars—are easily convinced and ashamed . . . and justly punished. But idolaters all over the world are ready to cry out . . . "Great is our Diana!" And however a heretic . . . has some checkings and convincings in his own conscience, yet both Papists and Turks, Jews and Pagans [who] are serious have trampled over posts and prisons, torments and deaths, to keep their consciences. Third, without some order of civility . . . [and] some civil officers of justice to punish those four sins especially, it is impossible that men can live together as men (and not beasts or worse). But notwithstanding several religions in one nation, in one shire, yea, in one family, if men be . . . but truly civil, and walk but by the rules of humanity and civility, families, towns, cities, and commonwealths in the midst of spiritual differences may flourish. . . .

The nineteenth question: whether Asa did well in bringing the people into covenant, since (as the Examiner said), he might thereby have made many turn hypocrites, [because] the people swore with all their heart?[10] And although hypocrisy does follow, yet this flows from the corruption of the hypocrite, and not from the holiness of the command. . . .

I ask whether [just] as to force the consciences of the unwilling is a soul rape, so to force the ignorant, profane, and unregenerate nations into a pretended holy fellowship and communion with God be not ten thousand fold more unholy and unrighteous than to force into the beds of any men of

10. Asa was a king of ancient Judah credited with a period of religious reform (2 Chronicles 15).

honor . . . impudent whores and strumpets? Would the proposer style their commands holy, just, and good did the matter concern his own bed? . . . I ask how much infinitely sweeter are God's methods, delighting only in a willing people? How sweet are the paths of the Lamb of God, Christ Jesus, whose true messengers are maidens (Prov. 9), who with virgin chastity and modesty invite poor sinners to the heavenly feast and banquet? And because there are not only rivers of pleasures at the right hand of God, but rivers of fire and brimstone for the obstinate, they [who know] these terrors of God persuade, pull, and compel poor sinners as brands from the everlasting burnings. . . .

The two and twentieth question: if God was to be blessed for putting it into the heart of a heathen magistrate to make the laws for religion (Isa. 7:27), [does] he come not nearer to a curse [who] would take out of the heart of a Christian magistrate the advancement of true religion, and persuade him to give a toleration to the chief enemies of religion, idolatry and heresy? . . .

I ask whether the plain English of not tolerating the idolater and heretic has not been in all ages since Christ Jesus the not tolerating indeed of *Christ Jesus* . . . , both in his own person and in his followers, the hunting or persecuting of him out of the world? Was ever any of the prophets esteemed so great a heretic from the Jewish religion as Christ Jesus was? Was there ever such a blasphemer of God (as the high priest esteemed him) . . . ? And do not the many books of martyrs . . . set forth that under this hood and vizard the devil has cast the saints into prison (Rev. 2)? He has watched to devour the man-child (Rev. 12) and hunted the . . . spouse of Christ Jesus. . . . And the great whore, pretending that she drinks the blood of heretics, has been drunk with the blood of the saints and witnesses of Jesus (Rev. 17). Hence will not reason suspect a murderous snare in the law pretended against thieves, robbers, and whores and yet most commonly falling upon none but honest and faithful, chaste and modest persons? Are not these engines worthily questioned which, pretending to take none but birds of prey and wolves, yet ordinarily catch nothing but harmless doves and sheep and lambs?

If it be said [that] idolatry and heresy are the chief enemies of religion, I ask, first, if those very famous religions which have pretended themselves the truest in the world have not been found the greatest idols? Second, grant them to be the greatest enemies, yet since enemies are of two sorts, spiritual and corporal, I ask whether as corporal weapons are proper against corporal, so are not spiritual weapons only proper against merely spiritual adversaries? Third, could Christ Jesus so forget himself as to not take sufficient order for spiritual weapons against all his spiritual enemies? In a battle . . . , how apt are men to charge generals and commanders if ammunition be wanting? Yea, in that case, how justly may men complain . . . that powder was said to be wanting in their own ships . . . ? And shall it be imagined that the last will and Testament of the Son of God, . . . whose gifts which upon his triumph in heaven he set upon men, should leave his army . . . unprovided, so that in the very day of the battle they must be forced to the forge of the Philistines to borrow swords, halberds, guns, pikes, prisons, and halters against idolaters and heretics?

Fourth, I may end and ask . . . if blessed are Christ's peacemakers and Christ's persecuted (Matt. 5), how nearer to a curse does he come [who] brings not buckets to quench, but bellows to kindle, the fire of God's jealousy against state inventions, the fires of persecutions and [the] hunting of Christ's saints, the fires of devouring wars among the nations for the respective religions and consciences? How nearer to a curse does he come who, under a cloak of Christian magistrate, true religion, zeal against idolaters and heretics, shall conceal a dagger . . . stabbing at the heart of God, his Christ, his Spirit, his saints, his pure worship—yea, and at the heart of all civil peace and civil magistracy, and civility itself!—throughout the whole world?

And therefore lastly I ask whether these two Examining Worthies shall not be wrapped up in the everlasting arms of blessedness itself, while they improve their talents uprightly and impartially, in the further examination of this fire of zeal in question? Yea, and whether not only these two honorable Senators, but the most renowned Senate of the world (the Parliament itself) shall not be truly crowned with the laurels of true nobility . . . while they candidly and impartially examine whether these things are so or no?

CHAPTER EIGHT

The Hireling Ministry None of Christ's

or, A Discourse touching the Propagating the Gospel of Christ Jesus Humbly Presented to Such Pious and Honorable Hands, whom the present Debate thereof concerns

During his second return to London in 1652, Williams was drawn into the controversy surrounding the long-established practice of taxing citizens to support the clergy. The chaos of the Civil War had suspended the practice temporarily, but in the relative calm of Cromwell's protectorate, Puritan leaders demanded that the government resume exacting tithes from all citizens to underwrite clergy salaries. Protestant Radicals, however, objected to being forced to support clergy not of their religious communities. Given Williams's discomfort with "national churches" and state support of religion, it is no surprise that this treatise rejects the practice of forced tithes and a "hireling ministry" as both bad for the church and inappropriate for the state.

In this Discourse are briefly touched these Particulars:

1. The national and parishional constitution of churches is found to be the grand idol of the nation.

2. The enforcing of the nation to such a constitution is the greatest soul oppression in this nation.

3. The hireling ministry attending upon such assemblies or others is none of the ministry of Christ Jesus.

4. The universities of the nation, as subordinate and subservient to such ministries and churches, are none of the institutions of Christ Jesus.

5. It is the absolute duty of the civil state to set free the souls of all men from that so long oppressing yoke of such ministries and churches. Yet,

6. Ought the nation and every person in it be permitted to see with its own eyes, and to make free choice of what worship and ministry and maintenance they please, whether parochial or otherwise?

7. The apostolic commission and ministry is long since interrupted and discontinued. Yet,

8. Ever since the beast Antichrist rose, the Lord has stirred up the ministry of prophesy, who must continue their witness and prophesy until their witness be finished, and slaughters probably near approaching accomplished.

9. The provocation of the Holy Eyes is great in all courts throughout the nation by millions of legal oaths, which if not redressed, may yet be a fire kindled from His jealousy; who will not hold him guiltless [who] takes his name in vain.

10. The free permitting of the consciences and meetings of conscionable and faithful people throughout the nation, and the free permission of the nation to frequent such assemblies, will be one of the principal means and expedients . . . for the propagating and spreading of the Gospel of the Son of God. . . .

Being desired by some loving friends to cast in my mite as to that heavenly proposition of propagating the Gospel of Christ Jesus, I am humbly bold to propose these conclusions. . . .

The two great prophets of God's revealed counsel, Moses (the Servant) and Christ Jesus (the Lord), as they have both declared to us a creation, a Creator, the shipwreck of mankind, the restoration, [and] the Restorer, so have they both revealed to us a visible company of the holy worshippers of this one most glorious Creator and Redeemer, and that as for his own most glorious praise. . . . In order to [serve] God's visible worship, the Lord Jesus has broken down the wall of division between the Jews and the rest of the nations of the world, and sent forth his ministers . . . to all nations, to bring in (by the Gospel's invitation) proselytes, converts, disciples such as should eternally be saved, to begin that heavenly and eternal communion in heaven here in a holy and visible worship on the earth. This going forth of the true ministers of Christ Jesus is represented under the figure of the white troop

ers in the opening of the first seal, where the Lord Jesus in his first messengers rode forth upon the white horse, . . . to conquer in the souls of men.[1]

[But] from the [6th chapter] of Revelation to the 19th, we hear no more
of those white-horsemen, that is (as I conceive), of the apostles or messengers of Jesus Christ, the whole stream of the intervening prophecies . . . in-
sinuating a total routing of the church and ministry of Christ Jesus, put to
flight, and retired into the wilderness of desolation. During the dreadful
Apostasy and Desolation,[2] the Lord has not left the world without witness, but has graciously and wonderfully stirred up his holy prophets and
witnesses, such as were before the Waldensians, . . . the Wicklevists, the
Hussites, the Lutherans, the Calvinists (so called), who have as witnesses
prophesied and mourned in sackcloth . . . and panted and labored after the
most glorious rally thereof, and Restoration. . . .

The world divided into thirty parts, say our ablest cosmographers, as yet
but five of thirty have heard of the sweet name of Jesus [the] Savior. His
messengers must yet go forth into the other twenty five, after the downfall of
the papacy, when also at the fullness of the Gentiles (or nations) coming in
shall be the joyful raising from the Dead of the accursed and yet beloved nation of the Jews (Rom. 11; Rev. 18 and 19).

The civil state of the nations being merely and essentially civil, cannot . . .
be called Christian states after the pattern of that holy and typical Land of
Canaan, which I have proved at large in *The Bloody Tenent* to be a non-such
and an unparalleled figure of the spiritual state of the church of Christ Jesus,
dispersed yet gathered to him in all nations. The civil sword therefore cannot rightfully act either in restraining the souls of the people *from* worship
or in constraining them *to* worship, considering that there is not a tittle in
the New Testament of Christ Jesus that commits the forming or reforming
of his spouse and church to the civil and worldly powers. . . . No man ever
did nor ever shall truly go forth to convert the nations, nor to prophesy in
the present state of witnesses against Antichrist, but by the gracious inspiration and instigation of the Holy Spirit of God. . . . In the present state of
things, I cannot but be humbly bold to say that I know no other true sender
but the most Holy Spirit. And when he sends, his messengers will go, his
prophets will prophesy, though all the world should forbid them.

1. Revelation 6:1–2.
2. By this Williams refers to the beginning of Constantinian Christianity.

From the former conclusions we may first see upon what a false sent or word our fathers and ourselves have run as to the true ministry appointed by Christ Jesus. How many thousand pretenders have been and are (Protestants and Papists) to that Grand Commission [in] Matthew 28: "Go into all nations, teach and baptize"? In the poor small span of my life, I desired to have been a diligent and constant observer, and have been myself many ways engaged in city, in country, in court, in schools, in universities, [and] in churches in Old and New England, and yet cannot in the holy presence of God bring in the result of a satisfying discovery, that either the begetting ministry of the apostles or messengers to the nations or the feeding and nourishing ministry of pastors and teachers . . . are yet restored and extant.

It may then be said, what is that ministry that has been extant since Luther and Calvin's time? Especially what is that ministry that has been [so instrumental in the hand of the Lord, to [the] conversion of thousands? answer, the ministry of prophets or witnesses, standing with Christ Jesus against his great corrival and competitor, Antichrist (Rev. 10:11). The whole *Book of Martyrs* . . . is nothing else but a large commentary or history of the ministry of witnesses during all the reign of the Beast to this day. Look upon Berengarius with the saints enlightened by him, look upon Waldus with his Waldensians in France, Wycliff in England, John Hus, Jerome of Prague in Bohemia, Luther in Germany, Calvin in Geneva—what were they but the holy prophets of Christ Jesus in those parts, and other places and countries. Now examine their witnesses in two particulars. Negatively, wherein they witnessed against the false, against the usurpations and abominations of Antichrist; and therein they were the infallible witnesses and prophets of Christ Jesus, preaching and oft times suffering to the death for his name' sake. But view them in their positive practice and worships, as they have assumed and pretended to such and such ministries, titles, churches, and ministrations, and there is not one of them—no not Calvin himself, the greatest pretender to church order—but the Father of Lights, in our times of light has been graciously pleased to discover their great mistakes and wandering from the first patterns and institutions of Christ Jesus. . . .[3]

3. Williams's point here and in the following section is that in the time of Constantine, the apostolic succession of authority to commission churches was severed, so that in Williams's own age no true church of Christ existed. Instead, faithful Christians gathered in enclaves of "scattered witnesses," among whom Williams counted the groups and figures mentioned here. Williams's failure to locate a true extant church in his time was both a product and motivation of his extreme separatism. For more on Williams's radical ecclesiology and its effect on his dedication to religious liberty, see W. Clark Gilpin, *The Millenarian Piety of Roger Williams* (Chicago: University of Chicago Press, 1979).

The Sins of the Hireling Ministry

Wherein have the former and latter ministries been defective? I answer, in all these four: their gifts, their calling, their work, [and] their wages. First, in their gifts, for notwithstanding they pretend to the apostles' commission and to succeed them (Matt. 28), yet they have never pretended to the gifts and qualifications of such a ministry, nor have they ever been able to clear up those two foundations of the Christian religion (Heb. 6), the doctrine of baptism and the laying on of hands. Second, notwithstanding that some plead their succession from the apostles or messengers, yet are they forced to run into the tents of Antichrist and to plead succession from Rome, and neither such nor others which plead their calling from the people can prove to my conscience, from the testimony of Christ Jesus, that either Christ's succession did run in an Antichristian line or that two or three godly persons might first make themselves a church and then make their ministers, without a preceding ministry from Christ Jesus to them, to gather and to guide them in such their administrations.

Third, the work of that commission (Matt. 28) was exercised and administered to the nations . . . and the world, but all our professed ministrations former and latter have been carried on . . . for the converting of a converted people. For if we grant all Protestant nations to be Christians, and so act with them in prayers as Christians and the children of God, how can we pretend to convert the converted, and to preach to them to convert them? One or [the] other must be denied, [either] that they are converted, or if unconverted, that we may offer up Christian and spiritual sacrifices with them. No herald, no ambassador sent to a city or army of rebels did ever . . . perform such actions of state with those rebels, which represents or renders them in a capacity of honest and faithful subjects. O, the patience and forbearance and long-suffering of the Most High, whose eyes yet are as a flame of fire!

Fourth, in their wages (whether by tithes or otherwise) they have always run in the way of a hire, and rendered such workmen absolute hirelings between whom and the true Shepherd, the Lord Jesus (John 10), puts so express and sharp a difference. So that in all humble submission, I am bold to maintain that it is one of grand designs of the Most High to break down the Hireling Ministry, that trade, faculty, calling, and living by preaching. . . .

But is not the laborer worthy of his reward? I answer, there is no reward . . comparable to a hundred fold (though with persecution) in this life, and eternal life in the world to come, to all that deny themselves in this life and do, teach, and suffer for the name of the Son of God. More strictly and particularly I answer,

First, he that makes a trade of preaching, that makes the cure of souls and the charge of men's eternal welfare a trade, a maintenance and living, and that explicitly makes a covenant or bargain (and therefore [says], "no longer penny no longer *paternoster*, no longer pay no longer pray, no longer preach, and no longer fast"), I am humbly confident to maintain that the Son of God never sent such a one to be a laborer in his vineyard. Such motions spring not from the living and voluntary spring of the Holy Spirit of God, but from the artificial and worldly respects of money [and] maintenance. . . .

Second, as to the laborer worthy of his reward, I answer [that] we find no other pattern in the Testament of Christ Jesus but that both the converting (or apostolic) ministry and the feeding (or pastoral) ministry did freely serve or minister, and yet were freely supported by the saints and churches—and that not in stinted wages, tithes, stipends, or salaries, but with larger or lesser supplies, as the hand of the Lord was more or less extended in his weekly blessings on them.

Third, when either through poverty or neglected support and maintenance failed, yet still they eyed . . . the good of the voyage and the battle (the common cause of the Lord Jesus), and their own hands day and night supplied their own and others' necessities. And this was and will be the only way of the laborers of the Son of God. . . .

The Universities Perpetuate the Errors of the Hireling Ministry

We may hence see our great mistakes, both of ourselves and our forefathers, as to the pretended seed plots and seminaries for the ministry, the universities of Europe and . . . this nation. For although I heartily acknowledge that among all the outward gifts of God, humane learning and the knowledge of languages and good arts are excellent, and . . . therefore that schools of humane learning ought to be maintained . . . and cherished, yet . . . *in ordine ad ministerium*, as to the ministry of Christ Jesus, they will be found to be none of Christ's, and that in many respects.

First, as to the name "scholar," although as to humane learning [it is in] many ways lawful, yet as it is appropriated to such as practice the ministry

. . . it is a sacrilegious and thievish title, robbing all believers and saints who are frequently in the Testament of Christ. . . . This title is so much theirs that both men and women believing were called scholars (Acts 9). . . .

Second, as to their monkish and idle course of life, partly so genteel and stately, partly so vain and superstitious, that to wet a finger in any pains or labor is a disgraceful and unworthy act. But the church is built upon the foundation of the apostles and prophets, who were laborers, fishermen, tentmakers, Jesus Christ (although the Prince of Life yet) a poor carpenter. . . . Yet in his time the Lord Jesus, whose is all power in heaven and earth, will spew out these seminaries of hirelings and mystical merchants out of his mouth, as he has done their fathers, the superstitious and bloody bishops before them. . . .

Fifth, as to their being prepared and fitted by these means, as in a way of apprenticeship, to set up the trade and way of preaching, the science or faculty of spiritual merchandise, . . . [the] trade of selling God himself, Christ Jesus, the Holy Spirit, heaven and hell, and . . . their own souls, and the souls of thousands. . . .

But extraordinary gifts be ceased, [it is objected], how shall now the people of this nation be supplied with ministers, but from such seminaries of learning which fit men both with learning to know and eloquence to utter the heavenly mysteries? Or would you have the people be of no religion at all, mere atheists, without God, without his Word, without a ministry?

I answer . . . , far be it [for] me to derogate from that honorable civility of training up of youth in languages and other humane learning, whether in the city of London or other towns and cities. All that I bear witness against is the counterfeiting and sacrilegious arrogating of the titles and rights of God's saints and churches . . . as also against their sacrilegious and superstitious degrees (as they call them) in the profession of divinity, as if they only knew divinity, godliness, [and] holiness. By such skill in godliness and by such degrees, [they] might succeed the ancient scribes and Pharisees in the uppermost seats in synagogues and feasts . . . as the only masters and teachers of religion and godliness, and all this in the way of the hireling dividing the whole land for gain. So that there has not been room (without some special and extraordinary privilege and license) for the poorest cottager to live in England, out of the bishop's diocese and the priest's parish and payments.

Civil Government Not Responsible for Enforcing
National Religion but for Protecting Free Religion

Therefore, . . . in all humble reverence and due submission to the higher powers, I affirm there was never [a] merely civil state in the world (for that of the Jews was mixed and ceremonial) that ever did or ever shall make good work of . . . a civil sword in spiritual matters. . . . I acknowledge with thankfulness that many heavenly spirits in King Edward's and Queen Elizabeth's days (and since that) have been forming and reforming the . . . nation's religion, worship, and ministry. Doubtless intentions were holy . . . , labors great, and God's mercy and pity and patience infinite, yet experience long and ever has told us that there was never a nation yet born in a day to God, that the bodies of all nations [are] part of the world, and although the Holy Spirit of God in every nation where the Word comes washes white some Blackamores, and changes some leopards' spots, yet the bodies and bulk of nations cannot by all the acts and statutes under heaven put off the Blackamore's skin [or] the leopard spots. Oh, why then should the wisdom of so many ages, still each after another, be preached (by the prevailing hirelings of each time, again and again) into the self-same delusion of washing the Blackamore?

There is not a town nor a parish nor a person in England but judge themselves Christian, and to that end challenge the right [to] and use of a minister *(in sacris),* [someone] (as in all religions in the world it is) to serve the Deity they worship, *ex officio,* as sacerdotes or holy persons for and with them, in prayers and holy rites. This mine eyes have often seen among thousands of the wild yet wise Americans, who yet (alas) as all the nations of Europe and the world are utterly incapable of forms and ministers or officers of Christian worship, while yet in their natural and worldly capacities. . . Yet . . . I desire uprightly to be far from diverse weights and measures in the things of God (especially), and therefore I desire not that liberty to myself which I would not freely and impartially weigh out to all the consciences of the world beside. And therefore I do humbly conceive that it is the will of the Most High and the express and absolute duty of the civil powers to proclaim an absolute freedom in all the three nations, yea in all the world (were their power so large), that each town and division of people, yea, and person, may freely enjoy [whatever] worship, ministry, [and] maintenance to afford them [that] their soul desires.

To this end, I am humbly bold to offer that it is not the will of the Father of Spirits that all the consciences and spirits of this nation should violently . . . be forced into one way of worship, or that any town or so-called parish in England, Scotland, or Ireland be disturbed in their worship by the civil sword ([whatever] worship [that might] be). If the people freely choose that way of worship, and ministry, and maintenance they walk in, yea if they will freely pay them the tenths or fifths, I shall not envy their ministers' maintenance nor disturb either minister or people's conscience by any other sword but with that spiritual sword of two edges, the sword of God's Spirit, the holy Word of God. . . .

Therefore . . . if it shall please our most noble governors to . . . take off the . . . soul yokes of binding all persons to parochial or parish forms, permitting them [instead] to enjoy their own belief, whether within or without such parish worships, parish maintenance, parish marriages, parish burials, by which the souls and consciences of so many have been [bound] in life and death . . . , if they shall please so far . . . to permit impartially all consciences (and especially the consciences, the meetings, and assemblies of faithful and conscionable people, the volunteers in preaching Christ Jesus) . . . [to] peaceably frequent and repair to such spiritual meetings and assemblies as they do the parish churches, [then] I am humbly confident that as to the point of converting souls to God (so far as the present state of Christianity can be so promoted), the souls of thousands will bless God more than if millions of hirelings were sent abroad from all the universities both of popish and Protestant countries.

. . . Upon the grounds first laid, I observe the great and wonderful mistake [of] both our own and our fathers as to the civil powers of this world, acting in spiritual matters. I have read . . . the last will and Testament of the Lord Jesus over many times, and yet I cannot find by one tittle of that Testament that he had been pleased to have accepted a temporal crown and government, that he would have put forth the least finger of temporal or civil power in the matters of his spiritual affairs and kingdom. Hence must it lamentably be against the testimony of Christ Jesus for the civil state to impose upon the souls of the people a religion, a worship, a ministry, [an] oath (in religious and civil affairs), tithes, times, days, marriages, and burials in holy ground. . . .

What is then the express duty of the civil magistrate as to Christ Jesus his Gospel and kingdom? I answer, I know how woefully that Scripture, "Kings shall be thy nursing Fathers,"[4] has been abused, and elsewhere I have at large discussed that and other such objections. At present I humbly conceive that the great duty of the magistrate as to spirituals will turn upon these two hinges: first, in removing the civil bars, obstructions, hindrances, in taking off those yokes that pinch the very souls and consciences of men. Such as yet are the payments of tithes and the maintenance of ministers they have no faith in. Such are the enforced oaths (and some ceremonies therein) in all the courts of justice; such are the holy marriages, holy burials, etc. Second, in a free and absolute permission of the consciences of all men in what is merely spiritual, not the very consciences of the Jews nor the consciences of the Turks or Papists or pagans themselves excepted. . . .

State Support of Ministry Necessary to Neither Religion nor Public Morality

But under the pretense of propagating the Gospel of Christ Jesus, it may be said, what horrible opinions and spirits will be vented, as woeful experience hath manifested. I answer [that] offensive opinions are of two sorts some savoring of impiety, and some of incivility. Against the first, Christ Jesus never called for the sword of steel to help the sword of the Spirit . . . , and therefore if a world of Arians deny the deity of Christ Jesus, if a Manichean his human nature, if the Jews deny both and blasphemously call our Christ a deceiver, nay, if the Mahumetans the Turks (the greater number by far of one religion in the world) . . . prefer their cheating Mahomet before him what now? Must we rail, revile, and cry out "blasphemers [and] heretics!"? Must we run to the cutler's shop, the armories and magazines of the cities and nations . . . , or must we fly up to heaven by prayers and curses to fetch down fire upon the persecuting captains and their fifties? This do the nations, this do false Christs and Christians, but this did not . . . the Lamb of God, the Lion of Judah's tribe, who with his Word and Spirit alone . . . will either kill or save the gain-saying opposite. The second sort, [that is], opinions of incivility, doubtless the opinions as well as practices are the proper object of the civil sword, according to that Magna Carta for the civil magistrate, Romans 13. . . .

But if the civil state enjoin not the maintenance of the ministry . . . , what

4. Isaiah 49:23.

will become of the ministry of the Gospel and the souls of men? For if each man's conscience be at liberty to come to church or not, to pay the minister or not, the profane and loose will neither pay nor pray, but turn atheistic and unreligious. . . . I answer, although the loose will be possibly more loose being at more liberty, . . . yet however it is infinitely better that the profane and loose be unmasked than to be muffled up under the veil and hood of traditional hypocrisy, which turns and dulls the very edge of all conscience either toward God or man. . . . It is [also] not to be doubted but that each conscience, the Papists and the Protestants, both Presbyterians and Independents, will . . . strive, for not only their conscience's but credit's sake, to excel and win the garland in the fruits of bounty.[5]

Conclusion

The *summa totalis* of all the former particulars is this: first, since the people of this nation have been forced into a national way of worship, both popish and Protestant (as the wheels of time's revolutions by God's mighty providence and permission have turned about), the civil state is bound before God to take off that bond and yoke of soul-oppression, and to proclaim free and impartial liberty to all the people of the three nations, to choose and maintain what worship and ministry their souls and consciences are persuaded of—which act, as it will prove an act of mercy and righteousness to the enslaved nations, so is it of a binding force to engage the whole and every interest and conscience to preserve the common freedom and peace. However, [it is also] an act most [suitable to] the piety and Christianity of the holy Testament of Christ Jesus.

Second, the civil state is humbly to be implored to provide in their high wisdom for the security of all the respective consciences—in their respective meetings, assemblies, worship, preaching, and disputing—and that civil peace and the beauty of civility and humanity be maintained among the chief opposers and dissenters.

Third, it is the duty of all that are in authority, and of all that are able to countenance, encourage, and supply such true volunteers as give and devote themselves to the service and ministry of Christ Jesus in any kind—it [is]

---

5. In other words, Williams assures his critics that moral competition will keep the diverse consciences striving for goodness.

the duty and will be the practice of all such whom the Spirit of God sends upon any work of Christ's . . . to work as Paul did among the Corinthians and Thessalonians, [rather] than the work and service of their Lord and Master should be neglected.[6] Such true Christian worthies (whether endowed with human learning or without it) will alone be found [to be] that despised model which the God of Heaven will only bless. . . . And if this course be effected in the three nations, the bodies and souls of the three nations will be more and more at peace, and in a fairer way than ever to that peace which is eternal when this world is gone. . . .

An Appendix as Touching Oaths, A Query

Although it be lawful (in case) for Christians to invocate the name of the Most High in swearing, yet since it is a part of his holy worship, and . . . therefore proper to such as are his true worshippers in Spirit and Truth. . . ; since it ought not to be used but most solemnly, and in most solemn and weighty cases . . . ; since it is the voice of the two great lawgivers from God, Moses and Christ Jesus, that in the mouth of two or three witnesses (not swearing) every word shall stand—[therefore, we may ask] whether the enforcing of oaths and spiritual covenants upon a nation promiscuously, and the constant enforcing of all persons to practice this worship in the most trivial and common cases in all courts (together with the ceremonies of book and holding up the hand), be not a prostituting of the holy name of the Most High to every unclean lip; and that on slight occasions, and taking of it by millions and so many millions of times in vain, . . . whether it be not a provoking of the eyes of his jealousy who has said . . . that he will not hold him . . . guiltless that takes his name in vain.

---

6. By working "as Paul did among the Corinthians and Thessalonians," Williams is referring to Paul's habit of financially supporting his own ministry by working as a tentmaker.

CHAPTER NINE

George Fox Digg'd out of His Burrowes

Or an Offer of Disputation on Fourteen Proposals made . . . unto [George] Fox
then present on Rhode Island in New England

Of the many religious sects that took advantage of Rhode Island's policy of religious freedom, no group caused Williams more consternation than the Quakers. As a Calvinist, he could not stomach their theology, with their emphasis on the "inner spirit" and corresponding dismissal of external religious authority (including, it seemed, the Bible). But what bothered Williams even more was the Quakers' socially deviant behavior, which included disrupting church meetings and occasionally appearing naked in public. In 1672 George Fox, the leader of the Quaker movement, visited Rhode Island on a public preaching tour. Williams challenged Fox to a theological debate, but by the time the invitation reached him Fox had left the colony. In his place, three Quaker missionaries accepted Williams's challenge, and this treatise (published in Boston soon after) represents Williams's account of their protracted verbal duel, held over several days in August 1672, first in Newport and then in Providence. While most of George Fox *deals with matters of theology, Williams occasionally used the Quakers to illustrate his understanding of the delicate balance between freedom of conscience and a commitment to "civility," a common morality on which he believed public order depended.*

Williams's Desire for Civility in the Debate Proceedings

. . . I knew our aged governor, Mr. Nicholas Easton, and other magistrates (of [the Quakers'] judgment) would be there,[1] and so civil peace maintained, and I had a strange assurance given to my spirit from God in answer to my poor requests . . . that by moderation and patience I should conquer their immoderations and impatience. I therefore thought it in vain to spend time about a moderator. It is true they gave me no answer either by speech or writing concerning their coming on me at once, but to their seeming great advantage they constantly fell on me all at once, and one of them, William Edmundson, with grievous language and insulting.

When I came into the place aforesaid, I found three able and noted preachers amongst them, John Stubs, John Burnet, and William Edmundson, sitting together on a high bench with some of the magistrates of their judgment with them. I had heard that John Stubs was learned in the Hebrew and the Greek, and I found him so. As for John Burnet, I found him to be of a moderate spirit and a very able speaker. The third, William Edmundson, was newly come (as was said) from Virginia, and he proved the chief speaker, a man not so able nor so moderate as the other two. For the first two would speak argument and discuss and produce Scripture, but William Edmundson was very ignorant in the Scripture or any other learning. He had been a soldier in the late war, a stout portly man of a great voice, and fit to make a braggadocio (as he did) and a constant exercise merely of my patience. He would often vapor and preach long, and when I had patiently waited until the gust was over, and began to speak, then would he stop my mouth with a very unhandsome clout of a grievous interruption, so that sometimes I was forced to play the moderator, and to protest that such practices were against the sober rules of civility and humanity. It pleased God to help me with such patience to weather them, that John Stubs openly confessed twice that though some others had given them some interruptions, yet I had not done it. . . .

Incivility and Public Punishment

Again, it is true in Christ Jesus [that] there is neither bond nor free, male nor female, and consequently no master nor man, no father nor child, no

---

1. By "judgment," Williams refers to the fact that Governor Easton and some of the leaders of the town of Newport were themselves Quakers.

king nor subject, but all are one in Christ Jesus and the second birth (as all are of one kind in the first Adam and the first birth). Yet first, how full is the Holy Scripture of commands and examples of God's children giving respectful words and titles and bowings, even to persons that knew not God? Fox grants difference of gifts, [but] . . . however they hypocritically lie and pretend to honor all men in the Lord, yet the Most Holy and Only Wise knows how proudly and simply and barbarously they have run into uncivil and inhumane behaviors towards all their superiors, the eldest and highest, how they have declared by principle and practice that there are no men to be respected in the world but themselves as being God's and Christ's. . . . Every nation, every shire, every calling have their particular properties or idioms of speech, which are improper and ridiculous with others. Hence these simple reformers are extremely ridiculous in giving "Thou" and "Thee" to everybody, which our nation commonly gives to familiars only, and they are extremely and insufferably proud and contemptuous to all their superiors in using "Thou" to everybody, which our English idiom or propriety of speech uses in way of familiarity or anger, scorn, and contempt. I have therefore publicly declared that a due and moderate restraint and punishing of these incivilities (though pretending conscience) is as far from persecution (properly so called) as that it is a duty and command of God to all mankind, first in families, and then in all [human] societies.

Having thus through God's merciful help gone through the 13th position . . . I hastened to the 14th proposition, the last of the seven at Providence.[2] They read it publicly: the spirit of the Quakers tends mainly to the reducing of persons from civility to barbarism; to an arbitrary government, and the dictates and decrees of that sudden spirit that acts them; to a sudden cutting off of a people, yea of kings and princes, that oppose them; and to as fierce and fiery persecution in matters of conscience as has been or can be practiced by any hunters or persecutors in the world.

I told them I could add more branches to this head, as to the peace and civil societies of mankind in the world, but I remembered my promise of brevity. And [Edmundson] was often reminding[3] me, saying, "Is this thy quarter of an hour?" For I believe they stood here upon coals and were not willing that I should insist upon my full quarter. . . .

2. Williams structured his attack on the Quakers as a series of propositions, which he then laboriously discussed over the course of several days.
3. Originally "remembering."

I told them that in our native country and in all civilized countries, civility—courteous speech, courteous salutation, and respectful behavior—was generally practiced, opposite to the carriage of barbarous and uncivilized people. . . . [Of] such a spirit was Christ Jesus, even to his greatest opposites and to the greatest sinners. . . . We English were ourselves at first wild and savage Britons. God's mercy had civilized us, and we were now come into a wild and savage country, without manners, without courtesy, so that generally except you begin with a "What cheer!" or some other salutation, you had as good meet a horse or a cow! And has not the Quaker spirit been such a spirit among us? Have we not known persons formerly loving [and] courteous, and as soon as this spirit has come upon them, have not our eyes seen them pass by their familiars, their kindred, the elders and superiors, and though kindly spoken to not give a word or a look toward them? As if they were not worthy of a word or a look from such high saints! How like indeed . . . I have heard that the Quakers have commended the spirit of the Indians, for they have seen them come into English houses and sit down by the fire, not speaking a word to anybody. But this carriage of the Indians proceeds from a brutish spirit, for generally they have boldly come in without knocking or asking of leave, and sit down without any respect in word or gesture to the governor or chief of the family whatsoever—just the Quakers' general fashion and spirit!

Further I told them, that in some respect the spirit and carriage of the Quakers was worse than that of the Indians, for if they were saluted by the English in the highway or coming into a house, [the Indians] are very ready to receive your salutation kindly and return you another. But commonly we know that it is not so with the Quakers' brutish spirit. The Indians, morning and evening and upon all meetings, they give a respective and proper salutation to their own superiors, and sometimes in gesture as well as speech. Although the Indians are brutes in their nakedness (both men and women), yet they never appear (no, not [even] in private houses) stark naked as the Quaker men and women do. Yea, they so abhor such a brutishness (except it be in their mad drunkenness, for then they will be stark naked) that as to their female kind, they will carefully from their birth keep on some modest covering before them.

[William Edmundson] rose up and said they did abhor uncleanness as well as ourselves or any. Their women were sober, holy, and modest, and some of them would not endure to have a toe to be seen naked! But, he said if the Lord God did stir up any of his daughters to be a sign of the nakedness of others, he believed it to be a great cross to a modest woman's spirit, but the Lord must be obeyed. John Stubs immediately seconded him, and . . . said he had been a Quaker nineteen years and yet had never seen a woman naked, and some of the Quakers said to me aloud, "When didst thou see any of our women naked?" And another of them said, "We did not think that thou wouldst have been such a wicked man!" These two (though of the Quakers' spirit) yet of long time had been loving and respectful to me, but now they were enraged, so that I said to my antagonists, "Seeing that some heat is risen about these matters, I will if you please go on to the second branch of this 14th position."

Quaker Religion Leads to Anarchy

I told them that the second branch was *that the spirit of the Quakers tends to bring in an arbitrary government.* . . . I argued if it were true that all the Quakers were guided in all they said and did by the immediate Spirit of God . . . , then if they obtain higher or lower governors of their spirits, surely it shines clear that there is no need of laws for them to rule and act by. For they had no need of Scripture, seeing the immediate inspirations of God would not suffer them to err in judgment. . . . So, I said, much more might it be said of men's laws and writings, that surely they had no need of them, for what could be more just and equal, more pure and holy in all cases, controversies, and business, than the immediate voice of God?

[Edmundson] said, "Why dost thou fill people's ears with strange notions, as if the people of God called Quakers were a lawless people and would bring all government and all laws to nothing? We are for righteous government and righteous laws! We are not for any to rule by force." And more he spoke to this purpose.

I replied that he mistook me, [for] by an arbitrary government I did not intend a government ruling by force (for there could be no government in the world without the sword), but "arbitrary" I said came from *arbitrium*, which signified will or pleasure. And so my argument was that [for] persons immediately speaking from God, it was impertinent and profane to clog and encumber them with laws, for the voice of God . . . proceeded out of their mouth. . . .

Here stood up an aged man and as able as most in the company (though much of late adhering to the Quakers), T.A.,[4] and said, "Methinks there is weight in Mr. Williams's argument." He being a noted man and his voice very audible . . . , [Edmundson] was forced to take notice of his speech, and said, "Wherein is there any weight in it?" T.A. answered, "Why if a magistrate be immediately inspired by God, and speaks God's laws and sentence, surely there seems to be no need of any other laws." They saw they were in a pound, and I perceived it, and yet not being willing to grate on them but watching my time (as I was glad all along [to do]), I said to them [that] if they pleased I would pass on to the third branch: *That the Quakers' spirit tends to the sudden cutting off of people, yea, kings and princes that oppose them.*

I here told them that I must crave their patience while I must profess my fears, lest that spirit by which they were guided might run them upon their own and others' temporal destruction. I told them I thought they had no such thing in the thoughts or eye at present, but if power of the sword came into their hand, it was easy to imagine that whom their (infallible) spirit decreed to death, peasant or prince, if it were possible must be executed. William Edmundson said, "Thou here makest a false and lying charge against the people of God, who are peaceable and quiet and yielding to magistrates!" I replied [that] I charge them with no matter of facts, but I charge them and their spirit with a *tendency*. . . . My antagonists jointly bid me show them when any of the Quakers had done so. I answered [that] they spoke not to the point, for I did not charge them to have done so, but that their spirits tended to it. . . .

Edmundson interrupted me and spoke to this effect: "Why should we suffer this man thus to wrong the innocent people of God? We will measure him by his own bushel! For thy book declares thy approving of the killing of the king's father and—said where is the book?" At which word William Harris (a fire-brand of town, colony, and country) rose up and carried a book (which they said was mine) to William Edmundson. I perceived that Edmundson and Harris, who was for any religion and a malicious mortal enemy to all good, had been plotting, and I said openly [that] I knew what malicious bloody counsel had been between Harris and themselves but [that] they would find themselves befooled, for there was nothing in the matter but ridiculous malice. For all of us knew that Harris loved the Quakers (whom now he fawned upon) no more than he did the Baptists (whom

4. The identity of "T.A." is unknown.

he till now fawned upon), but would love any (like a dog for his bone) for land, which he had a long suit for, as was known to all the country and their cost. Hereupon Captain Green, Magistrate of Warwick, desired that such matters might be forborn, and others spoke to the same purpose, and J. Stubs and others are said to have spoken to Edmundson to forbear, so that the book was laid aside and delivered again to that malicious bloody soul, William Harris. I challenged them again and again to read and prove what possibly they could, which I knew was no more than some words applauding the Parliament's justice and mercy, which these bloody sophists would like wolves and foxes construe as my approving the king's death, which God knows I never approved to this day.

Upon this occasion I may now inform the reader how easily the malicious spirit of William Edmundson and William Harris met in one. Formerly no man amongst us had spoken more scornfully of the Quakers than Harris. Now he extremely privately and publicly fawns upon them, seeing them my enemies who had ever been his friend, and never his enemy but in his outrageous practices against town, colony, and country. He was a pretender in Old England, but in New my experience has told me that he can be one with the Quakers, Jesuits, or Mahumetans, for his own worldly ends and advantage. He is long known to have put scorns and jeers upon the eminent inhabitants of town and country. He has been notorious for quarreling, and challenging, and fighting, even when he pretended with the Quakers against carnal weapons—so that there stands upon record in the town book of Providence an act of disfranchisement upon him for fighting and shedding blood in the street. . . . In public writings he stirred up the people (most seditiously and desperately threatening to begin with Massachusetts) and to cry out "No lords! No masters!" as is yet to be seen in his writing; this cost myself and the colony much trouble. Then, as the wind favored his ends, no man cries up the magistrates more, not finding that pretence nor the people called Baptists (in whom he confided) serving his ends. He flies to Connecticut colony (then and still in great contest with us) in hopes to attain his gaping about land from them, if they prevail over us. To this end he in public speech and writing applauds the Connecticut charter and damns ours. . . .[5]

5. For more on William Harris, his economic ambitions, and his conflict with Williams, see Ola Elizabeth Winslow, *Master Roger Williams* (New York: Octagon Books, 1973), especially chapters 10, 18, and 19.

I had thought to have declared thus much publicly . . . , but now my Lord Edmundson grew hot and told me that I had charged the people of the Lord with many great and grievous charges, which he said I could not prove. . . . Therefore he warned me that, being an old man, I should not carry such a burden on my back to my grave, and (among other angry insults) he said he heard I had been a magistrate, and said I was a fit man to be a magistrate, that would so wrongfully charge the innocent. . . .

Definition of Conscience

. . . Conscience (in Greek, Latin, and English) signifies a knowing together, a reflection or looking back on a man's mind or spirit upon itself. In point of justification or pardon of sin, conscience looks upon a cursed rotten nature, then upon millions of sins of omission and commission, which how to satisfy an infinite justice for and to attain a new heart and nature is the high business and out of the reach or thought of that poor conscience, which every man—Jew or Gentile, civilized or pagan—comes into the world with. . . .[6]

The Light of Nature

. . . What is the light of nature but that light in which every man comes into the world with, . . . a light differing from that light which beasts, wild and tame, and birds and fishes have.[7] And [there is] a second light differing from what is natural, as that light revealed from heaven in the Holy Scriptures and infused into the souls of men by the Holy Spirit, or Power of God. What is the light of nature in man but that order which the most glorious

6. Note that Williams's definition of conscience here emphasizes its accusatory nature and reaffirms that conscience itself cannot make a person righteous. This was for him an important point, because it distinguished a Calvinist conception of conscience from the Quakers' notion of the "inner light," which they identified as Christ himself.

7. In response to the Quaker conviction that God's spirit resides within every person, Williams is at pains to distinguish natural knowledge—that is, a rational capacity for scientific and moral discernment—from supernatural knowledge, or the saving knowledge bestowed on human beings externally, by God's grace. In the process of rejecting the Quaker doctrine of divine immanence, however, Williams provides a glimpse of his own natural theology, on which is based his optimistic assumption that human societies can flourish without enforced religion. For more on Williams's theological anthropology, see James Calvin Davis, *The Moral Theology of Roger Williams* (Louisville, Ky.: Westminster John Knox Press, 2004), chapter 3.

former of all things has set (like wheels in clocks or watches) a going in all his creatures. . . .

In former years I have conversed with all the Indians of this New England by land and seas, and I have read the [first chapter] of Romans often, and . . . I find that first, there is generally in all mankind in the world a conviction of an invisible, omnipotent, and eternal power and godhead. . . . I find all men confess that the will or word or mind of God is pure, and as they could come to know it is to be adored, kept, and observed, and that it was ever and is wickedness to sin against it. All mankind have the law, or without it [they] are persuaded that some actions are naught and against God's will, as to steal [or] to murder. . . . I find in all mankind a conviction that God is just and powerful and brings plagues and punishments upon persons and nations for those gross sins of adultery and murder. [But] I could never learn . . . that ever any man living or all the counsels of men could ever know or learn four things, but as revealed by God by extraordinary ways . . . or the ordinary of his holy records and the doctrine of them opened and preached: 1. how to pacify God's justice; 2. how to resist the devil's tyranny; 3. how to worship God; 4. how to get true blessedness, here and in the world to come. . . .

The natural truth or light is received within by a natural light or understanding. The civil and moral light or truth suits and agrees with those moral and civil convictions of the natural light and understanding. Hither to nature's light will reach. . . . All light or truth—natural, civil, or divine—comes from without and is received by the internal faculty according to the capacity, nature, and measure of it. All truth or falsehood, light or darkness, is first espied by the watch or sentinel, or Comprehension. From thence it is conveyed to the court of guard, where Captain Reason or his Lieutenant, Common Sense and Experience, take examination, and Memory keeps a record of proceedings which go on by degree to actions.

When I say it comes from without, I intend not that truth or light comes any other way from without, as by force and ravishment. I say no other way than there is a door and room and receptive faculty within willing to receive, and to make it welcome. . . . Natural truth, or morals [and] civil matters, are soon received by all natural and moral understandings. . . . But when we speak of supernatural, heavenly, and eternal matters, of spiritual things to be discerned spiritually, what a difference is there as between heaven and earth. . . .

CHAPTER TEN

Selected Letters

To the Town of Providence, 31 August 1648

*In 1648 opposition between William Coddington and Samuel Gorton threat-
ened to overwhelm Rhode Island. Each man gathered backers from the four
towns and refused to participate in the newly chartered government. In addition, William Arnold and his allies already had offered to place their property
under the jurisdiction of Massachusetts, which was all too eager to encroach
upon Rhode Island's claims and assert jurisdiction (and orthodoxy) in the
troubled colony. Likely out of town at his trading post, Williams wrote this letter to his fellow citizens to suggest arbitration as a way to extinguish their political disputes and to avoid intervention by either king or colonial rivals.*

Worthy friends,

That ourselves and all men are apt and prone to differ is no new thing, in
all former ages, in all parts of this world, in these parts and in our dear native country and mournful state of England. That either part or party is
most right in his own eye—his cause right, his carriage right, his arguments
right, his answers right—is as woefully and constantly true as the former.
And experience tells us that when the God of peace has taken peace from the
earth, one spark of action, word, or carriage is . . . powerful [enough] to kindle such a fire as burns up families, towns, cities, armies, navies, nations, and

kingdoms. And since, dear friends, it is an honor for men to cease from strife, since the life of love is sweet and union is as strong as sweet, and since you have been lately pleased to call me to some public service and my soul has long been musing how I might bring water to quench and not oil or fuel to the flame, I am now humbly bold to beseech you by all those comforts of earth and heaven which a placable and peaceful spirit will bring to you, and by all those dreadful alarms and warnings either amongst ourselves in deaths and sickness, or abroad in the raging calamities of the sword, dearth, and pestilence, I say I humbly and earnestly beseech you to be willing to be pacified, willing to be reconciled, willing to be sociable, and to listen to the (I hope not unseasonable) motion following.

To try out matters by disputes and writing is sometimes endless. To try out arguments by arms and swords is cruel and merciless. To trouble the state and lords of England is most unseasonable, most chargeable. To trouble our neighbors of other colonies seems neither safe nor honorable. Methinks, dear friends, the colony now looks with the torn face of two parties: the greater number of Portsmouth (with other loving friends adhering to them) appear as one grieved party, [and] the other three towns (or greater part of them) appear to be another. Let each party choose and nominate three [representatives]. . . . Let authority be given to them to examine every public difference, grievance, and obstruction of justice, peace, and common safety. Let them by one final sentence of all (or the greater part of them) end all, and set the whole into a unanimous posture and order. And let them set a censure upon any that shall oppose their sentence. . . .

Let me be friendly construed if (for expedition) I am bold to be too forward in this service, and to say that if within twenty days of the date hereof you please to send to my house at Providence the name of him whom you please to nominate, at your desire I will acquaint all the persons chosen with place and time, to which in your name I shall desire their meeting within ten days or thereabouts after the receipt of your letters. I am yours, mournful and unworthy, Roger Williams

To Governor John Endicott, 1651

Williams wrote this letter, appended to The Bloody Tenent Yet More Bloody *when it was published the following year, to protest the treatment of three Bap-*

tists (including John Clarke) who were caught and punished in the summer of
1651 for unauthorized preaching in the Bay Colony.

Sir,

Having done with our transitory earthly affairs (as touching the English
and the Indians), which in comparison [to] heavenly and eternal you will
say are but as dung and dross, let me now be humbly bold to remember that
humanity and piety which I and others have formerly observed in you, and
in that hopeful remembrance to crave your gentle audience with patience
and mildness, with ingenuity, equanimity, and candor, to him that ever truly
and deeply loved you and yours. . . .

Sir, it has pleased the Father of Spirits at this present to smite my heart in
the very breaking up of your letter. This death's head tells that loving hand
that sealed it, and mine that opens your letter, that our eyes, our hands, our
tongues, our brains are flying hence to the hole or pit of rottenness. Why,
therefore, should not our letters, our speeches, [and] our actions be as may
become our last minutes, our deathbeds? If so, how meek and humble, how
plain and serious, how faithful and zealous, and yet how tender and loving
should the spirits and speeches be of dying and departing men?

Sir, while something of this nature I muse over your death's head, I meet
in the entrance of your letter with this passage: "*Were I as free in my spirit as
formerly I have been to write to you, you should have received another manner
of salutation than now with a good conscience I can express. However, God
knows who are his, and what he is pleased to hide from sinful man in this life
shall in that great Day be manifest to all.*"

Sir, at the reading of this line (I cannot but hope that I have your leave to
tell you), the speech of that wise woman of Tekoah to David came fresh into
my thoughts: "Speaks not the King this thing as one that is guilty?"[1] For will
my honored and beloved friend not know me for fear of being disowned by
his conscience? Shall the goodness and integrity of his conscience to God
cause him to forget me? Does he quiet his mind with this—"God knows
who are his? God hides from sinful man, God will reveal before all?" Oh,
how comes it then that I have heard so often, and heard so lately, and heard
so much, that he that speaks so tenderly for his own has yet so little respect,
mercy, or pity to the like conscientious persuasions of other men? Are all the

1. 2 Samuel 14:13.

thousands of millions of millions of consciences, at home and abroad, fuel only for a prison, for a whip, for a stake, for gallows? Are no consciences to breathe the air but such as suit and sample his? May not the Most High be pleased to hide from his as well as from the eyes of his fellow servants, fellow mankind, fellow English? And if God hides from his, from any, who can discover? Who can shut when he will open? And who can open when he that has the key of David will shut? All this and more, honored Sir, your words will warrant me to say, without any just offense or straining.

Object. But what makes this to heretics, blasphemers, seducers, to them that sin against this conscience (as Mr. Cotton says) after conviction?[2] What makes his to stabbers of kings and princes, to blowers-up of Parliaments out of conscience?[3]

First, I answer [that] he was a tyrant that put an innocent man into a bear's skin and so caused him as a wild beast to be baited to death.[4] Secondly, I say [that] this is the common cry of hunters or persecutors, "heretics, heretics, blasphemers!" And why, but for crossing the persecutors' consciences . . . , whether Turkish, Popish, [or] Protestant. This is the outcry of the pope and prelates, and of the Scotch Presbyterians, who would fire all the world to be avenged on the sectarian heretics, the blasphemous heretics, the seducing heretics—had it not pleased the God of heaven who bounds the insolent rage of the furious ocean to raise up a second Cromwell (like a mighty and merciful wall or bulwark) to stay the fury of the oppressor, whether English, Scottish, Popish, Presbyterian, [or] Independent.

Lastly, I have said much and lately, and [have] given particular answers to all such pleas in my second reply or answer to Mr. Cotton's washing of the Bloody Tenent in the Lamb's blood, which it may be is not yet come to your sight and hand. It is true, I have to say elsewhere about the causes of my banishment: as to the calling of natural men to the exercise of those holy ordinances of prayers [and] oaths, as to the frequenting of parish churches under the pretence of hearing some ministers, as to the matter of the patent and King James's Christianity and title to these parts, and bestowing it on

2. A reference to Cotton's insistence that it was allowable, even necessary, for the church to punish those who persist in beliefs contrary to "fundamental" doctrines of faith after being admonished by church leaders. See *The Bloody Tenent* for Williams's reply to this argument.

3. Probably a reference to the Gunpowder Plot of 1605, when Catholic terrorists attempted to blow up King James and the Parliament during a state address.

4. A reference to a method of recreational torture in the Roman Empire, where Christians would be dressed in bearskins and released to a pack of dogs.

his subjects by virtue of his being a Christian king. At present let it not be
offensive in your eyes that I single out another, a fourth point, a cause of my
banishment also, wherein I greatly fear one or two sad evils which have be-
fallen your soul and conscience. The point is that of the civil magistrate
dealing in matters of conscience and religion, as also of persecuting and
hunting any for any matter merely spiritual and religious.

The two evils intimated are these: first, I fear you cannot after so much
light and so much profession to the contrary (not only to myself, and so often in private, but before so many witnesses), I say I fear you cannot say and
act so much against so many several consciences, former and later, but with
great checks, great threats, great blows and throws of inward conscience.
Secondly, if you shall thank God that it is not so with you, but that you do
what conscience bids you in God's presence, upon God's warrant, I must
then be humbly faithful to tell you that . . . strong delusions . . . have seized
upon your very soul's belief, because you prize not, love not the endangered
persecuted Son of God in his despised truths and servants.

Sir, . . . I know it is impossible for the otherwise piercing eye of your understanding to see into these things, for it is discolored, as in some disease
and glasses. It is impossible for your will to be willing to see, for that's in a
thousand chains resolved . . . to spend your dearest heart's blood in your
way. Yet with God all things are possible, and they that laughed the Lord Jesus to scorn when he said, "the damsel is not dead but sleeps," were afterward confounded, when they saw her raised by his heavenly voice.[5]

His holy pleasure I know not, nor do I know which way the glory of his
great name will more appear—either in finally suffering so great a fall and
ruin of so strong a pillar, that flesh may not glory but that his strength and
glory only may be seen in weakness; or else in your holy rising and reviving
from the bed of so much spiritual filthiness and from so bloody a mind and
lip and hand against all withstanders or disturbers in it, so that the short re-
mainder of your candle may hold out to the world the riches of his mercy at
whose words the holiest of his servants ought to tremble and to work out
their salvation with fear and trembling. I say . . . I know not which way he
will please to raise his glory. Only I know my duty, my conscience, my love,
all which force me to knock, to . . . cry at the gate of heaven and at yours,
and to present you with this loving and loud and faithful . . . sound of a few

5. A reference to Jesus' healing of the daughter of Jairus: Luke 8:41–56.

grounds of deeper examination of both our souls and consciences uprightly and impartially at the holy and dreadful tribunal of him that is appointed the Judge of all, the living and the dead.

Be pleased then, honored Sir, to remember that that thing which we call conscience is of such a nature (especially in Englishmen) that as once a pope of Rome (at the suffering of an Englishman in Rome) himself observed, although it be groundless, false, and deluded, yet it is not by any arguments or torments easily removed. I speak not of . . . the multitude of all nations, which have their ebbs and flows in religion (as the longest sword and strongest arm of flesh carry it). But I speak of conscience, a persuasion fixed in the mind and heart of a man, which forces him to judge (as Paul said of himself, a persecutor) and to do so and so, with respect to God [and] his worship. This conscience is found in all mankind, more or less, in Jews, Turks, Papists, Protestants, and Pagans. . . .

Sir, I am far from glancing the least countenance on the conscience of Papists, or on some Scotch and English Protestants, who turn up all roots and lay all level and in blood for exaltation of their own way and conscience. All that I observe is that boldness and confidence, zeal and resolution, as it is commendable in a kind when it seriously respects a Deity. So also, the greatest confidence has sometimes need of the greatest search and examination. . . .

Secondly, it is so notoriously known that the consciences of the most holy men, zealous for God and his Christ to death and admiration, even in our own country (and in Queen Mary's day especially), have been so grossly mislead by mistaken consciences in matters concerning the worship of God, the coming out of the Antichristian Babel, and the rebuilding of the spiritual Jerusalem, that I need but hint who they were that penned the [Book of] Common Prayer. . . . I say, who were they that lived and died . . . zealous for the bishoprics, and some too zealous for their popish ceremonies against the doubting consciences of their brethren, at which and more we that now have risen in our fathers' stead wonder and admire how such piercing eyes could be deceived, such watchmen blinded and deluded.

But (thirdly) we shall not so much wonder when we lift up our trembling eyes to heaven and [remind][6] ourselves . . . that our thoughts are not as the thoughts of our Maker, that that which in the eyes of man . . . is of high and

6. Originally "remember."

sweet esteem stinks and is abomination to God. Hence, such worships, such
churches, such glorious professions and practices may . . . ravish themselves
and the beholders, when with the piercing eyes of the Most High they may
look counterfeit and ugly and be found but spiritual whores and abominations. . . .

The Maker and Searcher of our hearts knows with what bitterness I write,
as with bitterness of soul I have heard such language as this to proceed from
yourself and others who formerly have fled from [and] cried out against
persecutors! "You will say, this is your conscience. You will say, you are persecuted . . . for your conscience. No, you conventiclers, heretics, blasphemers, seducers. You deserve to be hanged! Rather than one shall be wanting to
hang him, I will hang him myself! I am resolved not to leave a heretic in the
country; I had rather so many whores and whoremongers and thieves came
against us!" Oh sir, you cannot forget what language and dialect this is, . . .
the same unsavory and ungodly, blasphemous and bloody [words] that the
Gardiners and Bonners (both former and later) used to all that bowed not to
the state's golden image of whatsoever conscience they were.[7] And indeed
Sir, if the Most High be pleased to awaken you to render to his holy majesty
his due praises, in your truly broken-hearted confessions and supplications
you will then proclaim to all the world that whatsoever profession you made
of the Lamb, yet these expressions could not proceed but from the Dragon's
mouth.

Oh, remember . . . that you have now a great prize in your hand, to bring
great glory to his holy name, great rejoicing to so gracious a Redeemer. . . .
great rejoicing to the Holy Spirit of all true consolation, whom yet so long
you have grieved and saddened. . . . Your talents are great; your fall has been
so [also]. Your eminence is great; the glory of the Most High in mercy or
justice toward you will be great also. Oh, remember it is dangerous combat
for the potsherds of the earth to fight with their dreadful Potter.[8] It is a dis-
mal battle for poor, naked feet to kick against the pricks.[9] It is a dreadful
voice from the King of Kings, the Lord of Lords [that says,] "Endicott

7. Stephen Gardiner (ca. 1483–1555) and Edmund Bonner (ca. 1500–1569) were Catholic bishop
in England during the reign of Queen Mary and were responsible for much of the persecution o
Protestants during that time.
8. Jeremiah 18.
9. This sentence and the next are a paraphrase of the encounter of Saul (later the Apostle Paul
with the risen Christ on the road to Damascus: Acts 9. See also Chapter 5, note 6.

Endicott, why huntest thou me? Why imprisonest thou me? Why finest, why so bloodily whippest, why wouldest thou (did not I hold thy bloody hands) hang and burn me?" Yes, sir, I beseech you to remember that it is a dangerous thing to put this to the maybe, to the venture or hazard, to the possibility: Is it possible (may you well say) that since I hunt, I hunt not the life of my Savior and the blood of the Lamb of God? I have fought against many several sorts of consciences; is it beyond all possibility and hazard that I have not fought against God, that I have not persecuted Jesus in some of them?

Sir, I must be humbly bold to say that it is impossible for any . . . men to maintain their Christ by the sword and to worship a true Christ! [It is impossible for men] to fight against all consciences opposite to theirs and not to fight against God in some of them, and to hunt after the precious life of the true Lord Jesus Christ! Oh, remember whether your principles and consciences must in time and opportunity force you. It is by worldly policy and compliance with men and times (God's mercy overruling) that holds your hands from murdering thousands and ten thousands, were your power and command as great as once the bloody Roman emperors' were. . . .

But oh, poor dust and ashes, like stones once rolling down the Alps, like the Indian canoes or English boats loose and adrift, where stop we until infinite mercy stops us, especially when a false fire of zeal and conscience drives us, though against the Most Holy and Eternal himself? Oh, remember the black catalogues it has pleased the most jealous and righteous God to make of his fiery judgments and most dreadful stokes on eminent and remarkable persecutors even in this life. It has been his way and course in all countries—in Germany, France, and (especially) England—whatever their pretenses have been against heretics, rebels, schismatics, blasphemers, and seducers. How has he left them to be their own accusers, judges, and executioners, some by hanging, some by stabbing, some by drowning and poisoning themselves, some by running mad, and some by drinking in the very same cup which they had filled to others?

Some may say, "Such persecutors hunted God and Christ, but I, but we . . . ." I answer, the Lord Jesus Christ foretold how wonderfully the wisest of the world should be mistaken in the things of Christ, and a true visible Christ Jesus! "When did we see thee naked, hungry, thirsty, sick, and in prison?"[10] How easy, how common, how dreadful these mistakes!

10. Matthew 25.

Oh, remember once again . . . that every gray hair now on both our heads
is a . . . warning . . . to prepare us for the weighing of our last anchors, and to
be gone from hence as if we had never been. . . . Sir, I know I have much pre-
sumed upon your many weighty affairs and thoughts. I end with a humble
cry to the Father of mercies, that you may . . . commune with your own
heart upon your bed, reflect upon your own spirit . . . , that no sleep may
seize upon your eyes nor slumber upon your eyelids until your serious
thoughts have . . . fixed, first, on a moderation toward the spirits and consciences of all mankind merely differing from or opposing yours with only
religious and spiritual opposition; [and] secondly, [on] a deep and cordial
resolution (in these wonderful searching, disputing, and dissenting times) to
search, listen, pray, fast, and more fearfully [and] tremblingly inquire what
the holy pleasure and the holy mysteries of the Most Holy are.

In whom I humbly desire to be, your poor fellow-servant, unfeigned, respectful, and faithful, R. Williams.

To the Town of Providence, January 1655

*This letter likely was written in response to a political crisis in Providence in the
winter of 1654–55. In November the town voted to establish a citizen militia
(probably in response to the growing Indian threat) and imposed fines on those
who refused to participate. Opposition to the militia evidently was intense, and
frequently cited as justification the freedom of conscience on which the colony
was established. The opposition included Williams's brother Robert, whose protest paper elicited the following response, in which Roger Williams insists that
liberty of conscience cannot excuse an abdication of critical social obligation.*

Loving Friends and Neighbors,

It pleases God yet to continue this great liberty of our town meetings, for
which we ought to be humbly thankful and to improve these liberties to the
praise of the Giver, and to the peace and welfare of the town and colony,
without our own private ends. I thought it my duty to present you with this
my impartial testimony and answer to a paper sent [to] you the other day
from my brother—*That it is blood-guiltiness and against the rule of the Gospel to execute judgment upon transgressors against the private or public weal.*
That ever I should speak or write a tittle that tends to such an infinite liberty
of conscience is a mistake, and [one] which I have ever disclaimed and ab-

horred. To prevent such mistakes, I at present shall only propose this case: there goes many a ship to sea, with many a hundred souls in one ship, whose weal and woe is common and is a true picture of a commonwealth, or a human combination, or society. It has fallen sometimes that both Papists and Protestants, Jews and Turks may be embarked on one ship. Upon which supposal I do affirm, that all the liberty of conscience that ever I pleaded for turns upon these two hinges, that none of the Papists, Protestants, Jews, or Turks be forced to come to the ship's prayers or worship, nor secondly, [be] compelled from their own particular prayers or worship, if they practice any. I further add, that I never denied that notwithstanding this liberty, the commander of the ship ought to command the ship's course, yea, and also to command that justice, peace, and sobriety be kept and practiced, both among the seamen and the passengers. If any seamen refuse to perform their service, or passengers to pay their freight, if any refuse to help in person or purse toward the common charges or defense, if any refuse to obey the common laws and orders of the ship concerning their common peace and preservation, if any shall mutiny and rise up against their commanders and officers, if any shall preach or write that there ought to be no commanders nor officers because all are equal in Christ, therefore no master nor officers, no laws nor orders, no corrections nor punishments—I say, I never denied but in such cases, whatever is pretended, the commander or commanders may judge, resist, compel, and punish such transgressors according to their deserts and merits. This, if seriously and honestly minded, may . . . let in some light to such as willingly shut not their eyes. I remain studious of our common peace and liberty, Roger Williams.

To the Town of Warwick, January 1665

In October 1664, the general assembly of Rhode Island approved a tax on the four towns to cover John Clarke's expenses in procuring the colony's new charter. When the town of Warwick refused to pay its share, Williams wrote this letter, insisting on the religious and moral obligations of citizens to honor their debts and contribute to the common good.[11]

11. Although an explicit date has been lost, Glen LaFantasie argues for placing the composition of this letter in January 1665, based on internal evidence that suggests that it was written in response to a prior letter in the debate over the Clarke tax, a letter dated December 1664. See *The Correspondence of Roger Williams* (Hanover, N.H.: University Press of New England, 1988), 540n1.

Beloved Friends and Countrymen,

My due respects presented with hearty desires of your present and eterna prosperity when this short life is over. I was resolved to have visited you my self this winter and to have persuaded with arguments of trust and love th finishing of the payments relating to His Majesty's royal grant and charter t us. But it pleased God to visit me with old pains and lameness, so that some times I have not been able to rise nor go nor stand. I pray your courteou leave, therefore, of saluting you with these few lines, and your favorable at tention to them.

On two hinges my discourse shall turn: first, the fairness and equity of th matter; [and second,] the damage and hazard if not performed. As to th first, the fairness of the matter, please you to hear two or three witnesse: The first is common honesty and common justice in common dealings be tween man and man. This gives to every man his due, a pennyworth for penny, and will cry shame upon us that Mr. Clarke should be undone—yea destroyed and ruined, as to this world—for his great and long pains, faith fulness, and diligence, for which he ought in common justice to be faithfull satisfied and honorably rewarded. . . . These very barbarians, when the send forth a public messenger, furnish him out; they defray all payment: they gratify him with rewards, and if he prove lame and sick and not able t return, they visit him and bring him home upon their shoulders (and tha many scores of miles) with all care and tenderness.

At the first, Rhode Island, but afterward the whole colony, requested, em ployed, and sent to Mr. Clarke a commission and credentials sealed, wit which the king was satisfied and owned him for our public agent. Now le me say these two things which my eyes have seen. First, when I left M Clarke in England to negotiate the affairs of the whole colony, I saw wit what a low sail he stood along, with what content, patience, and self-denia which course I know he has continued, having received but little suppl from us nor of his own estate, which he continually wrote for. Second, at ou general assembly, when Mr. Clarke's accounts were fairly brought in of wha he had received and what he had borrowed (upon the mortgage of his hous and land) to go through our work, the assembly appointed a committee c able and judicious men to examine the accounts. Upon whole reports an upon their own further examination and consideration, they saw cause t agree upon a very moderate and equal sum to be raised throughout the col ony, to be discharged to him.

Worthy friends, it is easy to find cloaks and colors for denials and delays to any business we have no mind to [finish]. I have visited most of my neighbors at Providence this winter. Some say they are sorry and ashamed of the delay and promise to finish it with speed. Some few say they have done it. Some say they like not some words in the charter. Some say they will pay if all do. Some are against all government and charters and corporations. Some are not so and yet cry out against thieves and robbers who take anything from them against their wills. Some say they will see what became of their former payments before they will part with any more. Some will see the charter first, because they hear that Colonel Cartwright carried the charter to England with him.[12] Some say let those that sent Mr. Clarke into England at first pay him. And some say other things, but none say [anything][13] in my judgment which answers the witness of common honesty. For the sum and scope of His Majesty's royal grant and charter to us is to bestow upon us two inestimable jewels. The first is peace, . . . and the second jewel is liberty. . . . I confess it were to be wished that these dainties might have fallen from God and the king like showers and dews and manna from heaven, gratis and free, like a joyful harvest or vintage without any pain of our husbandry. But since the Most Holy God, the First Cause, has ordained second causes—means, agents, and instruments—it is no more honest for us to withdraw in this case than for men to come to an ordinary[14] and to call for the best wine and liquors, the best meats roasted and baked, the best attendants, and to be able to pay for all and yet most unworthily steal away and not discharge the reckoning.

My second witness is common gratitude, famous among all mankind— yes, among brute beasts, even the wildest and fiercest—for kindness received. It is true Mr. Clarke might have a just respect to his own and the

---

12. Connecticut's border disputes with both Rhode Island and the colony of New Haven, along with continued reports of Massachusetts's refusal to conform to English law, led King Charles II to send a commission of inquiry to New England in 1664. Colonel George Cartwright was one of the four members of the commission, which was instructed to settle the colonies' differences and pressure Massachusetts specifically to bring its Puritan government in line with royal expectations. The commission was accompanied by four ships and four hundred soldiers, which significantly raised tensions among the citizens of New England; but a year later the royal representatives left, having achieved little beyond the resolution of the boundary disputes. Neither did they leave with the Rhode Island charter in hand, contrary to the reports Williams cites.

13. Originally "aught."

14. An "ordinary" in the seventeenth century was an inn or tavern at which meals were served at fixed prices, often to higher-class clientele.

peace and liberty of his friends of his own persuasion. But I believe the weight which turned the scale with him was that truth of God, [namely], a just liberty to all men's spirits in spiritual matters, together with the peace and prosperity of the whole colony. This I know put upon him incredible pains and . . . anguish . . . which I believe a great sum of money would not hire him to wade through the like again. . . .

My third witness of the fairness of this matter . . . is Christianity, which we all . . . pretend to, though in various and different persuasions. This witness soars high above common justice and common gratitude, yes, above all religions. This not only speaks home for due payments and due thankfulness, but of doing good for evil, of paying blessing for cursing, of praying for enemies and persecutors, of selling houses and land, of laying down lives for others. Common justice would not, common gratitude would not, least of all will Christianity employ a public messenger to a mighty king and there leave him to shift for his living and means [in order] to go through so high a service. Nor [would they] leave him to . . . mortgage his house and lands to carry on our business, and then to forfeit and lose them—and lost they are (as all may see), except a speedy redemption save them. . . .

Give me leave, therefore, to mention my second part, or hinge, which is the hazard we run by not a free discharging. . . . If we wholly neglect this business, what will become of our credits? Will not our stink reach the nostrils of our neighbors, yea, of all the inhabitants of the world that hear of us? Rhode Island (in the Greek language) is an isle of roses, and so the King's Majesty was pleased to re-scent it. And his honorable commissioners, in their last letters to Massachusetts . . . , gave Rhode Island and this whole colony an honorable testimony. . . . Shall we now turn our roses into hemlock, our fragrant ointment into stinking carrion? Our own names . . . ought to be more precious to us than thousands of gold or silver, how much infinitely more precious the name of the Most Holy and Most High, and his holy truth of soul liberty among us. . . .

And yet if we imagine our mountain to be immovable by any wind or shakings under heaven, yet we must look higher, to the Most High King and Judge of the whole world, in whose most powerful hand we profess to be our breaths and beings, our ways and motions. He has whips and scourge for colonies and countries, nations and kingdoms, as we have felt in [New England] this last year and have dolefully heard from Old. . . . Worthy friends, the changes of the heavens and earth have been great and suddenly seen and felt by us all this winter. Let us not soothe and sing ourselves asleep with murdering lullabies. Let us provide for changes and by timely humilia- tion prevent them. For myself, seeing what I see over all New England, I can- not but say with David (Psalm 119): "My flesh trembleth for fear of thee, and I am afraid of thy judgments."

I remain longing after your present and eternal peace, R.W.

Index